THE JOURNEY

MARADONA, THE GENERALS AND THE ROAD TO NAPLES

By John Ludden

(The prequel to Once Upon a Time in Naples)

This book is dedicated to the Los Desaparecidos

'Diego Maradona's magical ability proved that fantasy can be effective, in a world that seems to condemn fantasy. For this alone he deserves eternal gratitude from all football fans.'
Eduardo Galeano

'Before Naples, there had already been a life lived.'

John Ludden

INTRODUCTION

The young boy who walks up to the church door couldn't have been more than fifteen-years-old. He appears no different to thousands around here his age. The dark skin, the long, messed up, scraggly hair-clearly of Indian heritage. This boy was on a life journey still in its infancy.

A road taking him many places. He will see the moon, the stars from all over the world, people will fall at his feet. This boy will become a God. He will rise, fall, rise and fall again. So far, the boy has only travelled the fourteen miles from his birthplace of the slums of Villa Fiorito, to Villa del Parque. A first step entering the church of the Virgin Child, making the sign of the cross, kneeling and thanking God for all he has been given. Slowly, the boy stands back up and kisses the crucifix around his neck, before turning to walk back out the door-the journey for Diego Armando Maradona, already a boy king in the neighbourhood and beyond,
continues on.

CHAPTER ONE
FROM ESQUINA WITH LOVE
Through the dust. The same, small, scraggly-haired kid with the ball at his feet could just about be seen through the dust being kicked up off the *Barrio* surface. Around him a cavalry charge of bigger lads, hardly visible to the eye, just a barrage of chasing, dirt-hidden shadows. All are yelling and shouting, 'Diego, Diego, stop it amigo, let us have a touch, come on man!' The little figure feints to go one way, two of them fall over-he then places the ball with great delight through the legs of another. A lady appears, one of the lad's Mother's, 'Diego!' she shouts, 'Time for supper, home now!' To the relief of the others the scraggly haired kid smiles and finally gives up the ball before running across. She playfully smacks her eight-year-old son around the head, 'You better not have been showing off Diego, your Father will have your hide.'
'No mum,' he replies laughing, 'I had my eyes shut most of the time to keep the dust out.

I was only playing with them.'

Diego Armando Maradona was born into a poverty-stricken family at the Evita Peron Hospital, in Lanús-an industrial district to the south of Buenos Aires. He was to grow up in a shanty town called Villa Fiorito. A known, breeding ground for assassins, pimps, priests and blessed luckily for one certain family-footballers. Diego was the first male child after four daughters to Diego senior, known as 'Chitoro' and his wife Dalma 'Tota' Salvadora. The girls names, Ana Maria, Rita, Maria Rosa and Elsa. Later, would come more siblings. Both parents hailed from Esquina, in the north-east of Argentina, close to the border with neighbouring Paraguay. Chitoro made a living as a fisherman and grazing cows. He also had a job as a porter loading crates and bales of fruits, cotton and rice onto the barges that operated along the vast *Corrientes* river. From there they were shipped to the port of Buenos Aires. It was a hard life, brutal even, the bosses at the transport company where Chitoro worked paid him when they felt like it. When there was no money, he and his brother, Cirilo would take out a wooden canoe fishing for pike, using the traditional traps of the indigenous *Guaraní* people. Chitoro lived in a self-built hut on the banks of the River, a lonely existence working dawn to dusk.
Until he fell in love with Tota.
Both were practically neighbours growing up only two hundred yards apart from each other on the riverbank. The two wasted little time getting married and soon, along came a baby girl, Ana Maria. Though they grew up in the same place, the same patch of ground, even, Maradona's parents came from different backgrounds. Whilst Chitoro's people were *Guaraní*. Tota's descended from the millions

of Italian immigrants who settled in Argentina during the late 19th and early 20th centuries. Both definitely belonged to the vast ranks of Argentinians knows as the *Descamisados*, (The shirtless ones). The poverty stricken, the working poor. The term was originally put on paper by the narrator in Victor Hugo's classic novel, Les Misérables to the 'Revolutionary Spanish masses.' Later, it was also used as an insult by the Argentine elite to describe the followers of Juan Peron, who served as President from 1946-1955, then again briefly from 1973-1974.

It was Tota's sister Sara, already living in Villa Fiorito, who claimed she should come to Buenos Aires and live with her family, claiming it would be better for the child. After discussing it with Diego senior, they agreed she go first and when the time was right, he followed. There, after an initial struggle, Tota finally found employment as a servant girl. Like so many Argentinians with her dark skin, job opportunities were scarce. Employers tended to look down on those who came to the capital from the countryside for a better life. The *Cabecitas Negras*, (The Little black heads), as they were referred to by the Argentine upper classes with utter disdain. It ultimately took Tota two years before she was reunited with her husband, when in 1955, he finally left Esquina, travelling by boat down river to be with his family. Slowly, together they made a new life in Villa Fiorito. You'd never have found it on any tourist map, for like so many similar, shanty towns, they were simply left to rot, the people living there fending for themselves. Chitoro worked all hours as a bricklayer, a labourer, mostly at a bone meal factory on the infamous *Riachuelo* stretch, alongside a filthy, black, horribly-polluted canal, that all but separated the rich and the poor of Buenos Aires. There was no fish alive in there, just dead ones, toxic waste, bubbling oil, chopped up human corpses. But nothing spooked Chitoro, it was never an option, for he had loved ones to feed and would take any job to put food on the table, for an ever-expanding family that eventually reached eight children. Chitoro and Tota were already blessed with four daughters, but he,

Diego senior, so desired a son.

Legends abound about Diego's birth, but there definitely wasn't no strange star over Buenos Aires that night, though some will always swear different. There were no angelic choirs, or divine shafts of light shining down onto the hospital, illuminating it in a floodlit haze! No hand of God handing the divine one over, (He would show later!), it was simply Tota being taken to the hospital after experiencing pain whilst dancing. 'I was with a very hard belly because of the contractions and my husband and sister-in-law, Ana Maria, told me that we had to leave quickly to the hospital. We walked three blocks to Fiorito station and from there we took the tram to Lanús. We got off a block and a half from Evita Hospital and I had a hard time standing, because the pains were so strong. I was already coming to the door when, I saw on the sidewalk something that shone, star-shaped. I crouched down to grab it.'

…Shortly after, Diego Armando came into this world kicking and screaming. It was Sunday 30th October 1960. El Diego was named after his proud, beaming Father who held him tight and despite the hellish trials and tribulations that would occur, he never truly let him go. Always there for his boy right until the end.

Home. Time past, over the years there would come to be ten people under a single rickety roof, with only three bedrooms at the Maradona home of number 10 Azamor street, 523 Villa Fiorito. A shelter/shack, made out of rusty scrap metal, bricks, stone and pieces of cardboard. Yet, despite such hardships it remained a house filled with love and fun They had no electricity, no real bathroom, or running water, just the rain that seeped through the roof. Diego once recalled, 'You could get more wet inside than out!' The Maradona's would use empty, twenty-litre oil tubs to fetch water from a tap down the street dragging it back to the house. 'In my house there was no running water. So, when Mom had to do the dishes, or we had to bathe, she would send me to get some water in the tubs to fill them.'

Don Diego worked every hour God bothered to send and more, the young Maradona never forgot this. 'I saw other kids had new trainers and toys, we couldn't afford them. It gave me a healthy envy, the one next door had the bike that I couldn't even dream of. But I saw my dad come home every day from work, his back was killing him. This told me I could never expect anything. You had to fight for it. For us, it was enough for my old man to bring the milk and that we could eat.'

There was also no Police station in Villa Fiorito, for fear of it being besieged. If the authorities ever did enter the dangerous wastelands of the shanty town, they would be bussed in, it would be with a deadly purpose, numbers and menace, God help any poor *porteno*, (Port kid), who got in their way. To survive in such an environment, you had to live on your wits. Be streetwise. As a small kid, Diego made a little money for the family pot by making kites, selling scrap, empty bottles, tins, opening taxi doors, catching cockroaches in factories-anything for a few Peso's more, but always ensuring he never did it on somebody else's patch. Otherwise? Diego would later claim having to stay sharp at so young an age taught him a sense of cunning. *Viveza.* Something only the ragged youth of Villa Fiorto, or kids from similar slum towns could truly understand. Pulling that stroke nobody saw coming, using your head to make a small mound of beauty out of a mountain of shit. In years to come such a state of mind would serve Diego well on the field and off it.

Maradona's earliest memories was just football. Foremost, being given a beautiful leather ball by cousin Beto Zarate-bought with his first pay check. Diego was just three-years-old, he would sleep with it tight to his chest every night. Or, later, if sent on errands, a barefooted Diego would keep the same ball up in the air all the way, even crossing a railway bridge and back, watched along the way by stunned admirers. If coming home from school, the *Remedios de Escalada de San Martin,* opposite Villa Fiorito railway station, he would do similar with an orange, an apple, anything slightly resembling a ball! Already, the love affair that would last a lifetime was in a first bloom.

'If you're going to play football Diego, do it after five o'clock!' would shout Tota, as her son and his *compadres* ran around like lunatics chasing the ball, or more normally Diego in the mid-afternoon, Fiorito blazing, sun. His parents noticed this, realising maybe more in hope that their son was, if not destined, quite likely to play football for a living. It was one of the few ways to escape from the ghetto, so they tried to help him achieve this in any manner possible.

'I think I was mum's favourite,' said Diego. 'When there was pieces of meat on the table, the biggest one was always for me and my sisters would fill up their plate with salad. The poor chewed lettuce like crazy! Also, she defended me to death. I disobeyed her once and went to play football, even though she had told me to stay home. I came back with my trainers a mess-they had cost so much to buy, all dirty and broken. My old man went mad and grabbed me for a beating, but mum came running, lifted his fingers off me and said, 'If you touch my son, tonight when you sleep, I'll kill you!'

Secretly, Tota always prayed silently that her Diego would go on to be an accountant, but the reality was not many accountants hailed from the badlands of Villa Fiorito. Tota's love for all the children knew no limits, even to the detriment of herself going hungry. Something Diego never forgot, 'At thirteen-years-old, I suddenly realised that my Mother had never suffered a stomach ache, She never had a stomach ache, she just wanted us to eat. Every time the food would come out, she would say 'My stomach hurts'. What a lie! It was because there was not enough to go around. That is why I loved my old lady so much.'

It was to be a close, childhood amigo who with a kind act began the journey to the stars for Diego Maradona. Diego and Goyo Carrizo played together on the *Siete Conchita* in Villa Fiorito, *(Seven Little Pitches)*-only a couple had nets. These were nothing more than rough patches of land surrounded by broken wire fences, cleared of rubbish, bricks and rubble to at least resemble a modicum of a pitch. They were tough, barren, surfaces that blew up dust storms when the boys were in the midst of their games. Nearby, a battered, old rail freight truck would rattle past, the long, haul of carriages seemingly never-ending. No grass seeds hardly ever grew in Villa Fiorito, but unknowingly, amid the desperate poverty, it had given birth to a footballing miracle, a boy king from the gutter, the likes of the world had never seen before.

Goyo was already training with Argentinos Juniors boys' team, when he mentioned to the coach that he should take a look at his friend, for Diego was better than him. Such modesty made the well respected Francisco Cornejo agree to let Goyo's amigo come along for a trial. It was December 1968, on first sighting of Diego Maradona, Cornejo couldn't believe his own eyes. It was an auspicious start to the legend, as the rain lashed down in torrents, meaning they were denied using the Argentinos Juniors club courts. Instead, Francisco Cornejo took them to Saavedra Park, twenty five blocks away. When the boys began to play, Cornejo watched on open-mouthed at the new kid.

'He was small and skinny, doing things with the ball an eight-year-old should not have been able to do. In that little time he was playing in Saavedra Park, Diego showed what he would do all his life.'

'You stay!' Maradona recalls it. 'Goyo said to me, 'When I was at Argentinos Juniors last Saturday, I heard they wanted new guys.' So, I ran home and told Mom. It was a Thursday. I stood at the door of the house, against the wire, hard as a statue, waiting for my old man to come back from work. When he turned up, I asked him, 'Will you take me on Saturday to the trials?' I begged him. He couldn't answer because he was so tired. So, I waited until the next day and tried to insist. Still, he was unsure. We went together to the Carrizo's, which was a long way off and he talked to Goyo's dad. When we came back, already late, just us two, I still wasn't sure. 'Okay, I'll take you,' he said! The night before, I dreamt only of the trials The next day on waking up, it was raining heavy. Even though my old man had promised me I could go, we just couldn't afford to spend money on the bus tickets, if, the training was suspended...So, we just set off walking-then, we found out the trials were off because of the rain, but instead they were going to practice in Saavedra Park, which wasn't too far away. Suddenly, a friend of dad's shown up in a van and he said he would take us. I went and played, afterwards the coach Don Francesco said to me,

'You stay!' Maradona always claimed how much he owed to Chitoro.

'My dear old man, we didn't talk much. And he beat me-it was another time, but I owe him everything. When he was so exhausted and weary from work, dad would take me on the bus to Argentinos for practice, I would hang up on the handrail and stand under his arm, on his toes to hold him, because he would fall asleep standing up! Without him I would never have become the ten. Never.'

  Cornejo did some homework to find out where this little wizard came from. Diego had been turning out for a Fiorito neighbourhood team Estrella Roja, set up by Diego senior. He had a good chat with Chitoro, who took an instant liking to him, giving permission for his son to continue training. Cornejo would stand close to tears at times watching this remarkable eight-year-old rascal, half the size of the boys he was playing against running rings around them. It was akin to a religious awakening. The beginning of a journey for Diego Maradona that would touch the heights of heaven and at times fall to the near depths of hell. Already, even at such a precocious age, it was clear to Cornejo, as the little one dropped a shoulder to elude a defender, skipped past a flailing tackle, before firing past a helpless goalkeeper, that he had been sent something truly magical.

Gracias Goyo! He always adored Diego. 'Sometimes we did things that we weren't supposed to do. We used to dodge fares on the trains and buses, so we had enough money for a pizza and a coke after the games. But, we weren't all bad, after matches we always stayed together to talk about the games-where he went I went. We were inseparable. They were great memories that I will never forget. God gave us different paths to follow. He gave Diego a path of fame and fortune, otherwise he would be living like me unable to escape from the poverty of our childhood. That's why I say we had different destinies, because my path has remained poverty.' At just nineteen-years-old, Goyo injured a cruciate ligament in his right knee so badly when playing football, that it put paid to any semblance of a career in the game. He never left the childhood home in Villa Fiorito. Instead, Goyo became resigned to watching his amigo from afar setting off on a blazing journey to the stars, crashing, burning, then soaring once more...

Goyo's youngest child is called Diego Armando.

CHAPTER TWO
CEBOLLITAS: THE LITTLE ONIONS

Argentinos Juniors were founded in 1904, by a football-crazy gang of Socialists and Anarchist *compadres*, whose original name *Martyrs of Chicago*, came from the infamous Haymarket Riots of Chicago. These occurred on 4th May 1886, when a labour protest rally near Chicago's Haymarket Square turned deadly, after someone threw a bomb at the police. Eight people were killed as a result of the violence that day, despite a lack of evidence against them, eight Labour activists were convicted in connection with the bombing-four were hanged, the others given life jail sentences. The following season as the football club grew, it was decided to change their name to something less radical, one more friendly-wise to supporters. Argentinos Juniors came into being, just five years later, they joined the Argentinian Football Association. Argentinos made their new home in the central *barrio* of La Paternal. From the early days till the present, no more than in the sixties, money had always been tight, so they raised their own footballers, building a fine reputation for youth development. Argentinos Juniors also were known for their attacking football, whatever the circumstances-which were usually fighting relegation, the rare occasion apart, such as 1960, when they finished third in the Championship. That year as the season entered its final stretch, Argentinos remained in with a good chance of actually winning the title, before being hammered 5-1, at the big city boys of River Plate. Back in their box, Argentinos continued to survive on faith, hope, charity, prayer and when a decent player was turned out of *Los Cebollitas*, (The Little Onions), they sold him. A proud history, if one unsuccessful.

  The journey began for Diego on the number 28, a battered, old green bus out of Fiorito, then, on a number 44 to Las Malvinas, where Argentinos Junior were based. In all, it took him two hours, but for a kid from the shanty towns who had seen little of life outside his neighbourhood, the big city for young Diego must have been a real eye-opener. Over the *Alsina* bridge crossing the *Riachuelo*, out of Lanus and Villa Fiorito, into the capital

Buenos Aires. Cornejo had arranged for him to train at *Los Cebollitas*. The word was already spreading. After making his debut, rumours grew wildly of a magical boy who could make a ball sing. The touchlines began to fill up as hundreds came to watch after hearing fantastic tales of him in action. Asked constantly where the young Maradona came from? Francisco Cornejo always replied with a smile, 'Diego must have come from another planet!' He was a phenomenon. People watched, but couldn't believe their own eyes as this youngster ran amok in games taking on and beating sides on his own. More, many more from across the provinces came to catch a glimpse of this kid from Villa Fiorito, who was being hailed with an almost Christ-like zeal. The genie was not so much out the lamp, but careering around Buenos Aires on a magic carpet. 'They say people witness at least one miracle in their lives,' Cornejo later wrote. 'Diego was clearly mine.' So special was the youngster's talents, doubts emerged amongst opponent about his true age when they came to play. Some even suspected that due to Maradona's short status, he may even have been a dwarf? Cornejo did have a false name when it was needed for the boy. Diego Montanya! Mostly though, to prove this nonsensical talk was rubbish, Diego was ordered to produce identity papers as evidence more than once to still-disbelieving opposing coaches, as he then went on to destroy their teams. With a gentle swish of a paint brush, the first strokes were being painted on the canvas of *El Pelusa,* (The scraggly haired one). 'Diego Maradona was the best painting of my life,' said Cornejo.

 It was around this time, he started taking the youngster to see a recommended doctor of sorts called Cacho Paladino, who claimed to be a specialist in building up body muscles. It was said Paladino worked with many sports people, mostly boxers and footballers. His methods were claimed to be dubious at best, but purported to show positive results in the short term. Maradona was placed on a course of drugs-pills, vitamins, more worryingly injections. Palodino himself later admitted that what he prescribed to patients was mostly trial and error. Some definitely had terrible side-effects later in life. These visits to Palodino became a regular occurrence for Diego, who believed they were just part of the process required to help him achieve his dream. The truth being it wasn't normal, far from it, making the boy think this only incurred him to do so right throughout his career. Like any other who witnessed him play, Palodino knew he was in the presence of greatness. His advice to Cornejo was, 'Take a piece of Diego now'. A signature on a piece of paper, the back of a cigarette pack, anything to keep him in the ring, before the family forced Cornejo out and other bigger dogs moved in to reap the treasures to surely follow. Already, River Plate had come calling with gifts to Diego's home, but had been given short shrift by Chitoro. He, maybe more importantly, Tota trusted their son with Cornejo and his assistant Jose Trotta, another so integral to *Los Cebollitas* and Diego's early development. It would be in Trotta's dependable, rusty old, ramshackled, bus that the team would travel to away matches around the provinces. Both he and Cornejo made sure none of their boys ever went hungry, for they knew the majority came from desperately poor families-such as Diego's. When he joined the team, both Chitoro and Tota travelled to every match to watch their son on the bus. VIP's! Cornejo would drive, whilst the Maradona's would sit chatting in the back with the boys and the affable Trotta. 'They were beautiful times,' remembers Cornejo.

'The wind in the face and the bustle of the boys around me, singing, making jokes. No one thought about the kids in terms of business, or money. At that time, everything just felt much more romantic, purer. None of them ever quizzed me asking how much they could make by signing their child to another club. Not even Diego's parents-who eventually realized that he was gold dust. For Don Diego and Dona Tota, it was all about trust and the fact their son wanted to stay with me. People always asked why I never made a contract with Diego's parents, they tell me that if I had, I would have been a rich man. I tell them this wasn't done, because it just never felt right to do so. I've always believed that.'

On reaching his teenage years, Maradona started to turn out as a ball boy at Argentinos Juniors home matches-one time during the interval, he was handed the ball and told, 'Go on the pitch and entertain the crowd!' As Diego began to perform, huge roars of delight erupted from the terraces. These swiftly turned to gasps of utter disbelief, even moments of shocked silence, as they watched the young boy, this kid from the badlands of Villa Fiorito before them, treat the ball as if he was the magician and it the servant. It was no simple display of ball juggling, this was Maradona. So, it became a regular occurrence that was loved by Diego and the crowd. No more so than one time against his boyhood team Boca Juniors. Even as the second half was due to begin, many supporters continued to clap, shouting for him to stay on the pitch. Soon, the entire stadium was on its feet chanting, *'Que se quede!'* ('Let him stay on!'). Unable to resist, Diego persisted to the delight of the crowd and the utter astonishment of the two teams who waited in the tunnel to restart the second half. He continued to provide an adoring audience with an audacious encore. Diego would later say, 'It felt like I touched heaven with my hands that day.' Shortly after, Diego even appeared on a television entertainment show performing first his remarkable tricks with a ball, then an orange! As the audience shouted for more, he was thrown a bottle and continued to keep that up in the air, until finally being told to take a bow. As the applause roared loud, this wasn't so much a rising star, but a blazing comet. Exceptional never did Diego Maradona justice.

Jorge. It was a friendship formed in early teenage years that lasted a lifetime of madness and wonder. Once upon a time in Buenos Aires, in the early 1970's, there was a boy named Jorge Cyterszpiler. Jorge was a huge fan of the Argentinos Juniors soccer club, a common sight stood behind the goal cheering loud. He would watch enthralled as his brother Juan Eduardo who was ten years older played for the team. Jorge had been adopted by the Argentinos players, as a sort of mascot-a good luck charm. He was a soft, fat kid, bullied, cursed by polio, forced to use crutches. When Juan Eduardo got near the goal, or scored, Jorge got so excited he would drop the crutches and fall over. Yet, still he would continue to cheer, the sight of the bushy-haired younger Cyterszpiler's manic enthusiasm became a memorable feature of Argentinos matches. Tragically, when Jorge was twelve-years-old this all stopped.
Juan Eduardo was kicked in the leg during a match, a freakish, yet horrific accident, developed a haemorrhage-and it killed him. Jorge truly worshipped his brother, watching football became simply too painful with Juan gone. Instead, he grieved, shutting himself off in his

parents apartment in La Paternal, no longer interested in the game, slipping fast into deep depression. One day, friends called claiming something, absolutely crazy. They spoke of a new kid from another planet performing for *Los Cebollitas*, who could do things with a soccer ball no one had ever seen before. At first, not interested, such was their great insistence for him to go with them, Jorge finally went along. With huge reluctance, still nursing a broken heart, he stepped once more into the world of football.

In doing so Jorge found a new vocation in life, for playing that day was a fourteen-year-old called Diego Maradona. After finding the courage to introduce himself to the young Diego, an enduring friendship between the two began. The raggedy kid from the dustbowl shacks of Villa Fiorito, the middle-class boy of Jewish-Polish refugees, from one of the leafier, suburban areas of Buenos Aires. Many a night, Maradona escaped the hardships of the shanty town to stay over at his new friend's house. The family was affluent and cosmopolitan, beyond anything Diego had experienced. Jorge's parents opened their home to him. It was as if he filled the space their dead child had left behind. The boys would talk until the early hours about hopes for the future. An unlikely double act, one close, nonetheless, sharing a wish to be the best at what they did. After securing for himself a business degree, Jorge Cyterszpiler was asked by Diego Maradona to become his manager in all matters financial. A touched Jorge said yes whole-heartedly to his amigo, together their journey to the stars began. Maradona trusted his friend implicitly with not just the hard-earned dollars, therefore, more importantly, the financial security of his family. Nothing to him mattered more.

There was already a feeling in the air-a sense that Diego Maradona even in his early teens was being fast-tracked for something quite extraordinary. People were bowing to his every whim-normal rules didn't seem to apply. Schooling grades, a tick where there should have been a cross. Passing exams when he wasn't even there. One time, Jorge Trotta visited Diego's headmaster after hearing stories the boys grades were being affected because of his absenteeism over football activities. Trotta explained to the headmaster who himself was an Argentinos Junior supporter, just how good-highly rated Diego was. He gave him a ticket for a *Los Cebollitas* game on the following Saturday. Come the day, the headmaster turned up, watched the little onions win 4-0, with Diego scoring three, one when he dribbled around half the opponents team to score. After the game, the headmaster spoke to Cornejo and Trotta and was moved to tears. He told them not to worry about Diego's grades, duly passing him in all his early exams. The boy was also given some books to read at home to give the impression he was keeping up with his studies. This was the extraordinary effect a young Diego had on grown adults when they witnessed him performing on the football pitch. A kid hardly out of his teens causing them to act like starstruck virgins.

Also, Diego experienced small acts of kindness, that if he was a simple kid in the neighbourhood, just would never happen. Diego walking past a grocery store, the owner seeing him would make a point of coming racing out with a bag of vegetables for his family. Grown up strangers staring on a bus, as if they were in the presence of someone unworldly. This kid was fifteen-years-old.

CHAPTER THREE
COMMUNIQUE NUMBER 23

'As many people as necessary must die in
Argentina, so that the country will again be secure.'
President Jorge Rafael Videla

Away from Villa Fiorito and Diego's world.
 Shortly after 3am, on Wednesday 24th March 1976, a coup
d'état, long in the planning, swift and perfect in its
execution occurred. Two hours before sunrise, the
Presidential palace at *Casa Rosada*, in Buenos Aires was
surrounded by tanks, as a small band of ambitious senior
military officers seized power from a crumbling, Isabelito
Peron's, civilian government. Immediately, the Argentine
Congress was dissolved and Peron placed under house
arrest. All the armed forces were involved. Commanding
the Army, General Jorge Rafael Videla, the navy, Admiral
Emilio Eduardo Massera, the Air Force, Brigadier Orlando
Ramon Agosti. A psychopathic trio set to drag Argentina
through the gates of hell. For this was no normal
government taking control, more of a heist. Uniformed
gangsters masquerading as Politicians, interested only in
power, lining their own pockets. But, there was a problem-
they were inheriting an Argentina tottering on the brink of
financial, social collapse. Peron's government had lost
control, so stricken had it become with corruption and
greed. Her inner circle disgraced by alleged close links
with South American drug cartels, wild rumours
abounding of cocaine-fuelled parties at *Casa Rosada.* Such
stories though would appear and sound like children's
fairy tales compared to what was coming.
  Argentina. A country that had torn itself apart from
within. Inflation soared to near incredulous levels of over

six hundred per cent, social unrest was rife, escalating by the day. Student demonstrations frequently exploding into all-out riots. Strikes were rampant, bringing the economy to its knees, the left-wing guerrillas, the *Montoneros*, whom had sworn an oath to fight to the death in their revolution against the establishment. Engaged in ferocious battles against the military that had brought the country to the brink of a civil war. No prisoners. Kidnappings and assassinations of government and police officers, in retaliation for the killings of their own by death squads, ·became daily events. Terrible atrocities committed on both sides. Argentina was blazing out of control. Such mounting chaos handed the three Generals the perfect opportunity to grasp the moral, high ground to seize power, restore order. Martial law was swiftly declared. Trusted senior officers imposed upon the boards of every organization. From banks, newspapers, televisions stations, even the national ballet. In order to maintain power, keep the rich in riches, the poor had to be kept in order. Wages were frozen, trade unions abolished, strikes banned. Millions of so called 'dangerous' books burned. The people had to be kept downtrodden, obedient, silent, the problem of the troublesome political-left would be solved by simply annihilating them, as the unholy threesome embarked on a killing spree, the likes of which even this blood splattered continent had never witnessed.

The military governor of the province of Buenos Aires, General Suarez Mason was quoted as saying, 'First we must kill all subversives, then their sympathisers, then those indifferent. Finally, we must kill all those whom are timid.' Lists were made, names selected, the round-ups began. It came as little surprise that the first act of the new regime was to issue a nationwide ultimatum for military and civil police to employ a shoot to kill policy, if any 'Subversive' activity was witnessed. The Generals grandly declared plans for their brave new world calling it the *Proceso de Reorganizacion,* (The National Reorganisation Process). Woe betide any whom stood in their way, for the murderous state of mind that existed within the leadership, summed up by a chilling statement made by General Videla shortly before the coup occurred.

'As many people as necessary must die in Argentina so that the country will again be secured.'

Videla proved true to his word, as the most brutal and sadistic period in Argentina's history grimly unfolded. Two days after they came to power, it was announced that General Jorge Rafael Videla had been designated as President of Argentina. In his first address to the nation the new leader duly declared,

'One historical cycle ends, another one begins.' State controlled newspapers, magazine articles spoke of him having, 'A deep, religious belief.'

'A wonderful devotion to his family and a favouring for English tailoring.' Videla was portrayed as a gentleman, splendid in army uniform. Photographs appeared everywhere of him gracefully drawing his sword at military parades. Videla, modest, successful, a man of discipline, valour and sacrifice. A true Argentinian hero. In reality the man behind the charade was a murdering sadist. Privately, the relationship between the Generals was derisory at best with the public masks of togetherness an illusion for the masses. It was all about feathering their own nests with the age-old human traits of greed and power influencing every move they made. The Junta robbed and plundered. Then, like all men of similar ilk, they filled up their private Swiss bank accounts in preparation for a quiet retirement far away from the past, in a foreign climate.

If not killed before…

Only a week after the coup occurred over three thousand substantial bank accounts were emptied. As men they differed from night to day. Between Air force chief Agosti and Navy Admiral Massera, there existed an open animosity. Whilst Agosti portrayed himself as a stout Roman-Catholic, a family man, Massera, codenamed 'Zero' to the security forces, was a playboy. A sharp tongued, bon-vivant who lived life to the full. Massera ensured loyalty by allowing those responsible for his safety a share of the Junta's ill-gained spoils.

'The boys must be compensated for the risks they run,' he claimed.

His rivalry with Agosti occasionally flared out of control, but with President Videla assuming the role of peace-keeper, they always found sufficient common ground and made their plans accordingly. For much work needed to be done, as this was the time of *Guerra Sucia,* (The Dirty War).

Under the false pretext of eliminating the *Montoneros* ,the Junta unleashed a wave of terror across Argentina. In a sinister development, green Ford Falcons supplied to the Junta by foreign car manufacturers were used by hooded snatch squads to raid homes in the dead of night, taking away unsuspecting victims. These vehicles came to epitomize the horror of the times. Chief amongst the guilty, Ford and Mercedes Benz executives who used the clampdown to rid themselves of troublesome Union delegates. One, Ford Motor plant 25, even had their own clandestine detention centre run by the military. There, for weeks and months on end, political prisoners were held until transferred to secret torture centres from which there was never no return. But it wasn't just in the car industries that these dreadful events occurred, places such as shipping yards, factories, universities and schools. All encouraged by the ruling powers to purge so-called 'undesirables'. Also, in a concerted attempt to scare and intimidate the population from any act of protest, armed soldiers arrived at selected people's houses to rob them. Other innocents pulled over in their vehicles for no apparent reason and beaten senseless. Most horrifically, some simply disappeared, never to be seen again. The clean-up of alleged 'state enemies' began immediately, but it didn't stop there. Men and women who simply didn't conform to the regime's ideals were disposed of in increasingly large numbers, relatives were advised not to cause a stir. People snatched off the street, from their homes, even arrested on the bus in broad daylight. 'They must have done something to be taken,' would be whispered by people, whom were simply scared to death of what was occurring. So, a strange, murderous, reality carried on unabated, with most simply shutting their eyes, or turning the other way.

Communiqué number 23. Against this terrifying backdrop of state-sponsored thuggery, there remained the small, if complicated matter of a football game taking place far away in Poland. Touring in Eastern Europe, Argentina had just beaten a formidable Soviet Union side 1-0 on a snow-covered pitch in Kiev. It was only on arriving in Poland they received news of the coup. On the evening of the 24th, Argentina were due to face the Poles in Chorzow, but the manager Cesar Menotti, *El Flaco* (The Thin One), and his players had grave misgivings about the rationale of the match taking place with all the turmoil back home. Menotti's personal politics meant he was totally opposed to the coup, but also wise enough to keep his own counsel. If the Generals had wanted a loyal disciple to carry out their wishes, they could not have picked a more reluctant, or unlikely one than the chain smoking, forty-year-old Menotti.

He was simply inherited.

Born in the traditionally radical-liberal city of Rosario, (home also to Che Guevara), the lean, gaunt, figure of Cesar Menotti hated their guts and the Generals knew this. Theirs' was to be a partnership hardly born in heaven, more a mutual loathing, but standing together for the greater good of Argentina. To the outside world it appeared a strained relationship. To those on the inside they watched, waited for the inevitable implosion. For it was a train wreck of a partnership. These were also changing times on the pitch. Not for Menotti, the brutal mentality that had scarred Argentina's mid-seventies football. Defensive tactics, thuggish, win-at-all cost displays were abandoned, for here was a man whose heart though scarred by what was occurring in his country, remained a footballing romantic. Cesar Menotti's Argentina had one tactic. Attack! *La Nuestra*, (Our style), the people's football. Not with brutal force as had become the way, but back to the angels with dirty faces. The ball players of yesteryear, the likes of Osmar Oreste Corbatta, Humberto Maschio, Omar Sivori, Antonio Angelillo and Osvaldo Cruz. These the forefathers of the Barrios, the *portenos'* of their day playing for hours on end perfecting tricks and technique, alongside crumbling, remnants of factories, broken down shacks, century old railway lines. *El Flaco* wanted fast, free and flowing-swift, one-two passing from midfield. Cutting a swathe through packed defences, this was how they would take on the world. With weary eyes that had seen and also enjoyed far too much, (Cesar loved a party!) A constant worn-down expression in a well-lived in face, Cesar Menotti carried the hopes and dreams of an entire nation on such slim shoulders. But there lay Menotti's problem. How do you serve two masters, one you loathed, one you adored? The Generals and the people. To do so *El Flaco* made peace with his conscience to make a pact with the devil. One that would test him to the limits.

When orders were finally received from Buenos Aires, via the Generals, through the AFA telling the team in no uncertain manner that they must play to boost 'National morale', he remained silent. Of the hundreds of ultimatums, decrees, memos and orders issued by the Junta in those first hours of coming to power that contained the words 'Prohibited', there was only one that mentioned 'Permitted'. *Communiqué number 23*, stated, 'Live coverage of the Argentina v Poland football match would be 'permitted' to go ahead.' That in essence, life would carry on. So, on a day when television was allowed to show nothing more than a static picture of the national coat of arms, when crimes against all decency were being committed, a simple game of football let people, at least for ninety minutes, breathe a little more easily. The famous saying that 'Football is the opium of the masses' had never been more apt, or more terrifying than in this instance. The lights went out in Argentina, in the darkness lurked evil beyond words. Yet, there remained that one last grasp of normality, for in front of 60,000 Polish supporters, Menotti's side won a hard-fought contest 2-1. Come the following morning, one of Argentina's best-selling newspapers *Clarin*, declared on its front page, TOTAL NORMALIDA. (Total Normality).

Just beneath it was written 'Argentina derroto a Polonia.' (Argentina defeat Poland). It was if the Generals themselves had scored the goals to claim victory. All proved good practice for the headline writers, because on the near horizon the greatest show on earth was coming to their shores. The eleventh World cup finals on Argentine soil, presented the regime with a God given chance to extol the virtues of their *Proceso* de *Reorganizacion,* help cleanse the stench of death haunting the everyday, sinew of Argentine life. For the Generals it was truly a gift from the footballing Gods of FIFA, one they intended to take full advantage of.

   Across the world, Human Rights organisations such as Amnesty International pleaded with FIFA to reverse their absurd decision, move the tournament. Many nations threatened boycotts, all to no avail. Money as ever won out over common sense and decency. That Argentina could never afford an event of this magnitude was irrelevant to Videla and his henchmen, for the Generals had already decided to not just host the competition. By all, any means necessary,

   they were going to win it.

CHAPTER FOUR
BLINDED BY THE LIGHTS

La Paternal Stadium. Buenos Aires. On Thursday 20th October 1976, just ten days before his sixteenth birthday, Diego Armando Maradona's meteoric rise through Argentinos Juniors ranks culminated in a first team debut in the Argentine First Division, the clan were there to witness it. His entrance came from the bench midway through the second half against Tallares de Cordoba. Unknown to the youngster, in the crowd that day was also *La Albiceleste* coach Cesar Menotti, who had heard all about this latest little angel with a dirty face and wanted to see for himself if the fuss was worthwhile. With Argentinos 1-0 down, Maradona ran on and the cheers from the terraces rang loud in his ears. With Diego it was never the simple narrative of history books, more tales born of myth and fable, indeed, legend has it that with his first touch he nutmegged the San Lorenzo defender Juan Cabrera. Many have cast doubt over whether this actually occurred, but just a few years ago a photo emerged to show it!

Wearing the number sixteen shirt, Diego impressed with some dribbles, but overall was dealt with by the Tallares defenders, failing to stop Argentinos losing. Post-match, an emotional Maradona spoke only of the magic and wonder of what he had experienced with his reception and being on the pitch. 'Today feels like I held the sky in my hands.'

El Gráfico wrote, 'Not even the surprising inclusion of the skilled and intelligent ex Cebollita Maradona was enough to resolve the problem'.

An incident occurred as Diego was leaving the ground, a tearful old man was so overcome at watching him make his debut, that he wanted to give Diego the bike that he had rode ten miles on to watch the match. The young Maradona kissed him on both cheeks, shook his hand, but refused point blank to accept the gift. This being just one of the countless examples of the hysteria and idolatry surrounding *El Pelusa*.

So, it began, the real world of professional football. This wasn't *Los Cebollitas*, where according to Maradona's accounts, a notebook given to him by Francisco Cornejo years later, between 1973-1974, they won 136 matches in a row. The fourteen-year-old Diego simply had no equals at that level, running riot, turning not just defenders inside out, but causing all who watched him to shake their heads asking, 'Who was this kid?' He swiftly became known as the best of his age in the country. Just a year later through a staggering rise through the ranks, Maradona found himself up against fully grown men every week, brutal in their trade, some even with evil in their hearts determined to do everything not be embarrassed by this wonder boy-who with a ball at his feet had the power to reduce them to stooges. Streetwise as Diego most certainly was already on the pitch, there were times he would need eyes in the back of his head when up against monsters-not all he could slay.

Maradona would spend five seasons at Argentinos Juniors, scoring in all 115 goals in 167 appearances. The first occurred just two weeks after his sixteenth birthday against San Lorenzo, on 14th November 1976, at Mar del Plata, in the *General San Martin.* Only 1335 spectators were present inside the sparse stadium bearing witness to history being made. Both teams were struggling around the bottom of the League, it was poor stuff to watch and the fans were letting the players know. At half-time the score stood at 1-1, enter Diego, who immediately made a difference. Playing wide-right he led from the front and for one so young exhilarating to watch. His first goal said to have been a snapshot of things to come as Maradona took on the Lorenzo defence going past three players, before placing a low drive into the corner of the net. All achieved with such consummate ease. The game finished 5-2 to Argentinos, with most of the goals scored late on, as the home side spent that time chasing Diego around like some slapstick comedy. Come the final whistle, he was embraced by his teammates and acclaimed by the local supporters hanging off the fences applauding him, trying to get a closer look at this little waif who had just left their team broken and embarrassed.

Slowly, as the weeks went on more glimpses of Maradona's magic were unveiled to all of Argentina's delight. Cesar Menotti even selected Diego for the national squad. A bewildering rise from the slums to surreal heights happening so very fast. Maybe too fast? The limelight already was in his face. Just a boy's face, his every move followed. It wasn't so much superstar status, he had been handed, more a saviour. Diego Maradona was already being blinded by the lights. Expectations being lumped on his teenage shoulders were quite literally unmeasurable. The 1978 World Cup being held in Argentina, even at just sixteen-years-old, Maradona's name was being put forward by the nation's newspapers, magazines, radio and television media as Menotti's secret weapon to win it.

CHAPTER FIVE
A THOUSAND BULLETS

It was a most beautiful morning in Buenos Aires when they killed the General. Just when he thought it was all over, they dragged him back in.

General Carlos Omar Actis was fifty-one-years-old, when he received the dreaded call from his President. A military engineer by trade, only recently retired, Actis found himself summoned to meet Jorge Videla at the *Casa Rosada*. He suspected if the rumours circulating were true, his services would be required for one last call of duty. After shaking the President's hand, Videla told him straight out that he wished him to return. Preparations for the *Mundial* were in a mess, close to disaster even. They had just two years before the world arrived on their doorstep. Strikes had been banned on pain of firing squads, those thought to be communist subversives were warned not to show their faces on the sites, or they would have their heads cut off. Videla explained they possessed the tools for the job, but just needed someone to link the dream with reality. A respected figure amongst the men whom everyone would fall behind. This was clearly no request, Videla told Actis it was time to dust down his uniform and return to duty as head of *EAM. (Ente Autuartico Mundial 78).* (The World Cup organising committee). Knowing he had little choice, Actis agreed, but demanded that the navy and the air force, fierce rivals of the army, not be allowed to interfere.

It didn't take long before he discovered blood couldn't be found in stone, for there simply wasn't enough money in the pot for the Junta's grand design. He was no maker of miracles, Argentina was in the midst of a financial meltdown, inflation spiralling out of control. The smell of blood, cordite-revolution in the air. A merciless civil war raging on the streets between the authorities and the *Montoneros*. A battle for the Argentine soul being fought in the towns and cities with no sign of the violence relenting. There was something else also-a problem that drove Actis even closer to despair. Despite promises made by President Videla, he found himself continually undermined at every opportunity by a Vice-Chairman forced upon him by the same man. A Navy officer, Captain Carlos Lacoste. A cousin of Videla's. A man of unbridled ambition, streetwise, able to walk and converse with both kings, paupers and FIFA. Presidents or drug lords. Lacoste crossed these worlds with limitless ease. He was a fixer, a pimp, a parasite, also a cold bloodied murderer. All things to all men, except Actis, who never trusted the Captain and was certain his every action and word were being reported back to the Junta leaders. He was right.

Trouble was brewing…

Actis' initial policy of attempting to keep a tight hold of the purse strings meant progress proved painfully slow, for he refused all attempts to spend sums of money Argentina could ill-afford. Lacoste fought him on this all the way, but was forever overruled, always told the same by Actis, 'I'm in charge, stay out if it!' Lacoste was not to be thwarted, many times he acted individually against Actis' orders. No more so than when behind the General's back, Lacoste began preparations to install a new domestic colour television transmission system. When a furious Actis found out he immediately halted Lacoste's plans. Following this the incensed navy man received a mauling from the head of one of the tournaments main sponsors Adidas. It's owner Horst Dassler was raging. They had just sold to him and Coca Cola the *'Event of the decade!'* Only, because of Actis' stubbornness, the world would now have to watch on black and white screens? Dassler threatened Lacoste that unless it was sorted, Adidas would pull out spelling disaster for the *Mundial*. It had reached an impasse, something had to be done. The Captain met with Admiral Massera and a decision was reached. Lacoste told Massera to leave it with him, the problem would go away. Forever. A simple nod from the Admiral, all preparations were made.

General Actis was becoming increasingly edgy. After a disastrous meeting with FIFA to discuss an ever-worsening, desperate agenda of ailing budgets, all had not gone well. Frustrated FIFA officials reported their discontent to the Junta, who fumed at being shown in a bad light by Actis' stubbornness. Admiral Massera had already relayed Lacostes' concerns and his own annoyance to Videla over Actis, but was told to just stay calm, that he would ultimately succeed. By this time Massera had already given the nod to Lacoste because he was convinced that when the deed was done, Videla would eventually come around to believe that sooner, rather than later, General Actis had to go.

Meanwhile, even knowing well it could cost him dear, Actis felt he had to act out of moral duty to save his nation from total bankruptcy. The final straw came with FIFA's insistence that they had to build an entire new stadium at Mar del Plata. He was also informed by the Junta that the thorny issue of a new colour

television system in Argentina, so the main sponsors Adidas, Gillette and Coca

Cola would look good on European television, had to be resolved. The price for such was just so beyond the pale that Actis finally snapped and planned to speak out at a major world-wide press conference, letting the media know of his grave misgivings. Although extremely wary of what may happen, Actis had still managed to totally misjudge the mood amongst the Argentine hierarchy, especially the megalomaniac Videla-who would view such an action as treacherous and unleash the dogs of war on his head. Actis fully understood the Generals had not taken kindly to the constant reminders of financial restrictions. They whom had expected golden stadiums to spring from Argentine dust like flowers in the rain had grown in murderous frustration. An endgame was drawing in for this rare breed in the seventies. A General of the Argentinian, military hierarchy who loved his country more than he cared for power and riches. An idealism that would cost him dear.

Shortly after 9am, on Thursday 19th August 1976, in Wilde, a south-east province of the Capital, Buenos Aires, General Omar Actis left home in his Chevrolet, heading for the military headquarters of *EAM*. As ever, he was early with a lot on his mind. Actis had been in charge for just a month and a half and already was close to exploding with the pressure and doubts. In just two days' time, he would be sat before the world's press to express his concern about Argentina's readiness for the tournament, Actis could only dread what would happen next? He pulled over in his car to watch a group of youngsters kicking a ball around on a nearby waste ground. Like all Argentinians, Actis adored football, himself a lifelong River Plate fan-such a simple game, a beautiful game, a religion for his people. Yet, such a poisonous weapon to control the masses. Used by the Junta to contort and control. A smiling General Actis wound down his window enjoying the thought of finally doing the right thing and hopefully grabbing a decent night's sleep for the first time in months. Suddenly, appearing from an opposing alleyway, a gang of figures dressed in construction overalls with their faces covered by protective helmets. They moved fast racing across to surround Actis' car-the General knew instinctively he was done for, closing his eyes. In a murderous shower of machine gun fire, they opened up at close range cutting him to pieces. Before fleeing, one of the hit-squad nonchalantly placed a hand-written note around his blood-stained neck reading, *'Actis has been executed by the 'Revolutionary Montoneros Army'*. Then, swiftly as they came, the assassins vanished, leaving Actis' body shot to pieces and strewn with a thousand bullets.

The General's worries over budgets over, his retirement permanent.

The stone in President Videla's shoe no longer pained, the path to the *Mundial* clear. *La Nacion* immediately blamed his death on the *Montoneros*. Retribution was swift, as the next day Junta death squads dumped thirty bullet-ridden, dynamited corpses in the insanely profound named town of Fatima, outside Buenos Aires. They claimed revenge for the murder of their General. Such was the shocking state of the bodies none were ever properly identified, but a leak by the authorities that these were the *Montoneros* assassins involved in the gunning down of General Actis was picked up and taken as fact, Yet, something didn't fit, such a swift and neat conclusion bore all the trademarks of a Junta hit. Also, quite strikingly the *Montoneros* themselves came out and denied Actis' killing was their doing. They had already issued a statement to say they wouldn't disrupt the World Cup. 'Estadio hombres y mujeres del pueblo.' 'We are men and women of the people.' It was unheard of for the *Montoneros* to break their word by gunning down a figure so blatantly associated with the competition. Many smelt a rat. One of the assassins had also stolen the General's watch, papers and money, something the *Montoneros* simply abhorred. Instead, the whispered accusations all pointed to one figure, though none dared say his name.

General Omar Actis' funeral was a paltry, low-key affair. Not for him the spectacular state-sponsored mourning, with all the added-on trimmings. No trumpets or bugles. No soldier driven, horse-drawn carriage. Instead, only a grieving family and a pitiful handful of low-ranking officers along with President Videla to pay their respects. A clear sign of the Junta's disillusionment with how Actis had gone about his job. One notable absentee, Admiral Massera, who swiftly set about putting one of his own men in charge of *EAM*. Hardly surprisingly, Captain Carlos Lacoste, soon to be a Vice-Admiral, was chosen to take the reins, he set about the task with an unbridled enthusiasm and relish. The press conference Actis was meant to give was instead hosted by Lacoste who was blunt and straight to the point. 'The 78 World Cup presents Argentina with two main challenges. One being infrastructure, the other, organisation. We shall succeed in both.'

Previous projects blocked by Actis were suddenly given the green light. None dared or even thought about saying no. Only later would they bother to count the cost. If ever. Money was found, begged, borrowed and stolen. No bank account left untouched. Soon, the stadiums started appearing, airports renovated, motorways re-laid. To appease the sponsors, a coloured television transmission was finally provided and the Captain became viewed by FIFA and sponsors, more importantly for him the Junta leaders as a miracle man. The word went out, Argentina was ready...

Two months before the tournament began, state radio stations and television channels received written orders prohibiting criticism of the national team.

Welcome to the 1978 World Cup.

CHAPTER SIX
TOUGH LOVE

Amore. It must be every young person's dream to be able to fight their way out of a poverty, stricken, childhood, where your mum and dad had worked like hell to put food on your table, the clothes on your back. Working dog hours for bastard bosses to the point where they were both mentally and physically exhausted-but still they grafted. The many kids they raised with love, tough love sometimes, but always with one intention. To keep them safe. Then comes the moment, the one you had dreamed about since you were three-years-old, clutching your football tight in bed, off cousin Beto, on 10 Azamor street, 523 Villa Fiorito. The blessed opportunity down to your blessed talent, when you buy your family a new apartment in the comfortable area of Villa Parque, Agerich street, Lascano 2257. Only four blocks away from the Argentinos Junior stadium. Handing the keys over to Don Chitoro and Tota, mum and dad, seeing their faces light up with pride, tears in their eyes, something else they both tried to and hide, but find it impossible-utter, sheer relief that the struggle was over, their boy was now the holy breadwinner, he had performed a miracle leading them to a new life. Initially, for Chitoro, the leap was just too far, he found it hard to adapt. So used to strenuous, long hours of work and little sleep, Chitoro at first kept to the hours of the bone crushing factory in his last job, keeping himself busy at their new home. As for Tota, she too, although thanking God every day, became even more aware of ensuring the family stayed close. Tota was paranoid about strangers trying to attach themselves to her children in efforts to befriend Diego. She trusted few outside the clan, it soon became apparently clear to Tota that whilst Villa Parque was heaven on earth compared to Villa Fiorito, even heaven came with hidden dangers on this journey with her fifth child to a new world.

It was a simple act of fate in a local grocery store that brought forward fifteen-year-old Claudia Villafane into

Diego Maradona's world. Tota was at the counter trying to pay for the food, when she noticed there wasn't enough money in her purse. Looking embarrassed with people around staring, Claudia stepped forward from the queue and paid the small shortage. So moved was Tota, she hugged the young girl, demanding to know her name and address so that the debt could be repaid soon as possible. It turned out Claudia lived only a stone throw from the Maradona's, later that day, Tota sent Diego round with an envelope carrying the cash.

 It was young love at first sight. The two swiftly became inseparable, where Diego went so did his girl for the next forty years. From Buenos Aires, Barcelona, Naples…There would be ups and downs, upsets, heartbreaks, marriage, children, monumental eruptions even, all born from a small, kind gesture in a grocery store. They had their first dance at the club social y Deportivo (Villa Parque social club) and have been dancing round each other, not always cheek to cheek since. Diego and Claudia. Amore.

 Now for tough love…

 On Sunday 27th February 1977, after only eleven appearances for Argentinos Juniors, sixteen-year-old Diego Armando Maradona pulled on his senior national shirt for the first time. At a packed *La Bombonera* stadium, with 60,000 present, this sacred turf, the home of Boca Juniors, Argentina took on Hungary with Diego on the bench. Come half-time, Menotti's side had gone goal crazy already winning 4-0. A hat-trick from winger Daniel Bertoni and one from the forward Leopoldo Luque. It had been a mismatch. Shortly after the interval, Luque added another to make it 5-0 and Menotti decided the time had finally arrived to unleash his young superstar. Argentina made a couple of substitutions, firstly, the future Tottenham Hotspur player Ricardo Villa came off for Jorge Benítez, then, as Diego Maradona came into view and *La Bombonera* erupted, on went Diego to a rapturous reception for the first of his ninety-one caps. 'MARADONNNA!' boomed out around the stadium! With just around thirty minutes to impress Maradona went straight on the warpath. He was quickly on the ball, brave, willing to take the Hungarians on, whom swiftly retaliated by handing out some dreadful tackling. From the touchline, Menotti watched, wincing heavily as Diego Maradona was clinically targeted. He also lost possession several times, clearly trying far too hard, but never stopped calling for the ball. When the opportunity was not on, Diego kept it simple. A team player, as the terraces sang his name it was clear a star, despite in its infancy, was being born before their eyes. When the time finally arose for Cesar Menotti's to announce his final World Cup 78 squad, there was little doubt amongst both the supporters and media that Diego would be in it, but the coach held grave doubts as to whether the youngster could handle the pressure of the ferocious intensity on the pitch and what would also be the emotional turmoil off it. A tournament on home soil that they simply had to win. The brief glimpses of what the Hungarian defenders had inflicted on Maradona would fade into comparison with the brutal treatment he could expect to receive off the Italians or Brazilians, to name just two. It was too much of a gamble for Menotti, he loved this kid and was not prepared to endanger Diego's fledgling career for a dangerous shot at glory, when already blessed with attackers such as Daniel

Bertoni, Leopoldo Luque, Rene Houseman and Mario Kempes. All this and besides, he was still just a boy? Call it tough love.

To gasps of shock, disappointment and no little anger across Argentina, Menotti's squad when announced did not include Diego Armando Maradona. It was indeed a courageous, even a kind act of mercy by the coach, one that ultimately paid off. Though at the time it wasn't viewed as such. Having already been named in Menotti's 25-man preliminary squad, Diego was taken aside and informed of the decision in the training base that he would not be making the cut. Maradona stormed out and sat crying his eyes out under a tree. 'How do I tell my dad?' he asked of an Argentinian reporter close to him, Carlo Ares. Diego raged, cried, tore into Menotti, immediately declaring he was retiring from international football. This, all at sixteen! The following week came an answer by pulling on the Argentinos Junior shirt and venting all his pent up frustration on poor Chacarita, scoring twice and setting up another brace as they won 5-0! The sheer anger from being snubbed clearly spurred Maradona on. His heart broken but determined to show Menotti that he had made a terrible mistake. A similar state of mind, of feeling wronged and a point to prove would show itself many times during his career, serving him well. Never more so than nine years later on a blisteringly, hot, June afternoon in Mexico against England in a World Cup quarter final. Maradona was at his pure best with a cause to fight for and with Menotti's decision hurting him like hell, leading the charge for Argentinos Juniors, whom were constantly fighting against the odds ignited the fires blazing inside this prodigious teenager. His dancing feet, blistering acceleration and fantastic finishing was already causing earthquakes both on and off the pitch in Argentina. The ground around him forever shaking with television cameras in his face, newspaper journalists desperate for a single comment. A kind of madness.

It was called being Diego.

CHAPTER SEVEN
THE MOTHERS OF THE DISAPPEARED: LOS DESAPARECIDOS
'Donde estan?'
'They are neither alive or dead. They are disappeared.'
President Jorge Videla

On Tuesday 30th November 1976, just eight months after Generals Videla and his henchmen came to power, twenty-five-year-old Nestor Di Vittoria, along with his wife Raquel, were snatched from their house by the secret police, disappearing into thin air. Nestor's fifty-one-year-old Mother Azucenza made desperate attempts with the authorities to find out what happened to them, but was met with only government indifference, deafening walls of silence. These people had been erased from public record with no official traces of arrests, or evidence of charges against them. Like ghosts, vanished from this earth. During her frantic and heart wrenching search, she came into contact with other Mothers and Grandmothers suffering the same plight. What began as a group of ladies coming together for a shoulder to cry on, to share their grief, swiftly became an organisation that would one day rock the very foundation of the Junta and ultimately in years to come help bring them to their knees. The decision was taken by the women to name themselves *Madres de Plaza de Mayo,* (The Mothers of the Plaza de Mayo). Situated in the very heart of Buenos Aires, the plaza lay opposite where Videla and his cronies held up at the *Casa Rosada*. Azucenza purposely chose this spot because of the political significance. Here was where it all began when the tanks first lined the roadside and the world changed overnight in Argentina.

Here would be where the women would no longer be ignored.

Here would be where they went public with the cause to find their missing loved ones.

Here would be where they ensured Videla and his uniformed Mafiosi heard them loud and very fucking clear. They each chose to wear a white scarf on their heads with the names of the disappeared inscribed upon it, representing purity and a Mother's love. The first gathering took place on a Saturday, soon they became weekly thirty minute vigils every Thursday afternoon. That first time, nervous and unsure, along with Azucenza Di Vittoria were twelve other brave ladies who simply couldn't take the silence anymore. On Saturday 30th April 1977, the women arrived in Plaza de Mayo clutching a letter which they intended to hand over to President Videla, demanding to know the whereabouts of their lost ones. Many of the women were terrified. Most came from small towns outside the city, some couldn't read or write, but all stood united. The authorities had forbidden any public gatherings threatening on pain of death. Once assembled at the Plaza, the police approached the women demanding they immediately vacated the area, or face arrest, even worse. Suddenly, led by Azucenza, they began grabbing each other in pairs, arm in arm, walking around the square in circles as if sight-seeing. It was sheer defiance. Thus, staying within the law and leaving the security forces at a loss what to do. So, they took photographs, filmed, soldiers with machine guns watched their every move from nearby, building rooftops. This was to be the first act of a movement that would shortly raise international awareness to the plight of the *Los desaparecidos*.

Tragically, each week their membership rose as the regime's blood lust grew and even more people were murdered. The authorities tried to mock, trivialize even their actions, calling them *las locas,* (the mad women). One Mother hit back at this claiming, 'Of course we are mad, they have taken our children.' They became emboldened. Even when the authorities arrested some of their numbers, the Mothers staged sit-ins at police stations. One time in Buenos Aires, when one of the members was snatched during a march, they found out her whereabouts, sixty Mothers stampeded into the police station raging, 'If you take one, you have to take us all!' At the centre of it always was Azucenza, a born leader. A stocky brunette who always carried a folder on her missing son, gently coaxing the other Mother's forward. Never back.

Their fame began to spread.

Articles began to appear in prestigious newspapers such as the Washington Post. Questions were being asked, 'Just what the hell was going on in Argentina?' The Generals decided this couldn't go on, plans were being made to end it. They considered the women to be politically subversive making them a legitimate target, at least in their eyes and when on Saturday 10th December, (International Human Rights Day), Azucenza placed the names of the missing in the newspaper *La Nacion,* it was the last straw, the call was made to round them up. Their man inside had done his duty, it was time to bring him home.

He was an actor, he was Al Pacino, he was Marlon Brando. He was twenty- seven-year-old Captain Alfredo Astiz, a member of Task Force 332, based in the Naval Mechanics School of *ESMA*. He was code named *El Ángel Rubio de la Muerte,* (The Blond angel of death). A specialist in the infiltration of human rights organisations . He never failed and once more had delivered to his Generals, more enemies of the state.

Alfredo Ignacio Astiz was born in Mar del Plata, on 8th November 1951. During the Dirty War, Astiz worked mostly undercover around Buenos Aires. He used the false name of Gustavo Niño. Astiz would join a group, gain their trust and then ultimately betray them to the dogs of the night. When enough information was gathered, he called time on his command performance, and the green Falcon Fords appeared from the darkness taking away the hooded prisoners, doomed to be tortured and murdered. One Mother back then who was looking for her son remembered Astiz well. The fair-skinned boy who called himself Gustavo Nino. 'He was a young man, well dressed, always very polite. We really believed he was the brother of a *desaparecido* and we felt very maternal and protective towards him. Azucenza especially. We used to surround him when the police attacked us in the square. We made a circle of Mothers to protect him. We used to say to him, 'Son, don't come. They'll kidnap you like they kidnapped your brother.'

On Thursday 8th December 1977, after a long stint undercover assuming the role of a heartbroken young man. Gustavo Nino, searching for his brother, Astiz organised the kidnapping of fourteen women associated with the Mothers of the Plaza de Mayo, plus Catholic nuns, Leonie Duquet and Alice Domon, whom had been helping out the

Mothers were also taken. They were all snatched from the church of the Santa Cruz, on the Holy day of the Immaculate Conception. None were ever seen alive again.

Azucenza Villaflor heard the news the next day. That night Azucenza's daughter recalled she was extremely agitated, saying to her, 'If I tell your Father, he won't let me do this anymore.' The following morning she went out to buy a newspaper, some fish for dinner. Later, witnesses said half a dozen armed men jumped out of Ford Falcons and grabbed Azucenza at a busy corner, with people watching, a block and a half from her home in southern Buenos Aires.

What happened to the women after being taken was unspeakable. They were dragged away, horribly tortured, some raped. Electric shocks would burn the prisoner's flesh. At the trial of one Argentine officer prosecuted for crimes against humanity revealed in 2005, the torturers liked to call these sessions 'barbecues.' Hell on Earth. The make-up wiped off, the acting over, Astiz was back as himself and witnessed torturing the French nuns in a cell by beating, half drowning them in water, before applying electrified, cattle prods to their breasts and mouths. Despite constant efforts by the French government to trace the nuns, all knowledge of them was denied by the Junta. Tragically,
by this time all the Mothers and the two nuns were dead.

Death Flights. a practice initiated by Admiral Luis Maria Mendia, usually after detention and torture. During 1977 and 1978, there were 180-200 death flights. Every Wednesday for two years, an estimated 1500 to 2000 people were murdered this way. In a sick side-show, lively music was sometimes played by the guards and the victims were made to dance for joy in celebration of the freedom that they were falsely told awaited them on being transferred. The prisoners were then vaccinated, injected with Pentothal and shortly after, a drowsiness/stupor would set in-from there the poor souls would be loaded onto army trucks and taken to an airfield. Pushed, carried into the waiting aircraft, stripped, then thrown naked out from thirteen thousand feet into the freezing waters of the South Atlantic or the River Plate. There were many in uniform whom refused point blank to have anything to do with these atrocities-mass slaughters. Soldiers on airfield guard later testified that they had seen many times, live people and corpses placed onto aircrafts ready for take-off, but it would always return empty.

Six month on from the original kidnappings of the women, the blond angel of death went back to work. He was sent to Paris spying on the resistance for the Mothers. There, he called himself Eduardo Escudero, this time around Astiz was recognised by an Argentinian forced into exile, his cover was blown. He next shown up working in the South African embassy in Paris, but all attempts to bring him to trial failed, as Astiz simply vanished once more. This creature of many faces.
Then,

in late December 1977, after several, heavy storms, unidentified corpses started to wash up on the Santa Teresita beaches, some 200 miles from Buenos Aires and were hastily removed by agents of the dictatorship, buried anonymously in mass graves at the General Lavalle Cemetery, in the capital. In March 1978, *Agence France-Presse* reported that the bodies found were believed to be the two nuns and several women of the *Mothers of the Plaza de Mayo*, but was never confirmed at the time by the

French government. Finally, in July 2005, the bodies were exhumed and DNA testing by an Argentine forensic team managed to identify the remains of Azucenza Villaflor de Vicenti and two other founders of the Mothers of the Plaza. Like their children they perished in the deep waters of the River Plate. Also, one of the French nuns was identified, Leonie Duquet. Autopsies revealed all died on impact. Azucenza's ashes were later intermed in Plaza de Mayo itself, an everlasting memorial to the lady's bravery and love for her missing son.

As for the blond angel of death? On 26th April 1982, Lieutenant Commander Alfredo Astiz surrendered to the invading, British marines in South Georgia, without firing a fucking shot. Obviously not fancying the odds when it came to someone able to fight back, the infamous Astiz threw his hands in the air and gave up. The French authorities applied immediately to question him about the disappearance of the nuns, Sisters Leonie Duquet and Alice Domon, but with relations between the United Kingdom and France not at their best during the South Atlantic conflict, this was denied and Astiz was repatriated home.

His luck continued to hold out when in 1987, Argentina passed the Pardon Law. An amnesty for all military and security officers involved in the Dirty War. Happily, the Angel's good fortune changed when in his absence three years later, a French court sentenced him to life imprisonment for the murder of the two nuns. The net was slowly, if painstakingly closing in, finally, after intense pressure, in 2005, justice caught up with him when the Argentine supreme court ruled that the inane Pardon Law was unconstitutional. The government immediately re-opened prosecution of seventies war crimes cases, with

Astiz amongst their top targets. At long, last Argentina was cleansing its stained heart. That same year he was detained on charges of kidnapping, torture and murder. The prosecution charges against Astiz were proved, the by-now, grey Angel of Death was convicted and sentenced to life imprisonment in Argentina, on 26th October 2011.

On Wednesday 14th June 1978, two surviving Mothers of the Disappeared, Graciela Lois and Lita Boitano, secretly entered the *Estadio Monumental,* during the second round match between Italy and West Germany. Staying hidden from soldiers, they made their way to both dressing rooms leaving leaflets and pamphlets on the player's benches denouncing the Junta and telling the story of their missing ones. *Los desaparecidos*. If caught, both women's fate was guaranteed, torture and certain death, yet they found the courage to try and expose to a wider world the truth about Argentina.

Such bravery.

The Mothers of the Disappeared were not going away.

CHAPTER EIGHT
A GOOD MAN IN BUENOS AIRES
'READ ALL ABOUT IT!'

1959. Hull born, British journalist Robert J. Cox was just twenty-six-years-old, when he first arrived in Argentina and was hired as a copy editor for the *Buenos Aires Herald.* An English language newspaper based in the capital. Cox was ambitious, a breath of fresh air, he had a way of bringing people along with him. His influence on a newspaper founded in 1876, was huge-a dusty, old publication stuck in the past had new life breathed into it. Cox had them change their design and reach-rising from a small community-oriented newspaper of the Buenos Aires English speaking community, to a nationwide, respected, national daily. In 1968, he was promoted to publisher, seven years later under his direction, the *Herald* moved to new and better premises with its own printing plant, in Buenos Aires, at 455 Azopardo Street. In Cox's hands, especially during the coming storm of the 1976 military Junta coup, whilst the rest of the media shut their eyes to the brutality and horror of everyday life in Argentina, the *Herald,* under the Englishman from Hull's direction, kept theirs's wide open. It gained huge prestige for standing up to much intimidation and threats from the Junta. At Cox's initiative, the *Herald* were the first to report on people going missing, the kidnappings, being snatched off the street by the authorities in broad daylight. Where elsewhere nothing was wrote about such shocking acts, the *Buenos Aires Herald* blazed out in indignation.

The telephone would ring in the Azopardo street office-Cox would answer and hear, 'You can't write about kidnaps and murders. Nothing, not a fucking word!' After speaking to fellow editors, he decided to carry on, do and be damned, Cox was going to publish all the cases in which a relative of a disappeared person made a complaint. Soon, as this became public knowledge, the Mothers of the disappeared descended en masse on the *Herald's* office to tell of their sons whom had been abducted. Azopardo Street was but a few blocks away from the Plaza de Mayo, with the *Herald* being the only newspaper courageous enough to help at the time, it was for them a single chink of light. Especially when the *Herald* put the Mothers on its front cover. No longer was the *Buenos Aires Herald* a simple publication for the British community, it became a beacon of hope for all Argentinians living in this horrific, dystopian nightmare. Cox would write the Editorial-the only part of the newspaper printed in Spanish. In there was the wicked-sweet truth against all the lies and damnations of the Military junta propaganda machine. Oh, they were beginning to hate Bob Cox from Hull so much.

Cox recalls, 'The day of the coup, they called to tell us it was forbidden to report on attacks or bodies found on the streets. People began to come to the newspaper. I asked them to request an *habaes corpus*. The Junta forbid any news of kidnappings or corpses without official confirmation, so we took the *habeas corpus* requests as confirmation. What was important to me, was to save people. I went to them with lists of names and said I would not put anything in the paper, if these people showed up alive. We were very lucky as some of these people were saved.'

Cox went to report on the meetings at Plaza de Mayo-the Mothers of the disappeared, at great risk to himself. He became good friends with Azucenza Villaflor De Vicenti, it was Cox who also personally discovered that the military were using the crematoriums at Chacarita cemetery to incinerate the *Los Desaparecidos*.

His card was being marked,

and in 1977, the authorities sent their thugs to the *Herald*'s office demanding he left with them. Cox remembers looking out of the window, down below was a Ford Falcon and a Peugeot with a driver looking as if he had just came off the set of a Spaghetti western. A Mexican bandit with crazy eyes and a swaggering moustache. He was taken to a detention centre-the grim realities of what was really occurring. Led down to a basement where the first thing you noticed was a huge Swastika hung on a wall. After being made to undress, they put Cox in a tiny cell, naked, leaving him there for hours. His detainment though had been duly noted by powerful figures in Buenos Aires, such as the American diplomat and good friend of Cox, Tex Harris, sent to Argentina by President Jimmy Carter. Harris immediately contacted Videla and made his feeling known. Such strong, international pressure worked, Cox was swiftly freed with no explanation. A lucky soul. From that moment, he and his family lived in a permanent state of threats that would eventually see them having to leave Argentina in 1980, but before that for a while, Cox remained a jagged thorn in the Junta's side. The jackals being held on a leash, for bigger jackals had informed them to 'Stay the fuck away from Bob Cox.'

They would in time though be let loose.

'The World Cup was a moment of horror and at the same time a moment of glory.' Bob Cox.

Come the 1978 World cup, Cox's friend Azucenza, along with many others of the Mothers and their close circle had been murdered, but still those left gathered at Plaza de Mayo, only the difference this time around, the world press were present to listen to their pleas. Many of them simply after a good story and here was one. Knowing there would never be a better time, on Wednesday 17th May 1978, an editorial appeared in the *Herald* that went off like a bomb at the *Casa Rosada*

'Although the presence of the Mothers of the Plaza de Mayo has been to a large extent ignored by the local press, they are part of the schedule of almost all visiting newspaper journalists and television channels. Their sad story has gone around the world. Their image on television screens will be the image of Argentina during the next Football World Cup.'

The world was coming to Argentine shores, in the Junta's eyes, Bob Cox was letting it be known in his fucking, English, kind of way where the bodies were buried. Patience, despite the gringo's saying Cox was untouchable, began to run dreadfully thin.

Still, the *Herald* went looking, asking questions no one else dared. They published the story of the kidnapping of forty-four-year-old journalist Julian Delgado, the editor of *El Cronista Comercial* and *Mercado* magazine. Delgado disappeared on Sunday 4'th June, just three days after the start of the World Cup. It was four o'clock in the afternoon. Delgado told his wife María that he would go out and get them something for tea. She never saw him again.

Nobody did. This article saw Cox sent for by the Argentine Interior Minister Albano Harguindeguy, at *Casa Rosada*. Another Junta hawk, deep up to his neck in blood and corruption. A furious Harguindeguy tried reprimanding Cox, claiming that Delgado had committed suicide. A few days before the World Cup began, he, along with thirty other top ranking editors and journalists, were summoned to see Harguindeguy and lectured on what could and not be published. He told them that the world was focused on Argentina, they had to present a 'Perfect image of the nation.' Now, Cox was back, taking no notice of the Minister's words, determined to carry on attempting to bring the Junta's dark atrocities into the full light of day for all to see.

Cox was like a dog with a bone-to Videla and the Generals, like a knife in the throat. He sent letters demanding information be released about the kidnappings of a family called the Eroles, then, two days later another letter wanting to know what had become of a high-school student called Alejandra Naftal, who had also vanished off the face of the earth?

Careful not to be tarnished with a 'leftish agenda' brush, a usual trick of the Junta, he also ensured the *Montoneros* were brought to task when needed be, Though clever with it, never more so, than a piece aimed towards a world-wide audience, as the circus of the *Mundial* drew ever closer. 'The visiting journalists will soon see that this is not Russia. The 'mad Mothers of Plaza de Mayo' wouldn't be allowed to be even close to the Red Square. You will see that Argentina is an exceptionally peaceful place, not at all similar to the ferocious military dictatorship on which they have been reading in the ultra- leftist press. But they will soon be able to ask embarrassing questions, such as why do they keep Professor Alfredo Bravo, the leader of human rights, detained without charge? And why has Adolfo Perez Esquivel been arrested more than a year ago without charge, a man opposed to the violence who had been nominated for the Nobel Peace Prize in 1976?'

Under Cox insistence, the *Herald* never stopped reporting on the Mothers of the Disappeared, as the World Cup continued on, there was ever increasing interest from the world press about these sad, broken-hearted, old ladies walking round Plaza de Mayo, clutching pictures of their missing sons, wearing white headscarves. 'One of the good things about the tournament will be that the international press will visit Argentina,' said Cox at the time. 'Journalists with quizzical minds will go hunting to find out just what's going on and will swiftly realise you don't just see world class football here, but also come to understand they kill people too.' Hardly the buzz words for any World Cup poster, one could only imagine the kind of furore these words caused at the *Casa Rosada.*

All came to a head one afternoon at the Plaza de Mayo, when in front of the world's television crews, some of the Mothers came forward to tell their stories before the camera. One, Enriqueta Maroni, spoke with tears falling, desperately after information about her two missing children, 'They have come to our houses, they have raided them, they have stolen everything they have wanted and they have taken our children. The Army has done that. That's, why we beg you, you are our last hope. Please help us, help us, please. You are our last hope.'

Alongside, the foreign media, the *Buenos Aires Herald* were also present, reporting and photographing everything they heard and saw. This received massive coverage from around the globe, specifically European television media. It was devastating stuff for the Junta to have to handle, anyone else, their carcass would have been dripping blood, chained to a cell wall, being cut to pieces.

'And when the journalists began interviewing the Mothers, two patrol cars appeared. The uniformed police approached the scene, but remained watching from the edges and then, plainclothes police intervened. Dutch television recorded a policeman insisting Mothers to 'circulate' through the square. They never did. …They kept telling their stories.'

Come Argentina's ultimate, footballing, triumph on 25th May, Cox wrote, 'The jubilation was so great that the massive celebrations of 1945, for the end of the war in Europe paled before the frantic joy that seized the twenty-six million inhabitants of the country.' He himself went outside with his wife Maud and their five children to celebrate the triumph. As all Argentina bathed in a euphoric, blinding, nationwide cascade of confetti, for a brief moment Cox thought maybe this could trigger a change?

He was wrong.

On Sunday 16th December 1979, Robert J Cox wrote his final editorial in the *Buenos Aires Herald.* Two days later, the Mothers replied in *La Prensa.*

'Thank you for being one of the very few journalists who showed through their professional actions, understanding for our pain and made us feel less alone.' Ultimately, with unrestrained venom, the dogs were finally let loose on Cox. An attempted assassination and kidnapping, left him little choice but to get out and in December of the following year, they finally left the country. A letter threatening one of his children, Peter, was the last straw.

'Dear Peter,

we know that you are worried about the things that happen to the families of your friends and that you are afraid that something similar could happen to you and your father. We do not eat children raw at breakfast. Considering the fear you all have and that your dad is a high-level journalist, who is more useful to us alive than dead, we have decided to send you this little note as a warning. For this reason and in consideration to the work your father does, we offer him and all of you, Peter. Victoria, Robert, David and Ruth, the option to leave the country, where you run the risk of being assassinated. Do what you prefer and tell 'daddy and mummy' to sell the house and the cars and to go work in Paris in another of the Herald's newspapers.'

Cox and his family moved to Charleston, South Carolina, where he became an editor of The Post and Courier, run by the same publishing group that owned the *Buenos Aires Herald*. In 2005, the Buenos Aires Legislature recognised him for his valour during the dictatorship. Robert Cox deserved a multitude of credit for shining a light on a nation ruled by monsters, for a while as the *Herald* stood alone, it was the traditional call of the newspaper to herald the news, 'Read all about it!'

No better ending for a good man in Buenos Aires.

CHAPTER NINE
EL CAPITAN

1977. When Diego Maradona made his international debut for the *La Albiceleste,* the hugely, respected, twenty-nine-year-old left back, the team Captain Jorge Carrascosa, gave him a couple of words to encourage as he ran on as a second half substitute and Diego was away! Carrascosa was Cesar Menotti's second Lieutenant on the field, his good amigo, his most trusted-two men alike in so many ways. Their footballing ideals, politics, both had sworn an oath to play for the people, not the diabolical, uniformed, murderous, scumbags, whom ruled above them causing untold misery. Menotti had no doubt that come *Mundial 78*, it would be Jose leading out his side to take on the world. Carrascosa was a ferocious, but fair competitor. They called him *El Lobo*, (The wolf). A player of great temperament, a superb leader of men. With him on the field, in their nation's most fateful hour, *El Flaco* would feel far more confident, but whilst he had made peace with himself for forming a pact with Videla and his horned devils, Carrascosa did no such things. Days before the squad was announced, he sensationally quit on the spot retiring from international football. The Captain, 'The soul of the team,' *El Flaco's* words, had thrown away the armband, for he had no wish to stain such a precious article with the dead Argentinians whom had already been murdered. Carrascosa had given up the opportunity to go down in history/folklore, as one of the great heroes. Instead, that honour would eventually go to River Plate's Daniel Passarella. Jose Carrascosa passed on such kinds of glory, for he needed to sleep at night. The story goes that on the evening before having to deliver his final list, Cesar approached Jose to see if there was any chance at all of him changing his mind. No thank you amigo' was the reply, that, was that. Menotti knew it was unwise, indeed worthless to argue the point. They shook hands, embraced and *El Lobo* walked away for good. 'Physically and technically I was fine,' recalled Carrascosa. 'But it was inside you, that you had to be fit. And what was happening made me sick.'

  Real doubts first took hold for him during the 1974 World Finals in West Germany, where the possibility of hanging up his boots early entered Carrascosa's mind. On 23rd June 1974, in the final games of the first round, Argentina needed to beat Haiti by three goals and pray that Poland overturned Italy. This duly occurred, but what stuck in Jose's throat was the fact his team mates had offered the Poles a $25,000 incentive to ensure the Italians were beaten 2-1. 'I must do my best without you giving me anything in return,' he later said. 'One must distinguish between things that are good and things that are wrong.'

So, it was come 1978, after thirty appearances for Argentina, that Jose Omar Carrascosa, let heart rule head and to the shook of all, maybe Cesar Menotti apart, stood down. The thought of being seen to carry the flag for one of the most frightening and despicable dictatorships ever witnessed on a blood-soaked continent, well used to playing host to uniformed maniacs drunk on power-obsessed with controlling a population for their own sick whims, was simply a game, a tournament too far. Just two years later, at the age of thirty-one-years- old, the wolf retired from the game altogether with his beloved Huracan. He left with no fuss, Carrascosa's final game came on Sunday 2nd December 1979. A silent hero for those who knew what lay behind the mask. A true *El Capitan,* whose heart was simply too big to go along with the grand illusion set to follow. His nation bent by terror to the knees, simply not allowed to look up on fear of having a bullet put through the head.

Jose lived with no regrets, for he saw the birth of Maradona in the blessed colours of *La Albiceleste.* 'I lived the joy of being the captain when Diego was born for the national team. I have a great affection for him.' He played against Pele for Huracan in a friendly against Santos. Experienced the beautiful cruelty of Johan Cruyff, in the 1974 World Cup Finals, as the Prince of *Oranje* tore them, Argentina apart. 'The three best footballers I have seen,' said Carrascosa. Summing up his decision to not play in Mundial 78, is best left to *El Lobo's* answer to the question asked him a million and one times.

'Why?'

'Because you must win or lose, but always with dignity,' he would reply.

'That's why I never regretted my choice.'

CHAPTER TEN
JUST AN ILLUSION

Burson-Marsteller: Death Inc

Everything can be made clean if you throw enough money at it.

So, it was the Argentinian Junta hired the New York, American advertising agency, Burson-Marsteller, to ensure come the 1978 World Cup, Argentina would appear to the rest of the planet, a South American paradise of love-a Garden of Eden. The hideous, bestial, states crimes hidden behind a plethora of shiny, happy, clappers and slogans. It could never have been a question of conscience with Burson, for when the bottom line was dollars, countless of them, tears like reality could be easily swept away. Hidden

'It is of paramount importance that Argentina begins to speak with one voice in the nations of the world. And that can only be achieved through a highly controlled communications program.'

This was part of a huge document the agency put together in order to convince the Junta that they were the go-to guys for such a heinous task. Little did Burson know the decision had already been taken by President Videla, alongside Massera and Agosti, to try and 'Clean up' their image. (Like wiping dog shit off your shoe).Welcome to Argentina, Burson-Marsteller. Watch you don't step on a murdered corpse as you celebrate your good-self on a winning presentation.

With serious complaints being fired at them from Human Rights organisations around the world, it was clear to the Junta, on one of the rare situations they could actually agree on anything, that specialists to counteract the serious 'Adverse propaganda' were required. In Mexico, June

1976, the agreement was secretly sealed with a $1.1million dollars contract to a subsidiary of Burson's, Comunicaciones Interamericanas SA.

'Twenty six Million Argentinians will play in the world Cup.'

This was swiftly changed by Argentinians to 'Twenty six million people will pay for the World Cup!'

For Burson-Marsteller, the country needed to go from black to white, hell to heaven in just a short period before *Mundial 78* began. They operated on the basic code of, 'It is not necessary to speak well of one-self, but it is necessary that others speak well of us.' A huge publicity blitz was organised. Burson listed from major countries, their top magazines, newspapers, radio and television stations. Plus a list of established journalists, editors, authors and other elite, media sources, who would needed to be invited to see the 'Real' Argentina. All on arrival would be handed documents and brochures, even a couple of Videla's recent speeches pontificating about the beauty of the Argentine soul. They would be taken for lunches, managed walks, guided tours. Plane and coach trips to the nominated, World Cup cities. Giving them a feel of a nation at peace with itself and the leadership. All those chosen to speak to the visitors, handpicked. Whilst, all the time, existing in the shadows, lurked an evil attempting to bury its true-self behind the blessings of Junta, favoured Catholic Priests. During the morbid clean up the number of murders, kidnappings and disappearances increased in fury. Behind the peace wall innocent people were being nailed upon it and tortured. These not the 'Personal experiences' talked of by Burson executives when speaking to the invited journalists from different parts of the world, asking if they had enjoyed their stay in Argentina?

An enthusiastic President Videla bought in wholeheartedly to the Burson-Marsteller project, come the summer of 78, this strange new world where the blood was wiped off whitewashed walls and the Mothers of the disappeared cried themselves to sleep at night, truly became the face of Argentina to outsiders. Any negative coverage abroad was challenged by Videla calling it 'Anti-Argentine'. The domestic press, with one blazing exception, the *Buenos Aires Herald*, wrote what they were told. Through this many Argentinians were cajoled, confused, if not personally affected, unsure just what to believe.

In the months leading up to the tournament, shanty towns and impoverished neighbourhoods, even just unsightly buildings were flattened-the residents forcibly removed by soldiers to keep them away from foreign tourist's eyes. Welcome to the land of oz.

Welcome to the world of Burson-Marsteller.

With their help Argentina was showing its best face, if by far the wrong one.

But, as they say.

Everything can be made clean if you throw enough money at it.

Buenos Aires. The *Estadio Monumental.*

The opening Ceremony.

It was a cold, but sunny day...

Thursday 1st June 1978. The Pope was good enough not to turn up, but did send his blessing from Rome, delivered by the Catholic Cardinal of Argentina, Juan Carlos Aramburu. The very same Cardinal who publicly disputed any notion of mass-murder by the Junta, making the astonishing claim that the nation's disappeared were in fact, 'All happily living in Europe.' To the awful backdrop of an out of tune military band, President Jorge Videla pinned a medal on the FIFA President Joao Havelange, thanking him for everything. A thousand doves of peace, though many didn't look like doves, more pigeons, were let free into the skies above Buenos Aires and not a five minute walk away, Argentina's Auschwitz, at *ESMA*, didn't even have the decency to shut the doors for a month. Also, a few miles further south, drugged, innocent people were being thrown alive into the River Plate from military aeroplanes at a great height to their deaths.

'At long last the world can see the true face of Argentina,' said Havelange.

How fucking true…

Hundreds of white uniformed children moved into position to choreograph the words *Argentina 78*. So, it began. This orchestrated propaganda on a grand scale, rumoured to have been organised by Josef Goebbels himself flashed around the world on television. As Argentinian blue and white swamped every orifice of the newly revamped *Monumental*, the other fifteen nation's flags, whom would be playing in the tournament were hardly seen, paraded that afternoon almost as an afterthought. As if the eleventh World Cup finals were already a foregone conclusion. As if? President Jorge Videla's welcoming address to the 80,000 crowd and world-wide audience met with little enthusiasm. His line, 'The tournament would be played under a sign of peace,' causing quiet, gasps of incredulity across the stadium. The Argentinian people clearly sending out a coded message to all whom were watching.

'For God's sake help us.'

It was an elegant building, a beautiful building.

In clear earshot of all that was occurring in the stadium, just a few hundred yards away, hidden inside the tree-lined campus of *Escuela de Mecanica de la Armada. ESMA*-the Navy-Officers School of Mechanics, or to give it the proper title, the regime's most obscene, concentration camp, all continued on as normal. Cattle prods were the first torture item used on arrival. This to signal a welcome to the prison. It was also used as a tool for rape, whatever your gender. Recordings of Adolf Hitler's speeches were played over speakers. The smell of urine and faeces overpowering from the tiny cells where existing prisoners, many hooded, weakened from infected, torture wounds waiting for their end. The state wanted vengeance, names, the guards set out to get them. The techniques used depraved. When it had been decided the prisoner was no more of use, they were stripped as earlier described with the ghastly murders of the Mothers of the Disappeared and the two French nuns, given pentothal to be drugged. From the detention centre, put on a plane to where the River Plate meets the Atlantic, a dark abyss and thrown into the ocean.

'They fell like ants,' claimed a former, naval Captain Emir Sisul Hess.

This was just the first floor of *ESMA*.

 The second, a maternity ward of hellish sorts, where Mothers gave birth, only to have their babies stolen from them straight away-they themselves were mostly murdered. The new born adopted by military families, friends of the Junta, or simply sold on to the highest bidder. Horror on a biblical scale. This was the largest, most well-known of these so-called detention centres across Argentina, that were in reality nothing more than concentration camps. The last call of the *Los Desaparecidos.* No mere football competition was going to let such important work of state stop. Indeed, whilst prisoners were chained naked onto bloodstained cell wall with electrodes attached to their testicles, being skinned alive, they could hear loud the roar of the football crowd. This was the reality of Argentina 78. What went on in these accursed buildings, an affront to humanity, equally depraved as anything ever witnessed. Of the 4,700 men, women and teenagers who entered *ESMA,* only a handful survived. One human rights worker was quoted as saying, 'Videla and his thugs could have taught the Nazis a thing or two.' There even existed an office set up by the navy supposedly to provide information on the whereabouts of missing people…Staffed by a naval priest.

Those trying so hard to expose the reality behind the illusion never stopped digging, but when sport and politics come together, the overwhelming stench of money and corruption is strong enough to hide any truth. Amnesty International tried all in their power under the slogan of, *Yes to Football, No to Torture!*

A poster of a football made from lines of barbed wire. Some players did refuse to go, such as the World Cup winning, brilliant, West German defender Paul Breitner-a fierce advocate of Human Rights. Also, the Dutch Prince of *Oranje*, their inspiration playmaker, the great Johan Cruyff. At that time undoubtedly the world's greatest player. Nearly three decades later, Cruyff let slip in a radio interview he never played in the *Mundial* because of any protest, the real reason for not travelling to Argentina had been for so long wrapped in a veil of silence. Earlier in

1978, there had been a kidnap attempt on him in Barcelona, where a rifle was placed at his head. That it failed mattered little, for the family were left traumatised after Cruyff's children witnessed all. Because of such there was no chance he was leaving them to travel to a banana Republic-fucked-up country, in the midst of a civil war. A place where assassinations and kidnappings were a common, everyday occurrence and run by a sadistic, regime appearing, seemingly, intent on stealing and murdering, anything or anybody, they could lay their hands on.

No wonder Johan decide to watch on the television.

As for his Holland? Before going to the World Cup, the Dutch players received detailed information about the atrocities that were taking place in Argentina. 'They all knew,' claimed Freek de Jong, of SKAN, the Dutch Humanitarian Organisation. The international midfielder Wim Van Hanegen said, 'If the people of SKAN call me, I will pass the phone to my dog.' Holland's ABN bank gave the Junta millions of dollars in credit, God knows where that ended up? The government had no problem of the heart selling them many Fokker planes that could have served to throw people alive into the River Plate. Finally, why should the Dutch players have been forced to take a stand, when on the day of the opening ceremony, their own ambassador in Buenos Aires declared that 'General Videla is a honourable man?'

Despite huge pressure to shift the tournament to Belgium and Holland, FIFA remained unmoved. Ultimately, the human rights stance was overlooked in favour of preserving the footballing, political/status quo, a gigantic money making scam. Videla, like many world leaders had little interest in football, but he saw an opportunity and jumped on anyone's throat daring to try and stop it.

CHAPTER ELEVEN
SAY IT AINT SO ANTONIO
ARGENTINA V HUNGARY (FIRST ROUND MATCH)

The *Estadio Monumental*. Friday 2nd June 1978. As the Hungarian coach edged ever closer to the stadium surrounded by supporters on all sides, the sheer passion, the desire for the home nation swiftly become apparent. It was scenes of frenzied madness that began as a whisper, one man, a lone voice on the sidewalk. Then, it grew until like a bomb exploding from the masses. *'ARGENTINA!'* Even the soldiers in charge of ensuring the Hungarian's safety joined in with their countrymen's chants. Thousands jumping up and down with eyes bursting out of their heads. Utter delirium. They banged on the side of the coach. They shouted insults, they made throat-slitting gestures caught up in the moment. The players on board watched on in astonishment. Finally, after what was deemed a suitable amount of intimidatory time, an Argentine military officer clapped his hands-a signal to clear the way for the coach to enter the stadium.
Job done.

Elsewhere, Argentina tv footage shown President Jorge Videla's cavalcade being swiftly ushered through a side-entrance. His blacked-out Chevrolet escorted by two motorcycle riders at the front and back, plus the added comfort of two jeeps fixed with heavy-machine guns, followed by a truckload of soldiers. All armed to the teeth with enough firepower to kick start another coup. With Videla was Admiral Massera and the head of Argentina's

World Cup organising committee, the newly promoted Vice-Admiral Carlos Lacoste. His had been a remarkable rise up the ranks since General Omar Actis' unfortunate demise. The cameras followed the three men step out of the car to a barrage of salutes, as they entered inside and out of sight.

   Across the *Monumental*, 80,000 people were slowly working themselves into a frenzy. A raging sea of blue/white flags. the two teams appeared from beneath the stadium into view, walking in line over the running track greeted by a vast, white, glittering snowstorm of ripped up paper dropping down from the grandstands. The Argentinian players gazed around with looks of sheer disbelief, maybe a little fear also. For such fanaticism on show can either cause sportsmen to aspire to levels of greatness, or see them fall from the stars shattering into a thousand pieces. The tall, hunched figure of Cesar Menotti briefly came into view, but swiftly disappeared again amidst a barrage of photographers and cameramen. The noise beyond reason-almost description. Like a jet liner passing ten yards above your head. This was the World cup.

This was Argentina 78.

The players lined up for the national anthems with Argentina's played first. As it began, the television cameras focused in on Videla and the gathered Generals in the VIP box, all stood like statues to attention. Sporting fresh haircuts, newly trimmed moustaches, wearing their finest attire. Some in uniform, all sparkling and polish, covered in medals and braid. Others wearing long overcoats. Their faces, solemn and sober. The world watching. The Hungarian anthem next up, well respected, polite applause. Almost time…

Cesar Menotti's Argentina were a team set up to go after teams with the onus most definitely on attack. A new era, a new Argentina. Foremost amongst them leading the charge, a dashing, leggy, twenty-six-year old centre-forward recalled from overseas playing in Valencia, Spain. Mario Kempes. On his slim, shoulders lay mainly the hopes, prayers and dreams of an entire nation. The players broke away for a brief warm up. Hungary were a decent team, already in qualification they had knocked out a powerful Soviet Union. In their twenty-two-year old's Andras Torocsik and Tibor Niyilasi, they possessed two of the best young talents in the competition. Menotti's men, already playing under immense pressure were going to be severely tested by a fine new Hungarian generation. Easily the best since Puskas and his Magyar cohorts rampaged through the early fifties. As the seconds were counted down, the Portuguese referee Antonio Garrido looked at his watch and blew to begin the contest, starting an extraordinary, at the same time wretchedly, dark, Argentinian tale.

Twelve minutes in Hungary drew first blood. A rasping drive by their midfielder Zombari, fumbled by the goalkeeper Ubaldo Fillol and from six-yards, to the horror of the home crowd, the darting Cspao fired into an empty goal! A biting, cold, chill of dread drifted over the entire stadium. The home team restarted, as did the crowd-like the arrival of thunder they exploded back into life. A rousing 'ARGENTINA!' roared from across the massed, terraces of the *Monumental* once more. Immediately, Menotti's men reacted to such passionate support driving forward in search of a swift equaliser. Newell Old Boys' Americo Gallego, Huracan's Rene Houseman and their little magician Osvaldo Ardiles, dominated midfield. The passing crisp and neat, lightning quick, effective. Consistently fed into the feet of Kempes and his side-kick hitman, Leopoldo Luque. It took only three minutes. A thunderous long-range shot by Mario Kempes rebounded off the Hungarian keeper Gudjar, for Luque to pounce. 1-1! All around joyful carnage! The game restarted, the Hungarians regrouped and it swiftly became apparent Lajos Baroti's men were a ferocious band, meeting the intimidatory, roughhouse, Argentine tackling with an eye for eye policy. Menotti may have managed to banish the defensive mindset of his team, but their traditionally, cynical ploy of hacking down opponents if they dared to have the temerity to go past them remained. It was a fast, moving, exciting, at times, brutal contest. No quarter asked or given by either team. As for the referee? Antonio Garrido had managed well up until that point, showing no sign of cracking, despite the blazing, furore raining down upon his head from the terraces. The second half saw little change with both teams going all out for another goal. The Hungarians matching the Argentinians in the quality of their football and ability in the dark arts when needed. The Magyars played mostly on the counter attack with the dashing Torocsik and the incisive, probing Niylasi horrifying the crowd whenever on the ball. Each time the two Hungarians moved into Argentina's half, it was greeted by deafening, piercing, whistles. Shrieks and cries from the terraces, even some breaking into prayer! Equally though for the host nation, their front two partnership of Mario Kempes and Leopoldo Luque were causing heart attacks amongst the Hungarians. The naturally left-footed Kempes, the right of Luque, blending at times to perfection. Both tall and powerful with each possessing great poise and technique, they cut a mesmeric, breath-taking sight, rampaging towards the Magyar penalty area, Seven minutes remained of what had been a fantastic, open, game of football. Many of the crowd by that time reduced to watching the match through their fingers as a goal for either team would surely win it. Argentina kept attacking in waves-a scramble in the Hungarian penalty box saw the ball run lose for the brilliant, Independiente winger, Daniel Bertoni, a Buenos Aires home boy, to flash a shot into the net. Madness erupted inside the *Estadio Monumental!* Total, unadulterated, fucking madness!

 The Hungarians cherry red shirts were on the turf, a wonderful attempt to stem the blue and white Argentine hurricane looked to have been for nothing. The frustrations clear also as they restarted. Andras Torocsik imploding, stupidly hurling a ball away, after being denied a throw in. Hardly a hanging offence, but in ungodly haste, the referee Garrido reached for his pocket and after receiving a first half yellow card, Torocsik was flashed a red. Ironic, because for most of the game the Magyar talisman had been subjected to the kind of tackles that erred worryingly toward savage by the South Americans. The electronic scoreboard displayed time almost up. Argentina were content to just keep the ball-the whistling and cries from the crowd for the referee Garrido to end their pain, came with an almost, tormented plea. Hungarian frustration spilled over when Tibor Niylasi snapped, lashing out at defender Alberto Tarantini, leaving him reeling in pain on the turf. Obviously still upset at seeing his teammate so unjustly ordered off, Niylasi simply nailed the unfortunate, curly-haired, if slightly unhinged, at times, Tarantini, in brutal retaliation. Off he tramped, head down. On the touchline the Magyar coach Baroti appeared devastated. Not only was this game lost, but his two best players for the next match against Italy. Ten days before the tournament began, after a friendly against England at Wembley, he had confided in journalist Brian Glanville that, 'Everything, even the air, was in favour of Argentina.' Something was in the air. Finally, it was over, the end of a magnificent, if, sadly, tainted contest. Antonio Garrido's whistle saw an eruption of emotion and joy amongst the crowd. The Hungarians players, those who remained on the pitch remonstrated with the Portuguese official, but he simply waved them away. High up in the VIP box, Videla and his fellow Junta members applauded a hard-fought victory and just maybe the criminally weak Garrido. A man in black, who for the rest of his life would never have to buy a drink in Buenos Aires again.

Down below on the running track, the lean figure of Cesar Menotti with the proverbial cigarette in hand. He pulled up the collar on his long, black overcoat, as the night chill began to bite deep. There was no punching the air or backslapping. Indeed, Menotti appeared oblivious to the hysterical scenes breaking out around him and simply walked away back down the tunnel.

El Flaco, knowing well the victory over an impressive, but now broken Hungary was one the they had gotten away with by the skin of their teeth. Much work remained to do for Argentina, whom were by no means a finished article, far from unbeatable. The Magyars shown the defence could be got at, much better sides lay in wait to test them, and end the dream.

In discussing the aftermath of the late Hungarian meltdown, many were whispering it had been given a huge, helping, hand from the referee. Had Antonio Garrido been bought? Overall, despite the clearly over the top decision to send off Torocsik, it appeared more likely

Garrido simply fell victim to the simmering, hellish, atmosphere, the enormous, pressure placed upon his head by the *Monumental* crowd. So, in all, it was more likely Garrido simply bottled it. After the victory against Hungary, one smiling Junta official remarked to Leopoldo Luque as they were leaving the stadium to board their bus that, 'This could turn out to be the group of death, as far as you are concerned.' Luque later recalled foremost on his mind at the time was not the football, or the fervid celebrations breaking out across Buenos Aires, it was that earlier in the day, the brother of a close friend of his had disappeared. His body later found by villagers on the banks of the River Plate,

with concrete attached to his legs…

CHAPTER TWELVE
LES MISERABLES
ARGENTINA V FRANCE (FIRST ROUND MATCH)
The *Estadio Monumental*: Tuesday 6th June 1978.

A miscarriage of justice? Robbed and cheated more so. After a first half at the *Monumental*, during which Argentina and France fought out a breathless, if scoreless encounter, the host nation were gifted a penalty by the seemingly hapless, Swiss referee Jean Dubach. After a narrow 2-1 loss to Enzo Bearzot's wonderfully, compelling Italy in their opening match, Michel Hidalgo's France was desperate for victory to stay alive in the tournament. The French had exchanged attacks blow for blow with Cesar Menotti's, rampaging outfit from the first whistle. As against the Hungarians, a sublime, wonderfully, open game of football broke out. With half-time almost upon them, the scoreboard showing forty-four minutes, thirty-three seconds, Mario Kempes surged forward from the centre-circle to leave a host of chasing French shirts in his wake. An electrifying Kempes chipped a delightful left-footed pass into the path of partner, Leopoldo Luque. As the noise level from the *Monumental* soared, Luque raced into the penalty area, steadied himself to fire when his path was suddenly blocked by the powerful, black, Marseille defender Marius Tresor. The quick-thinking Tresor had anticipated Luque's run putting his body on the line, between the forward and the French goal. Still, Luque attempted to get a shot away, but Tresor lunged to prevent this also-only to then fall. Wholly unaware and unable to stop his hand touching the ball. Frantic Argentinian arms went up demanding a penalty, though surely knowing their calls would be ignored for Tresor's, alleged, minor, indiscretion.

For it would have been like blaming a man getting wet because it was raining. Implausible and unthinkable, a travesty, if awarded. However, to rising French fears, Marius Tresor's foremost amongst them, Dubach appeared unsure. A full thirty yards away from where Tresor went down, he decided a second opinion was called for. In scenes of utter consternation, Dubach raced across to his Canadian linesman Werner Winsemann, who must have been thinking,

'Please God man, don't drop this one in my fucking lap!' The two officials conversed amid an atmosphere of unbridled, tension, Dubach astonishingly asked Winsemanne, 'Linesman, inside or out?' The incredulous Canadian stared at him, not really sure what to say. Before he could reply the referee attempted to return to the fray, only to be grabbed on the arm by Winsemanne. He whispered into Dubach's ear, 'Surely from my position that is not fair to ask me?' A clearly disturbed Dubach glared angrily towards the linesman. His integrity being so publicly questioned. He then pulled his arm away and to French horror and Argentinian joy raced back pointing towards the penalty spot! Mario Kempes, Americo Gallego and Osvaldo Ardiles raised their arms in celebration, the *Monumental* erupted! On the touchline, the French coach Michel Hidalgo smiled ruefully shaking his head in disgust. Different rules appeared to apply here in Argentina.

 The young *Les Bleus* Nantes playmaker, twenty-three-year-old Michel Platini walked across to Dubach clearly seen suggesting whilst pointing at Tresor, 'Just what was he supposed to do Ref?' A furious Platini had to be pulled away by team-mates. This was a midfielder who painted pictures when on the ball. His movement, touch and passing a delight to watch. At times in the first half, Platini had tortured Menotti's defence.

  It came down to a straight shoot out from twelve-yards between the Casablanca born-naturalised, French goalkeeper Jean-Paul Bertrand-Demanes and the beloved, home hero, Daniel Passarella. The Capitan of River Plate and Argentina. He never made no bones how to take penalty kicks, Passarella simply let fly, then prayed to God they flew in. Up he came to hit a thunderous shot past Bertand-Demanes, 1-0! In the press area, emotions erupted when Argentinian journalist jumped up in celebration and their French counterparts went for them. Dubach blew to end the half. In the VIP section, President Videla with Admiral Massera and General Agosti alongside him were on their feet clapping politely. For with the eyes of the world focused upon them it was only right to be seen as gentlemen. Meanwhile, left, right, over and below, thousands of their fellow countrymen indulged in bedlam!

The second half restarted. Appearing like they had been whipped into a frenzy by the cruel injustice which befell them, France charged forward. Playing incisively, delicate at times, but mostly, devastating, attacking football. Their team full of wonderful footballers. Balletic almost, rapier-fast. Bathenay, Six, Battiston and Lacombe all impressed. Their tousled, black-haired winger Dominique Rochteau, delightful, as he flew across the pitch leaving defenders queuing in desperate, attempts just to kick him! Above all, Platini, a truly special talent. It was he whom the crowd truly feared when in possession. As the home nation were forced further back, gasps of horror echoed loud whenever Platini received the ball. Yet, despite French pressure, Argentina retained a venomous ability to hit out on the break. The Tallares de Cordoba midfielder Jose Valencia smashed a ferocious thirty-five-yard, dipping volley that was tipped magnificently over his own crossbar by Bertrand-Demanes. Only then for the French goalkeeper to fall onto the post, seriously looking to have damaged his back. On ran the stretcher-bearers as there appeared real concern from French and Argentinian players alike. Another, unfair, striking blow for Hidalgo's brave team. A substitute keeper in the shape of experienced thirty-one-year old Domonic Baratelli was called for and the game continued. On sixty-three minutes, the French grabbed the equaliser their performance duly deserved. A swift break down the right-hand touchline ended with a lobbed shot from centre-forward Bernard Lacombe, that careered into the Argentine crossbar, rebounded and after an almighty scramble, fell to Michel Platini-who from eight yards hammered past Fillol into the top of the net.
1-1! An engulfing, fearful whisper etched with groans and whistles coveted the *Monumental*. As delighted and

relieved French journalists punched the air in the press box, justice at last, the home players appeared distraught. Alberto Tarantini received a comforting slap around the head from the Captain Passarella, who then roared out to his other *compadres,* whilst clapping his hands together 'Vamos Argentina!' On the touchline, Cesar Menotti watched on looking neither nervous, nor confident. His face etched in concentration, a simple drag of the cigarette, he just looked like Menotti.

Les Bleus came again! The French were swarming all over the home side, it appeared just a matter of time before the Argentinian rearguard cracked again. The ball treated with love and deep affection, passed amongst Hidalgo's exuberant team like a precious gift, as worried screams and piercing whistles from the terraces deafened, Indeed, more than worried, they were petrified. At the heart of this French masterclass, the magician Michel Platini. Always Platini. Such poise and a deft of touch. His sublime pass sliced apart Argentina, putting the winger Didier Six clear with just the keeper Fillol to beat. Time stopped in the *Estadio Monumental*-remember the magnificent finale in the Sam Peckinpah movie, The Wild Bunch? When Peckinpah slowed down the camera action, so the audience could relish even more the carnage and bullets fizzing and crashing into blood, splattered bodies. To let them experience more the agony and slaughter? Well, as the dashing Six fired goalwards and a nation closed its eyes, he missed! Six's left-foot effort flying inches wide of the far post. From just ten yards, the boy from Marseille had defaulted on his moment in time and appeared devastated. His long, black hair soaked with sweat. Six fell to the turf, but was immediately lifted up by Platini, who with a gentle pat on the head consoled him. Across the terraces, a collective sigh of relief, eyes now back opened, their prayers answered. Six's aberration greeted like 80,000 people had just been informed the imminent end of the world was cancelled for the foreseeable future. The minutes ticked down, fourteen remained-again, the French attacked, yet, albeit, sporadically, Argentina were coming back to life, hitting back on the counter. The noise level rose infinitely whenever they managed to break out. Their tall, dark players with hair flowing, the long legs eating up the turf like the finest, thoroughbred racehorses. Striding away. Kempes, Luque and Gallego roared on by a sweating, praying, fanatical, crowd. This was truly a magnificent football match. The passion and emotion from both on the field and off, overpowering.

Then, Bang! What a goal! France 1 Argentina 2 and the *Monumental* exploded in a rapture of delight! Leopoldo Luque had smashed a glorious, long-range shot into the net past the flailing fingertips of the French substitute keeper Baratelli, to ignite mass euphoria among his countrymen. A showering cascade of confetti thrown and dropping, glistening beneath the floodlights. A Niagara falls of sheer, unadulterated, Argentinian joy. Seventy-three minutes showed on the electronic scoreboard, as an image of a football danced in joy across it. A win and Argentina qualified out of the group, those were the stakes for Menotti's team. For France, an equaliser was required, if not, despite everything they had already given to *Mundial* 78, would be homeward bound. Left with nothing but sweat, tears and bitter memories of what could, and should have been.

The French restarted-on the touchline, a close to tears Hidalgo urged his boys for one last great effort. Platini took the ball as all Argentina braced for the onslaught. Just what had this devilish box of tricks Frenchman left in his locker?

The last stand. A rampaging Tresor charged forward laying off a pass for Didier Six, who from thirty yards exploded a sizzling, drive saved splendidly by Fillol, leaping high to push the ball around the post. The French were not yet done-Six appeared on a one-man mission to atone for the earlier miss. Wriggling like an eel through desperate, Argentinian challenges in the penalty area, finally making room to shoot-a retreating Luque back helping his defence tripped him up. Penalty! Again, in the press box, the French journalists were up screaming, demanding a spot kick. Salvation. The crowd held their collective breath, as all eyes turned towards the referee Dubach, who turned it down. No penalty? Six once more fell to his knees crying with frustration. A dismayed Tresor screamed loud into the Buenos Aires sky. A shocked Platini stood with hands on hips, shaking his head. Hidalgo, incandescent with rage on the touchline. It was the last act.

Dubach's full-time whistle blew loud and the *Estadio Monumental* erupted in a tumultuous heap. The manner of victory highly dubious, but no matter, for as the terraces danced in joy, Argentina were through. On leaving the pitch the French players tried remonstrating with Dubach, but he simply waved their protests away. As for the coach? He cut a desolate, defeated figure. Hidalgo later admitted to being, 'Sick to the stomach.' His team had played with great honour, there had been glory in defeat, but defeat all the same.

The songs of angry men echoed loud in Paris that night.

Later in the evening, the roads, streets and avenues of the capital were crammed tight with cars, vans and open-top trucks filled with flag-waving revellers. The deafening, beeping of horns that resonated across the city, competed joyfully with the ever-constant chants of 'ARGENTINA!' The soundtrack of the *Mundial*.

CHAPTER THIRTEEN
CLEAN HANDS
ARGENTINA V ITALY (FIRST ROUND MATCH)

Estadio Monumental. Saturday 10th June 1978. The referee Abraham Klein's was an astonishing tale bearing witness to the worst excesses of the world, a person could ever imagine. A life so less than ordinary. Born of Jewish blood in Timisoara, Romania, he survived prejudices, politics and the Holocaust to reach the top of his trade. Whilst so many of his family fell victim to the systematic Nazi extermination of his race; taken by cattle truck to Auschwitz, murdered in a manner beyond human belief, the young boy Klein survived by being smuggled by his Mother to start a new life with relatives in Holland. Here, a love of football helped him settle into new surroundings. An adoration of the beautiful game never equalled by a playing talent saw Klein settle for the man in the middle status.

His ball became a whistle.

He later moved to Israel, going on to become one of the finest referees of the late-sixties, seventies and early eighties. Respected as a fair, no-nonsense character, Klein refereed with a calmness and stern authority. Small in stature, huge in presence. In 1970, came his crowning glory. Mexico, Guadalajara, Abraham Klein stood tall and proud. He was thirty-six years old and about to referee his first World Cup match. To one side, the mythical yellow-shirted giants of Pele, Carlos Alberto, Rivelino, Jairzinho and all. The other, the World Champions. The gleaming, white-shirted lions. Bobby Moore, Bobby Charlton, Geoff Hurst, Gordon Banks and all.

This was FIFA's jewel in the crown between favourites Brazil and holders England, but the referee, an unknown? Many scratched their heads, who was this guy? A Jew from Israel handed the golden ticket? Prejudices abounded. One lowly, mealy-mouthed FIFA official not happy with Klein's appointment beforehand stated that 'Appointing him is like sending a boy scout to Vietnam.' Inwardly, Klein was nervous. He had refereed international games before, five in all, but never anything like this footballing royalty, a battle between the knights of the game. Not wishing to let the players see his shaking hands, Klein kept them in pockets at first, although before greeting both Captains, he wiped both clean of sweat and offered each a strong handshake.

Klein looked left and right, then blew the whistle to begin proceedings, from the opening moment to the last, he was immaculate, in what turned out to be one of the most iconic World Cup matches of all time. An enchanting encounter. Although being unknown to the Brazilian and England players, he swiftly earned their respect. Klein saw all, missed nothing. Pele was admonished gently, but firmly for a dive in the English penalty area. One look from Klein and he embarrassingly rose swiftly back to his feet. This a man clearly not to take liberties with and he received huge praise in its aftermath from both sides and FIFA.

The murderous events of the 1972 Munich massacre of the Israeli Olympic athletes, meant it was deemed not safe for Klein to partake in the 1974 World Cup finals in Germany. Death threats abounded. Fear of kidnapping and worse saw him forced to watch the tournament from afar on television. Four years on Argentina dawned and many experts viewed Klein as an outstanding choice to referee the final. Firstly, though, came the daunting prospect of Argentina and Italy in their final group match. Both countries had already qualified, but the winner remained in Buenos Aires playing at the *Estadio Monumental*. Thus, a victory for the South Americans was still so important, for to stay in the capital was essential. There was momentum in the *Monumental*. Inside a gladiatorial atmosphere, a cauldron of unerring hostility to the opposing team, anything went, it did and mostly in Argentina's favour. Events in the host's opening two contests meant all eyes were on the referee appointed who would have to keep his head, ignoring the hysteria that engulfed Menotti's team. FIFA were convinced in the principled, strong-minded Abraham Klein, that they had such a man. One who kept his head under immense pressure when all around him were lost amidst an air of unremitting madness.

The final whistle, Argentina 0 Italy1. Abraham Klein had been immaculate in both decision making and the ability to withstand the Argentinian verbal slings and arrows aimed upon his head, both on and off the pitch. In the most difficult ninety minutes of his career Klein was supreme. He rightly turned down two home penalty decision just before half-time, for which there was mounds of vicious abuse from the *Monumental* terraces that came raining down upon his head. Both were dubious at best and Abraham Klein, the boy from Timisoara simply stared the beast down. Come the interval, a stadium in uproar. Boos, whistles, shrieks and insults deafening the ear drums, but the courageous Klein was oblivious to all. He stood tall between his two linesmen before striding off, knowing the decisions taken had been just and correct. An opening period saw the Italians pinned back in their own half for vast swathes of the contest, as Menotti's men went forward with all the ferocity of a force ten gale at their backs. Both Kempes and his Captain Passarella, were only denied by the magnificent, goalkeeping of the legendary Dino Zoff. After two wins and performances of unusually, vibrant, attacking, football, Enzo Bearzot's *azzurri* had been forced onto the back foot, looking to counter-attack. On sixty-seven minutes, they broke out, their new young striker Paolo Rossi setting up the *Silver fox,* Roberto Bettega, to fire past Ubaldo Fillol, silencing the *Monumental.* For the first time in the tournament Argentina were behind. The last quarter saw the *azzurri* lock up and the shutters go down. *Catenaccio.* The South Americans sublime interchanging, one-twos, short passing, repeatedly coming unstuck against an Italian defence marshalled superbly by Zoff, with the likes of Juve's, Claudio Gentile, Antonio Cabrini and Gaetano Scirea in front of him. The explosive Mario Kempes found himself shackled, hunted down by the tentacles-like grip of the brutal Gentile. Libyan born, but with all the hallmarks of a traditional, top class Italian defender. Argentina's fire waned, by the time Abraham Klein's whistle resonated loud ending the game, the host nation had been served a dose of reality. This World Cup wasn't going to be handed them on a silver platter. Of the two nations, Italy appeared more equipped to go further, it would be they whom remained in Buenos Aires, whilst Argentina moved 300 kilometres away to Rosario, on the west bank of the *Parana* River. Before leaving the pitch, Abraham Klein stood with the ball, as players from both sides queued to shake his hand. Job done, pride and dignity intact.

In the VIP section President Videla and Admiral Massera offered polite applause, but the grim features spoke volumes for their true feeling. Stood behind them a worried, looking Vice-Admiral Lacoste. An angry Massera was seen to turn towards him and speak. Obviously inaudible, though no doubt something along the lines of,

'Don't you fuck this up Carlos.'

CHAPTER FOURTEEN
BROTHERS IN ARMS
ARGENTINA V POLAND (SECOND ROUND MATCH)

A Batalha de Rosário, (The Battle of Rosario). Fate's, larcenous habit of bringing people down from the stars to earth with sickening reality, had struck again, this time with Argentinian striker Leopoldo Luque. After scoring an unforgettable, late winner against the French, Luque dislocated his shoulder in the dying moments and was forced to miss the loss against Italy. However, such misfortune paled into comparison with what happened next. On hearing of his injury, Luque's younger brother Jose decided to drive to the team's training facilities to be by his side. Horribly though, tragedy struck when Jose's car crashed on the *San Isidro* Bridge, along the *Panamericana* highway and he was killed. For two days this grave news was kept from Luque, as he recovered in hospital from the shoulder injury received against the French. Finally, his Father arrived, along with Coach Cesar Menotti to break the terribly, sad tidings. Leopoldo was obviously distraught with grief at what had befallen his younger brother. More so, because following the France match, he experienced a frightening premonition that something terrible was set to occur. His teammates also came to support him, whilst his heartbroken Father returned to their family home in Santa Fe to sort out the funeral details. This was the spirit Menotti had bred amongst the squad. They were brothers in arms, both in life and death.

The sad loss of Luque on the team sheet meant more pressure than ever placed upon Mario Kempes. Himself, like Menotti, back home in Rosario, the city of his birth. A dangerous, experienced Poland team whom had finished above holders West Germany in the opening round, lay in wait with only one from the group going into the final. Peru, and Argentina's oldest rival made up the other. That would be the mother of all battles. The boys from the Copacabana, those devils in yellow shirts, the three-times, World Champions were coming to ruin Argentina's party and steal away the trophy.

Brazil.

Rosario. *Estadio Gigante de Arroyito*. Wednesday 14th June 1978. All that was experienced in River Plate's *Estadio Monumental*, the cauldron of noise and passion, was beaten in the far Southern provinces of Rosario. An atmosphere both intoxicating, intimidating, 40,000 Argentinians created a bear pit that in the end overwhelmed a brave, talented, Polish side. Again, refereeing controversy, with Kempes himself blatantly handballing on his own goal-line. A penalty was rightly awarded by the Swedish referee Ulf Eriksson, but the Argentinian forward received remarkable leniency from Eriksson, being allowed to remain on the pitch. Much to the Poles disgust. However, the chance was wasted horribly by their veteran captain Kazimierz Deyna, on his 100th international appearance. Ubaldo Fillol's earned his countrymen's undying gratitude by blocking Deyna's

weak shot. A miss leaving the Polish Captain shattered.
That apart, a fine contest was ultimately decided by the
genius of home boy

El Matador. Two goals, one a flying header from a left-
wing cross by Daniel Bertoni, met with fire and accuracy
by Kempes-guided with a craftsman's ease past every
Scotsman's favourite goalkeeper, Jan Tomaszewski. 1-0!
The Rosario terraces exploded, their boy had come home!
Mario Kempes had erupted at last upon the World Cup,
more importantly for the host nation, Argentina finally
resembled a side capable of taking on the very best in the
Mundial and beating them. Poland were gallant throughout
creating sufficient opportunities to steal a draw. Their
outstanding, attacking players in Boniek, Lato and
Lubanski all going close. It was to be the electrifying
Kempes who finally, finished them off. His second goal
coming eleven minutes from time. A wonderfully, darting,
run by the slender, but increasingly potent Osvaldo
Ardiles, saw him soar into the crumbling heart of Poland's
defence. Ardiles found Kempes, who from twelve-yards at
an angle drilled a bullet of a low-drive past a diving
Tomaszewski sealing the contest and sending the stadium
into meltdown. 2-0! So, ended a game in which the Poles
had contributed hugely, only to find themselves beaten by
a team driven by what they believed was their destiny and
a fanatical backing that verged towards unworldly. Cesar
Menotti's post-match, press-conference proved equally
hysterical, as all thoughts turned to the next opponents.
Arch-enemies Brazil were coming to Rosario in just four
days' time. The ferocious rivalry between these two age
old adversaries made other rivalries appear like minor
skirmishes. The Brazilians had already thrashed Peru 3-0
earlier that same day in Cordoba, after a slow start in the

opening rounds, they were finally clicking into gear. Much to Argentina's chagrin. A win for either team would all but guarantee them a place in the World Cup final. What if Brazil claimed a fourth title on Argentine soil? The Junta's worst nightmare, how would the people react? Wars had been fought over less in this part of the world. It simply was unacceptable. As the questions were fired bullet-like, a hundred microphones stuck within inches of his face, Menotti cut a composed, confident figure.

 He lit another cigarette appearing like the coolest man on the planet.

CHAPTER FIFTEEN
BROADCAST
'Attention, attention! Radio Liberación transmitting.
The voice of the Montonero Peronist Movement!'
Mario Firmenich

 For the duration of the 1978 World Cup, the Commander-in-Chief of the *Montoneros,* Mario Firmenich, had promised the Argentinian people they would cease armed hostilities, but never said anything about giving up the struggle to bring down Videla and his gang of murderous crooks. The guerrillas had come up with an ingenious plan to hopefully spread the word of their fight to the watching world, but not by guns, bombs, grenades or knives, it would be killing them by words. Words heard over the television coverage going out live across the planet. It was seven o'clock, on Tuesday 6th June 1978, the Argentinian national team were set to play their second, first-round group match against France, at the *Estadio Monumental.* The entire country, except those in the stadium and the poor souls detained by the state would be tuned into

Argentine station Channel 13. At first, sounding just like static/interference, but then, everybody watching on the above channel from far away as seventy kilometres, the nearby cities of Berisso and Ensenada, in the Buenos Aires provinces, they heard it! The *Montoneros* had taken over the airwaves! The image stayed live, but the commentary? That belonged to Mario Firmenich. It spread to other parts of the capital, no further, the signal not being strong enough. Firstly, a distant hum of the rebel anthem, the *Peronist March*, then, a voice. One that struck fear into the Junta's heart. As the confetti fell and the two teams appeared amidst a snowstorm of faith, hope and prayer, Firmenich's could be heard for up to thirteen minutes on local televisions. He spoke about, 'The painful reality of living in the lies of the military Junta.' And saying, 'It is the duty of every Argentinian to show the world the real Argentina.' As this occurred, all hell broke out over Buenos Aires with the security forces rushing around the city to find out where these broadcast were coming from. Truckloads of soldiers careering to various addresses emptying off, smashing down doors, but finding nothing. Just empty rooms, sometimes an unfortunate occupant who was handed a busted head off a rifle butt, maybe worse, so much worse if taken away to be questioned.

It never just ended there.

This command performance actually took place on the fifth floor of the Hotel La Plata, in central Buenos Aires, A transmitter was set up fed by the battery of a nearby Ford Falcon, with an aerial sticking out of the window. When the security forces finally tracked down the signal and came kicking the door off its hinges, the *Montoneros* had vanished, leaving behind only an 8-track tape and a message daubed in paint on the wall.

'Only the people can save the people!'

Vice-Admiral Lacoste raged with anger on being told of what had occurred-even more so when it was reported in some of the next day's national newspapers, More worryingly abroad, *El Pais* in Spain and the Mexican magazine *El Processo,* picked up the story. The one thing the Junta feared more than any other was their *Mundial* being hijacked by the *Montoneros* and exposing the true face of Argentina to the world. The hunt was on.

For the guerrillas it had been a huge propaganda coup, one that couldn't have worked out better if they had blown up the *Casa Rosada* itself!

This had not been the first time, for back in December 1977, the authorities seized a host of transmitting gear belonging to the *Montoneros* in a town called Villa Tesei. Information led them to a small factory that was raided by the army. They were quick to show off to the national media, claiming the captured equipment was to be used in the forthcoming *Mundial. The* raid was deemed a great success in their ongoing battle against the guerrillas.

'The efforts of the subversives to transmit during the World Cup has been left severely hindered'.

Step forward to Wednesday 14th June 1978. Towards the end of the first-half of the second-round match between Argentina and Poland, the *Montoneros* went live again, with Firmenich's voice heard distinctly over the commentary. This time on the Channel 10 television station, based in Mar del Plata. The transmission was so powerful that despite orders from the authorities to the channel to cut down on its emissions, the message was still coming through to many local areas. The guerrillas were operating from a sixth floor apartment on 3259 Simon Bolivar street, just eight blocks from the Channel 10 studio. For two hours they managed to broadcast, before word came their position had been compromised and off into the Mar Del Plata evening they fled. Mission complete!

Such had been the desperation of the army to find them, they were reduced to combing one by one the surrounding streets with radio direction finders-a job lot bought off the United States, last used in World War two. When the soldiers finally came across the apartment, they found the transmitter stuck to a living room window, facing the Channel 10 studios. Also, a special message for their boss daubed in paint.

'Argentina champion, Videla to the wall!'

It was to be the final broadcast of the guerrillas, but not the last battle, for the war would wage on with bullets and bombs once the last ball of *Mundial 78* had been kicked.

CHAPTER SIXTEEN
MEXICAN STAND-OFF
ARGENTINA V BRAZIL (SECOND ROUND MATCH)

In world football, there's probably no harder job than the Brazilian national coach, as thirty-nine-year old Claudio Coutinho discovered at *Mundial 78*. After a disappointing, opening 1-1 draw with Sweden, when Welsh referee Clive Thomas, entered World Cup folklore by disallowing Zico's last gasp header by blowing for full time, Brazil got infinitely worse. So much that after a torturous, second draw, a 0-0 against Spain, outraged fans were burning effigies of the unfortunate Coutinho back in Rio de Janiero. There were calls for him to be immediately sacked, as the three times winners stood on the brink of a humiliating, early exit. The head of the Brazilian football federation, Admiral Heleno Nunes, once a friend of the besieged coach, ran for cover distancing himself well away from the under-fire coach. Team selection was handed over to a committee. Overnight, Coutinho became a mere puppet. A proud man, he was forced to take a backward step in his duties. Nunes himself was under pressure from above. Like their southern neighbours, Brazil too was in the grip of a murderous, dictatorial, military regime. The miserable equal of Argentina's in how they did business. Unholy brothers in arms.

Finally, back on the pitch a narrow 1-0 win over a disinterested Austrian team that had already qualified enabled the boys from Brazil to reach the second round. After finding a semblance of their true form to thrash Peru 3-0, an old ancient foe awaited to do battle in Rosario.

It was the eve of the match against Brazil, at the Argentinian training complex in Rosario, the world media had descended and it resembled a siege. The air acrid, the smell of sulphur filled the room, for there had been serious Brazilian accusations that following the match against Poland, of Mario Kempes failing a drugs test and it being covered up. A livid Menotti was prepared to tear a strip off the Brazilian journalist who broke the story that became front page news across the world, but he never shown! Just as well for a ready-made posse of Argentinian hacks also lay in wait to lynch him. They were convinced it was a planted story designed to upset the *La Albiceleste*, especially their superb, in form striker Kempes, on the eve of the biggest match ever between these two great enemies. In a room packed to the rafters, amid a barrage of blinding flashlights and a cascade of raised voices, Cesar

Menotti finally appeared through a side entrance to take the questions of a rabid world media. He settled down, lit the proverbial cigarette and leaned back in his chair. Immediately, the grilling, or to give it a more accurate description, the interrogation began. Brazil's finest hacks aimed low, but with his typical laid-back style, it didn't take long before the Brazilians were becoming increasingly irate, as *El Flaco* swatted away their questions about the Kempes drugs claims with ease and a half-smile on his face. Only once did Menotti spark when informed that the Brazilian team coach said he had lost control of his squad, 'I think Claudio should concentrate on his own team, because from what I have seen, so far he has many more problems than me.' After a further hour of non-stop questions fired like bullets towards him, Menotti departed the stage, but not before receiving a standing ovation from his countrymen-and a fair few good riddance comments from their rivals-a fistfight broke out in the audience between an Argentinian and Brazilian journalist, but was swiftly broken up as tempers frayed. Nerves fraught.

There was a storm brewing.

Rosario. *Estadio Gigante de Arroyito*. 21st June 1978. Twenty minutes before kick-off, the Argentine dressing room was silent as a graveyard at midnight. However, the noise from the expectant crowds soared through the walls threatening to send them tumbling down. Like a never-ending crash of thunder, it echoed with deafening, intent the war cry of the Mundial.

'ARGENTINA!'

The battle of Rosario. The Brazilians supporters arrived in town by their thousands. A large, smattering of yellow and green evident on the terraces. They were defiant. Their drums beat loud but were drowned out amid the incessant, chanting of the host nation. That evening their boys had to show real guts standing up to an Argentinian side that once more included Leopoldo Luque. Menotti had fired up his side to the extent they were going to war with Brazil. It took Luque just twenty seconds to release some pent up frustration, as twice he charged into yellow shirts like a bull with a toothache. A stalemate swiftly ensued. A drab, if nerve-shredding first-half littered with endless stoppages for petty fouls. It was a Mexican stand-off, with neither daring to fire first. Only Mario Kempes appeared willing, letting fly twice from twenty yards, only to see both efforts land in the chest of Brazilian goalkeeper Leao. The interval came, went and shortly after Argentinian substitute Ricardo Villa took out the Brazilian Batista, by nearly cutting him in half with a sensational, wild lunge, after he had done similar to Villa's *compadre* Osvaldo Ardiles in the first half. Justice-South American style. The Hungarian referee Palotai daren't act to send Villa justifiably off, he just daren't! That apart, the stakes were simply too high for either team to contemplate a more open contest. The final whistle blew to end what never really started. A French journalist was quoted after as saying, 'Both teams were prisoners of their own fears.' A goalless draw suited all. Cesar Menotti stood to leave the Argentinian bench and shared a handshake with his opposite number Claudio Coutinho, whispering something in his ear. The Brazilian smiling as they walked off together. Everything now went down to the last round of matches. First up Brazil versus Poland, followed later that same evening, Argentina versus Peru in Rosario. A straight shootout. Many Argentinians remained far too nervous, scared even to call it.

Whilst others in the shadows were already ensuring, there would be no need to.

CHAPTER SEVENTEEN
A FISTFUL OF DOLLARS
ARGENTINA V PERU (SECOND ROUND MATCH)

'I would like to say just a word about human rights. The fights and dignity of human beings concerns us all and must be defended and enhanced. I'm convinced that the peoples of the Americas want a world in which citizens of every country are free from torture, from arbitrary arrest and prolonged detention without trial, free to speak and to think as they please, free to participate in the determination of their own destiny.'
Taken from an Address by President Jimmy Carter
to the UN General Assembly.
Wednesday 21st June 1978.

…As night time's veil drew across the dark, Rosario skies, a half moon made its first dramatic appearance of the evening and all Argentina held its breath…

On Tuesday 20th June 1978, that huge, soccer fan, Henry Kissinger arrived in Buenos Aires. He was greeted warmly, before being chauffeur driven around the city to meet with the cream of Argentine society. All the time chased by a fawning, not just local, but world press. When asked whom would win the World Cup, the *Good Doctor* replied without hesitation, 'I believe Argentina will be champion.' That said, a wave to the adoring crowds and Kissinger was away into the night. He had work to do.

Rosario. The *Estadio Gigante de Arroyito*. Wednesday 21st June 1978. Earlier that same day, Brazil had beaten Poland 3-0, meaning Argentina required a huge four goal haul against Peru to overtake them and reach the World Cup final. It was in this type of atmosphere that revolutions broke out, lynching became commonplace, if you were not prepared to die for the cause. The city of Rosario was on fire! As the Peruvian team coach arrived at the stadium, it was surrounded by chanting, manic-faced Argentinians screaming abuse at them, banging on the sides. Through the windows the footballers appeared fearful. The venom and bile towards them etched clear on faces, 'Don't you dare,' appeared to be the general feeling being hurled towards them. 'Don't you fucking dare!' Not surprisingly, their military escort had stopped, so the supporter's point could be clearly made before it moved off again. Elsewhere, another entourage of vehicles, but this one far larger headed by military motorcycles arrived outside the stadium. This carried former American Secretary of State, Henry Kissinger. By that time plying his dark, if masterful trade to the highest bidder, whilst also acting as an unofficial ambassador for his nation. The *Good Doctor* always spoke for the White House and his words had to be heeded by those who wished to keep the Gringo's goodwill in the joint war of the good guys against threatened, Communism expansion.

…*Operation Condor*. The CIA paranoia eating them up that the big, bad Russian bear was sneaking through the back door, one day soon their tanks lining up on the Rio Grande border. An agency that would stoop to any level protecting the hallowed dreams of their forefathers. Liberty for all, unless we didn't like you. Of bubble gum, hula-hoops, hot dogs, bud beers and all sweet American apple pie. Whose God was the star-spangled banner and their devil on earth, fucking Communism. A cause the CIA was willing others to die for. A human wall of bodies stretching across Central and South America. They sided with despots, drug lords and psychopathic Generals.

The ultimate endgame on that glorious day being the Soviet threat totally neutralised, a nuclear bomb with an American flag inscribed upon it reducing the Kremlin to ashes. With a kind hand, a vaccine and when needed beheaded corpses as warnings, they fought a silent war alongside men of monstrous, murderous egos. 'All necessary means' to ensure the war was won. To murder, rape, corrupt and bribe. A cruel play on words contrived to reveal its true measure in real life. The burning of a village, the screams of the tortured as the knife cuts deep. The look of sheer disbelief in a person's eyes as a pistol was aimed at their temple, before the trigger was pressed. A Mother's tears at seeing her dead son's body. 'All necessary means,'
that resulted in the fires of fucking hell.

They had the nerve to call it The '*Cold war*'? Arrogantly proclaiming themselves as the 'Land of the Free?' Then, try with all their almighty might to prevent others having the same freedom, because they wouldn't lie down before them. This two-faced front they showed to the rest of a world, that were mostly unaware just how decadent and savage the CIA tactics were in central and South America, to counter Communist aggression-both real and imagined. Few ever realised the lengths they went to, the depths sunk to prevent any Left-wing governments gaining the slightest foothold. The CIA ran a highly secretive facility in Panama, under the official title of the 'School of

Americas.' The SOA. There, officers and chosen men of so called 'Friendly' nations were trained in the dark arts of interrogation and torture methods. Also, how to kill and mutilate methodically, without mercy or contrition The gringos referred to it as 'Psychological warfare.' Through those doors to light the next fires in Latin America went future dictators, Generals and Colonels schooled in 'Counterinsurgency methods' (terror tactics). Assassins and torturers willing to ply their rancid trade in the name of 'Freedom.' Freedom?

Acting like John fucking Wayne in the Green Berets, striking like snakes in the night. The air was so thick with paranoia, Uncle Sam would've sided with the devil himself against the imagined, red hordes sweeping to attack them down Mexico way. Like a child in the night scared of that imaginary monster in the wardrobe, they refuse to believe there were no 'Commies' under their beds. So, the Americans waged secret wars with the battles not being fought out on North American soil, but on other continents. In cities, towns and villages, with other people's blood. In Bolivia, Chile, Peru, and Argentina.

Kissinger was in Buenos Aires that night of the Peru game. A close amigo of President Videla, brother's in arms against the red peril. The great Henry Kissinger, blessed by the Pope, lauded as a peacemaker, winner of the Nobel Peace Prize. A son of Jewish immigrants who settled in America. Who fought with great bravery against the Nazis for his adopted country in World War Two. How could a man from such a background be reduced to polluting nations like Argentina by bankrolling their psychotic Generals? Kissinger's past suggested he was a politician of rare ilk-the type who could move mountains when necessary on the world stage to bring warring nations together. To reason with them until a way to make peace was found. Kissinger brokered a deal between Hindus and Moslems, with India and Pakistan in 1971. He brought Israel and the Arab world around the table in 1973. The *Good Doctor* even managed to pull the Americans out of Vietnam, albeit with little dignity intact.

Then, he turned his eyes to Argentina. Always with the right amount of threats and promises he succeeded. Armed with an unholy military might and a treasure chest of used Yankee dollars, a wink to whoever that America never forgot her friends. A speaker of true substance, whose words always demanded to be heard, a deep voice that resonated common sense, those world-weary, wise eyes that saw through weak men. Kissinger never missed a trick. Trusted by the White House, like no other to carry their flag abroad. To dine with kings and Presidents, Prime Ministers, with mass murderers and sadists. All in the name of American foreign policy. The good old Stars and Stripes. Yankee, doodle, dandy painted on the side of a fucking bomb. Kissinger would shower whatever was required on those he needed to keep onside and drown in their own blood whoever dared to cross him.

So, unfolded Operation Condor. The CIA battle-plan to rid the Americas of all Communists and left-wing influence. Brazil, Bolivia, Peru and Uruguay, all were purged, but it was the spectacular success in killing President Salvador Allende, replacing him with General Augusto Pinochet in Chile, that became the role model for future operations. Destabilise, destroy and dethrone. The three D's. To be used further on down the road in El Salvador and Nicaragua, maybe even Mexico if the situation ever arose. In those parts a ruthless dictator only became problematic, when they turned their gaze towards Moscow. Otherwise, Uncle Sam rewarded loyalty with a blind eye-see nothing policy to the most frightful, brutal atrocities. So long as they knew the words to 'God Bless America' all were family. 'The greater good must always prevail,' said Henry Kissinger.

The greater good...

Argentina was a clear case in point. Videla, Massera, the rest of the goons in *Casa Rosada*-more of a Mafia, than a government. Although lacking the Italian's cunning in politics and matters of business, they were savages to be controlled, trusted to do the CIA bidding when their leash was tugged.

In the name of God, the family and the American way.

Amen...

Rosario. Doctor Kissinger was ushered out of his car and taken through a side-entrance into the stadium. There was himself, an entourage of personal aides and bodyguards escorted down a corridor, where waiting was President Jorge Videla's party. After a swift handshake and brief exchange of platitudes, they headed off to the Peru dressing room. On entering, Kissinger remained behind Videla, but clearly visible to the shocked Peruvian players, as the President addressed them. Videla spoke of a 'South American brotherhood' and, 'A sense of Duty to do the right thing.' All very ominous. 'Gentlemen, I just wanted to tell you this game tonight is one between brothers and in the name of Latin American brotherhood, I am here to share my hopes that things turn out well. Latin America will be watching you.'

The message clear,

think not tonight of the Peruvian flag, but instead of your lives.

It was also heavily rumoured an infamous Colombian drug lord, one of the heads of the Medellin cartel, alongside the legendary Pablo Escobar, Gonzalo Rodriguez Gacha, *El Mexicano*, (The Mexican), tried to influence the result of the match, but a suitcase stashed with cash was intercepted in the United States. Gacha was a huge soccer fan who would later go on to own one of Colombia's top clubs Millonarios. The story goes that in June 1978, a Colombian named José Fonseca packed a suitcase in Bogotá to travel to Lima on the Avianca airline, but due to a company error, that same suitcase was diverted to New York, where it was opened by the authorities finding $250,000, in $100 bills. The cash was duly confiscated going to a state court. There, Fonseca tried demanding its return, but failed. The Colombian government also put in a claim because of it having left Bogotá outside of their normal procedure, they too were denied.

Fonseca's suitcase was claimed to have been just one of a number of cash deliveries, that the Medellin cartel were willing to allegedly bribe the Peruvian team with. In return President Videla would grant them the opportunity to invest, launder profits-also to keep their huge fortunes safe in Argentine banks. Plus, future sanctuary in the country, if ever needed to keep them free of North American, or their own Colombian justice system. According to the chief of the Colombian anti-narcotics police, Colonel Jaime Ramírez Gómez, Fonseca was trying desperately to recover the suitcase in New York, for the money was the same above bribe, en-route to Lima. Ramírez said most of the money was contributed by Pablo Escobar, José Gonzalo Rodríguez Gacha and the Rodríguez Orejuela brothers, whom in 1978, ran the Medellín cartel.

Did the money ever reach the Peruvians?

Such an answer forever hidden amidst the dark intrigue and politics of South American soccer folklore. What is true that in later years, when the tables were being turned on the cartel, if one of the leaders fell, or was captured, their families always managed to find a welcome in Argentina. None more so than Pablo Escobar, whose wife and two children settled in Buenos Aires, after he was killed by security forces in Medellín, on Thursday 2nd December 1993. Maybe *Mundial 78* was the door that opened the door to all this? Then again,

maybe not?

Well past midnight, on the day of the game, the Peruvians were awoken by a sudden, emergence of an open-truck convoy-Argentinians circling their *concentracion* blasting out music, beeping horns and fans on board singing 'ARGENTINA!' for hours on end. The notion of sleep was impossible-no surprise, the security guards and military police had vanished, nowhere to be seen until it was over. That same afternoon, the bus taking the weary, Peru party to the *Estadio Gigante de Arroyito,* got lost several times on the way, with hostile crowds waiting to scream abuse at every turn off and corner. A simple journey that should have taken no more than thirty minutes, instead lasted over two hours, thus giving the players only an hour in the dressing room before the match began. Then, shortly before kick-off, who walked through the door…

Finally,

the teams took to the field in a blistering snowstorm of confetti. A whirling cascade of tickertape. High above a half-moon still shone in a black sky. Like a thief in an alley waiting for its next victim, skulking in the shadows. The noise, a crescendo, resonating like an explosion towards the heavens. A primeval scream, a longing. A desperate cry from the home crowd for their team not to let them down. The entire stadium an emotional wreck. High in the VIP section, President Jorge Videla seated next to Henry Kissinger. Alongside them Admiral Massera, Vice-Admiral Lacoste and General Agosti. They rose to their feet as the teams came into sight applauding politely. The national anthems performed by an Argentine army band. All pomp and braid. Both tunes blasted out rather tunelessly, as the intensity of the occasion clearly affected the musicians ability to concentrate fully. The Peruvian players appeared as one terribly uncomfortable in their plain red shirts. No flashing red stripe cutting across their hearts on that night, for this was the fix. Cesar Menotti headed to the bench as ever with the dying embers of a cigarette in hand, staring across at the madness breaking out on the terraces. People were praying, others, so hysterical in tears, all before a ball had been kicked. Menotti walked over and shook the hand of the grim-face Peruvian coach Marco Calderon. A good friend of his, Calderon carried the haunted look of one set to jump off a building. He accepted Menotti's hand, but clearly no words were exchanged. *El Flaco* returned to the Argentinian bench, lit up yet another cigarette and sat down.

Nothing of this was real, those who were the innocents in all this sordid drama, dancing and singing for a miracle, did so never knowing that once it was achieved, the dark curtain would again fall down over Argentina and reality would hit like a jackboot in the face. That all along they were mere pawns in a cast of millions, this epic swindle known as a footballing fiesta. The *Mundial*. Those people, the real Argentina were the real victims.

The warm-up balls were cleared off a pitch, covered in ripped-up confetti, as French referee Robert Wurtz checked his watch, signalled to the linesmen beginning the most controversial football match of all time. Argentina kicked off, but it was Peru who started the brighter-their rapid-like wingers Jose Oblitas and Juan Munante, whom had ripped apart Scotland in the earlier rounds appeared to be operating on backburners. The Peruvian's main tactic was just to constantly feed them the ball. Argentina were clearly nervous, their touch off, players guilt of repeatedly giving away possession. With just two minutes gone, an electric Juan Munante latched onto a Teofilo Cubillas through ball, to race clear into the home penalty area. Pushed wide of goal, being chased by a host of panicking Argentine defenders, around the stadium time stood still, as Munante took aim, firing a low shot that flashed past the goalkeeper Ubaldo Fillol, striking a post! Swiftly, as other Peruvians moved in for the kill, Passarella lashed it to safety. Mighty whistles, groans and sighs of relief filled the Rosario night air like a wild, sudden, gust of wind. Argentina were performing like eleven strangers, moments later the ball was again lost in midfield, this time around, the other winger Juan Oblitas careered past Passarella and his defenders going clear on Ubaldo Fillol's goal. Taking aim, the Peruvian let fly, his shot beating Fillol, but just so narrowly wide! A fearful hum of fear, of rising alarm fell across the Rosario terraces. There appeared for want of a better phrase, a real sense of dread that their team were bottling it. Marcus Calderon's team were in danger of sending Argentina's suicide rate through the roof. The television cameras cut over to the VIP area where President Videla shuffled nervously in his seat, whereas on the Argentinian bench, Menotti cut a worried figure as he stood screaming at Passarella to get a grip on his *compadres*. To slap a few heads together. Still, the Peruvians swept forward throwing caution to the wind, as they played their best football of the *Mundial*, since dismantling the Scots. Every pass from a red shirt aimed towards the rampaging Munante and Oblitas-their terrifying pace repeatedly tearing the home nation's rearguard apart. Twenty minutes passed and on twenty-one, Argentina scored.

 Taking possession from a one-two with Daniel Bertoni, Mario Kempes roared through the centre of Peru's defence. Like the parting of the red sea they opened up for Kempes, who took aim with his left foot, firing low to beat the diving keeper, Ramon Quiroga. 1-0! So, it began, with the stadium in uproar, amongst the Argentinian players there were few celebrations, for they still required three more goals. Kempes raced back to the halfway line, as they waited for the Peruvians to restart, their heads down, Calderon's men were in no rush, no point running headfirst into infamy, they would get there soon enough. Argentina went up a gear, Luque hit a post, River Plate's Oscar Ortiz clipped the bar. The home side were refused a penalty when Daniel Bertoni was brought down, Passarella came roaring upfield to head a Kempes cross narrowly wide. It just had to happen-a second goal arrived two minutes before half-time, when a corner was met by defender Alberto Tarantini's diving header finding its way in to the net past a fumbling Quiroga. Halfway there. An ecstatic Tarantini raced away punching the air-the crowd delirious. The stadium alight with newfound hope and expectation. Even on Menotti's face, there appeared a trace of relief. Across the terraces, the belief a miracle was back on after a horrific beginning had returned.

Half-time came, went and as the moon now hovered in all its majesty over the seaport of Rosario, the entire stadium danced through the interval. Four minutes into the second half, an increasingly, unplayable Kempes again combined with Bertoni, who from twelve yards unleashed a ferocious drive into the net. Ramon Quiroga could only stare and watch as the ball ripped past him. Argentina were closing in. Peru immediately substituted their Captain, Chumpitaz, who looked shocked at his withdrawal. Quiroga stood with hands on hips staring dismally at the turf. His fellow defenders around him like onlookers at a car crash, half daring not to stare, for none appeared capable of looking each other in the eye. 3-0. Menotti's men were trampling all over Peru, as once more they swarmed forward. *El Matador*, the electrifying, long-haired Kempes, headed down in the penalty area, for his unmarked partner-in-crime, Leopoldo Luque, to stab the ball into the net past a floored Quiroga, from four yards. 4-0! A roar like incoming thunder erupted across the terraces, as a lone soldier on the touchline fell to his knees in tears. Scene of delirium broke out not just in the stadium, but around the country. Once freed from the joyful clasps of his *compadres*, the scorer Luque stared upwards towards the dark heavens dedicating the goal to his recently, departed, brother Jose.

…At exactly the same time that goal was scored, 20:20, the car of the Argentinian Secretary of Treasury Juan Alemann, suddenly exploded in flames outside his house, in Amenabar street 1024, the plush neighbourhood of Belgrano, in Buenos Aires. Call the bomb, a gift, a message even from the Junta, one man in particularly. During the build up to the *Mundial,* there had been no greater critic of the amount of money spent than Alemann. New stadiums were built in Córdoba, Mendoza and Mar del Plata, another three that already existed were completely renovated. River, Vélez and Rosario Central. Brand spanking, gleaming, hotels appeared, routes and new communication systems built. The spending totally out of control. Like the deceased General Actis, he too thought it mad the size of the expenditure, one Argentina simply could not afford. A sum of $700,000 million dollars that Alemann publicly labelled at a meeting with the world media as, 'Complete nonsense'. A figure ten times over the original budget. Such negative comments infuriated the Junta, Alemann's words forced them into explaining what exactly such a monstrous amount of money had been spent on and where?

All roads led back to two men. Vice-Admiral Lacoste and his superior Admiral Massera-these two did not forget or forgive. Juan Alemann's card had been well and truly marked. In an interview for Argentine magazine *Revista Veintitres*, back in 2005, Alemann admitted that he knew at the time it was Massera who gave the order for the bomb, because of his constant criticism, he just couldn't publicly say so! A bomb with a kilogram and a half of explosives went off, such was the force of the blast it destroyed the ground floor of his home. Every window on the block was shattered by the detonation and a just a miracle nobody was killed. A message sent by Lacoste that he and the Junta had not forgotten what they regarded as his treason and the only reason they let him live was that his international status at organisations such as the United Nations, were such, they simply didn't need the hassle of another dead body to deal with…

  On the field, the footballing massacre continued unabated. Chance created, missed, but with all the certainty that the dimming stars would be followed by a rising sun, you just knew another was coming along soon. Twenty minutes remained when Rene Houseman steered the ball into an empty, Peruvian goal, after winger Daniel Ortiz's cross bypassed Quiroga at his near post. It was carnival time in Rosario, for any doubts that remained had now vanished. 5-0! A World Cup final awaited against Holland. The stadium awash with blue and white flags. In the VIP box, a content looking President Videla sat with arms crossed, Kissinger alongside him. Eighteen minutes from time, Luque made it 6-0! The Peruvian defenders all but stood and watched as the Argentinian forward took aim from twelve yards, with time to pick his spot, firing low past a clearly, distressed, Ramon Quiroga. The keeper was close to tears, for he knew what awaited him after this game. Quiroga was actually born in Rosario. Here at the crime scene of Peru's, greatest humiliation, *El Loco* had no doubt who was going to be public enemy number one after this fiasco for his adopted nation. The referee Wurtz ended the game, as the Peruvians scurried off quickly amid wild and fervent scenes of Argentine joy. Post-match, Calderon refused to speak to the press, choosing instead like his team to just get the hell out of Argentina. The prayers of a

God-fearing nation had been answered, the miracle realised. One hardly delivered by God, but the Generals. How did they achieve it?

It now appeared quite certain that President Videla ordered their supreme Mr fix-it, Colonel Lacoste to fix the result and secure Argentina's place in the final. Lacoste met with senior officials travelling with the Peruvian squad and they agreed a price, more so it was rumoured with a gun at their heads. 35,000 tonnes of grain were to be immediately shipped from Argentina to Peru, $50m of credits unfrozen and substantial bribes paid directly to Peruvian government ministers from accounts held by the Argentine navy. It was also claimed three member of the football squad were offered extra cash to enthuse the others. The players themselves paid just $20,000 each to take the fall. A paltry fistful of dollars for having to live with such shame for dishonouring the red stripe.

The Peruvians returned home in abject shame and fans were waiting for them at Lima airport with rotten throat, according to Chumpitaz, 'They shouted that we had been bought. The people were enraged, it was very sad.'

The boys from Peru did indeed pay a heavy price for their pieces of silver. Defender Ernesto Manzo got drunk one night in a Lima bar and told the entire sorry story to a pair of investigative Argentinian journalists. However, the next day when sober, Manzo went back on his wild tale, claiming he had made the whole thing up to simply keep the drinks coming. Goalkeeper Ramon Quiroga was another who spoke to the same reporters. He admitted something did go on in Rosario that just wasn't right. The following day a bomb exploded in the stadium where the keeper was playing. Nobody was killed, but the message clear. Keep your fucking mouth firmly shut. Others were not so lucky, tragically one man did pay the ultimate price. The coach Marcus Calderon never got over what happened in 1978. It haunted him. Rumours were in December 1987, Calderon was set to give an interview with an unnamed American newspaper to blow the entire scam wide open. Two days beforehand, the plane he was travelling on with his then-team Allianza Lima, inexplicably dropped out of the sky into the Pacific Ocean off the Peruvian coast. Forty-four people were killed, including Calderon. Silenced forever. To this day in Peru, the crash is shrouded in mystery with claims of conspiracies and cover-ups. In the continent of the blinding sun and its shadow, the truth is never easy, if indeed possible to discover. Argentina had made the final, the show went on, but at what price?

A sad, sordid and tragic tale.

CHAPTER EIGHTEEN
TOMB OF ANGELS
ARGENTINA V HOLLAND: THE 1978 WORLD CUP FINAL

'In hindsight, we should never have played in the World Cup. I strongly believe that.'
Leopoldo Luque

Estadio Monumental. Sunday 25th June 1978. A nation expected. Argentina awoke and despite everything their people were being forced to endure in everyday life. The horrors that came in the dark, the missing loved ones. The sheer evil of it all. As the team bus made its way through the Buenos Aires streets, people waved rosary beads, openly praying that Cesar Menotti's team delivered for them on this day of days. 'It was a crazy thing,' recalled

Menotti. 'They were on all sides, with the children, they were ahead of the bus. The players looked at each other like saying, 'Where do we go?' Incredible, there was a need. Some imbeciles say that we did a favour to the dictatorship, I could tell if I were as imbecile as them, that we also put three million people on the street, when there could not be more than three.'

The fallout, controversy of the 6-0 victory over Peru still raged with accusations flying, mostly from Brazil, whose team were now back home fuming. Elsewhere, more trouble erupted when the Argentine FA lobbied for a late, refereeing switch, arguing, inexplicably, but succeeding in claiming that the FIFA designated Israeli official Abraham Klein was an inappropriate choice, due to said political links between Holland and Israel. So, it was Klein shamefully missed out on the biggest game of his life and in came the Italian, Sergio Gonella. Said by many to be a lot weaker than the original choice. In charge of this fiasco was none other than Vice-Admiral Carlos Lacoste, it was no surprise the Generals wanted rid after Klein's masterful performance earlier in the tournament, the Argentina v Italy match. It was hard to believe that the likes of Videla, Massera and Agosti, a sadistic triumvirate, even this blood soaked continent had never witnessed stood on the verge of the greatest heist in football history.

In the Argentinian dressing room, Menotti told his team not to look up at the Generals in the VIP box, but the people on the terraces. It would be them whom they were playing for, not the regime. 'You're playing for your families and the people, not those sons of bitches!' A final rousing chant of 'Viva Argentina!' …They headed out.

· As for the Dutch? Their trip to the stadium from the hotel took far longer than it should have done, as they, like the

Peruvians, were given an unexpected, unwanted, guided tour of the Buenos Aires backstreets, where hostile crowds lined the routes. This continued all the way to the *Estadio Monumental*. Wired and wanting nothing more than to get stuck into the Argentinian team, matters hardly improved for the Dutch, when they were kept waiting a whole eight minutes on the pitch-side receiving the expected abuse, of whistles and derisory chants. Again, obviously a deliberate tactic to let them feel the full venomous wrath of 82,000 Argentinians intent on a lynching, if their night did not go well. Finally, to a tumultuous reception by a home crowd already whipped up into a frenzy, Argentina decided to emerge from the tunnel and the *Monumental* rocked! A snowstorm of confetti glittered like a million diamonds under the floodlights, in the Buenos Aires evening. A tidal wave of emotion-banging drums. The bouncing terraces full of dancing, tear-stained faces, so wound up with patriotic euphoria, their voices already choked, bone raw through roaring out their country's name. Argentina's mind games had not yet finished with the Dutch. A further twist in what was undoubtedly, yet another pre-arranged move, as the coin was tossed by Gonella, the South American players led by a passionate Daniel Passarella complained about Rene van der Kerkhof's plaster cast, that was protecting a broken bone, even though he had worn it on his wrist without complaint, since Holland's opening group game. All done to try and gain a modicum of psychological benefit by damaging the concentration and rattling Ernst Happel's team.

The fifty-seven-year-old Austrian Happel was one of Europe's great, coaching mercenaries. Tough, uncompromising, tactically brilliant, he had already led an extraordinary life. Born Vienna, in 1938, as an aspiring youth player, a defender at Rapid Vienna, Happel was forced to join the *Hitler Jugend*, (Hitler youth), but this was no Nazi, young Ernst refused to sing along to their songs and was kicked out. In 1943, he was conscripted and sent to the Eastern Front. Come the war's end, Happel was a prisoner of the American forces, but he escaped by jumping off a Munich train wagon and in a devastated post-war landscape, a bomb-ravaged Germany, it took him a long time to make his way home to Vienna. Once there, Happel took up playing once more at Rapid Vienna. Come 1978, a managerial career had already seen Happel take in Belgium's ADO Den Haag, San Francisco Gales, Feyenoord of Holland, The Spaniards of Sevilla, Club Brugge and now the Netherlands on the brink of a World Cup final. Happel talked rarely to the press, but did say 'We are optimistic, we do not know what the word fear means and we do not care what team Menotti chooses.' This was a tough and resilient *Oranje* bunch, full of world-class experienced players not to be pushed around, whom could play or fight you. Ruud Krol, Wim Jansen, Johan Neeskens, Arie Haan, the Van Der Kerkhof twins Rene and Willy, Johnny Rep. These were the type of character never to bow down. They had already lost one heart breaking World Cup final four years previously to West Germany, not again.

  With Passarella constantly yelling in his face, the referee Gonella cracked, initially ordering Rene to remove the plaster cast. Then, having suffered sufficient annoyance, the Dutch snapped! Enough was enough. Their Captain Ruud Krol telling his team, 'Come on lads, back to the dressing room!' He was no fan of their opponents and had experienced personally some of the lies that were being spread about the truth of what was really occurring in

Argentina, when a journalist from *El Grafico*, made up a letter that he had supposedly sent to his daughter back home in Holland.

'Don't worry, my daughter, about what they say about Argentina, it's all a lie. Argentina is the land of love. Everything here is tranquil and beautiful and the soldiers fire flowers from their guns.'

Chaos reigned, Krol recalled, 'It was unbelievable! An official from FIFA should have intervened. I'm convinced that both Argentina's later arrival on the pitch and the protest over Rene, were carefully planned. We had already warmed up and where we made a big mistake was not returning to the dressing room as we intended, even if it meant delaying the World Cup final by another thirty minutes. Our manager, Happel, had said when they complained to the referee about Rene, 'We'll go back to the dressing room,' but unfortunately, Neeskens translated his threat to the Argentinian players. And they told the referee. When he realised we were threatening to leave the pitch, he changed his mind and said that Rene could play. He did not want to take the decision which would have stopped the match, even if only temporarily. He knew the eyes of the world were on him and was embarrassed. We were very angry and that's why we were not concentrating properly in the opening minutes of the match. We should have played them at their own game and returned to the dressing room as threatened. Neeskens had said to their Captain, Passarella, 'If that's how you want it, you can play the World Cup final on your own' It was our mistake.'

Johnny Rep described the atmosphere as 'Boiling hell,' this, all before a ball was kicked-but the Dutch were not going to fall for the South American's antics. The situation was finally settled to some agree when the referee suggested another bandage to cover the plaster cast and to a watching world wide audience and all in the stadium, a modicum of peace was declared in the *Monumental*. It wouldn't last long. As the Dutch returned to the field, an angry Johan Neeskens turned to Rene Van der Kerkhof and declared, 'All right, let's go and get them!' Come the national anthems, the host team had been under instructions to turn to the VIP box and salute President Videla, instead, they did as their coach asked and faced the people. A brave act, one that if they won would be instantly forgotten by the Junta, but, heaven forbid Holland went home with the trophy, then all hell would have been let loose upon their heads.

'We will attack flat out,' claimed Menotti beforehand. 'Holland have superior, physical strength, but we will continue to take the same risks to go straight for victory. We have achieved more than I dared hoped for three months ago. The Final will be decided by possession. Holland's total football is probably unanswerable at its peak, but they have to get the ball from us first. I'm a little scared, but in spite of this,

we will attack from the start.'

The game kicked off and the well-orchestrated, if unsportsmanlike, pre-match, high jinxes of Menotti's team, meant it was never going to be nothing more than a footballing war. As many suspected, Gonella swiftly lost all control, that was if he ever had any in the first place. It was brutal beyond words-the tackles flew high and dangerous with all the fifty-fifty decisions going to the host nation, thus only increasing the already, ignited Dutch fury. The early skirmishes bordered on carnage. Jan Poortvliet sent Daniel Bertoni flying, Haan nearly caused a riot when he cut down Osvaldo Ardiles like a tree and Américo Gallego squared up to Neeskens in the fall-out. The Dutch were clearly riled, but still had the best of the first half. An early chance shown itself for Johnny Rep, when he headed past the Argentinian post missing by inches-causing gasps from the terraces. Holland came again, Wim Jansen's cross was misjudged by the home defenders, only for Rep again to take advantage, firing in a shot that was saved superbly by Ubaldo Fillol. A million rosary beads clutched. Their team like a deer in headlights, able to kick orange shirts, but not go past one. At long last, Argentina awoke. Daniel Bertoni broke clear, but rushed his effort, shooting badly wide of the keeper Jan Jongbloed's goal. Shortly after, Passarella had a header scrambled clear out of the Dutch six yard box. A lull followed with each team intent on crippling the other, until seven minutes before half time, Argentina struck first blood. It began with Osvaldo Ardiles dribbling clear of the midfield battleground-a beautiful sight, this slim figure, almost balletic, his dancing feet tangoing with the ball, skipped past two fearful, Dutch lunges, before finding Leopoldo Luque. A slip of a pass to the onrushing Mario Kempes, who took it in his stride before firing low under Jongbloed, creating scene of absolute mayhem across the *Monumental* terraces. Off soared Kempes with his arms raised on a surface covered in sparkling confetti. Some of it so thick you couldn't see the green turf. The noise of the crowd accompanying him like a rattling crack of thunder. 1-0 to Argentina! From the restart, Holland poured forward in search of an equaliser, but when players such as Ardiles were being booked for attempting to rip Rene Van Der Kerkhoff's head off as he tore past him, it became apparent Argentina were by this time beyond fired up! As the half closed, the host nation should have made it two when Passarella again caused havoc in the Dutch area, only for the ball to be cleared. Holland broke-Neeskens headed down to Willy Van Der Kerkhof, onto the Anderlecht winger Robbie Rensinbrink, who as time appeared to stand still in the stadium fired in a shot, only for Fillol to save with his feet. The *Monumental* breathed one collective, giant, sigh of relief. Gonella's whistle blew to end proceedings, Argentina were just forty-five minutes away from becoming World Champions.

The second-half swiftly turned into a game of cat and mouse with the Dutch pressing forward, Argentina sitting-looking to counter attack for that killer second goal. Hardly lock tight at the back, despite Daniel Passarella pulling fellow defenders here, there and all over, they definitely remained fallible. Rene van der Kerkhof ran clear, laid the ball back for Arie Haan, whose shot was deflected wide. Another effort by Haan, this time his speciality, a long rang drive was tipped away by Fillol-then, Bertoni was away, he squared the ball to the unmarked Luque, but Jongbloed was at his feet. The scoreboard ticked on as the Buenos Aires skies turned black. Still, Argentina led. Happel brought on his substitutes. The tall and effective centre-forward from Roda JC, Dirk Nanninga for Johnny Rep and defender Wim Suurbier for the exhausted Wim Jansen. With Nanninga on the park, Holland's tactics went from their so much admired, slick and swift passing movements, 'Total Football'. Players effortlessly interchanging positions, an intense work rate matched by a masterful touch and technique, at its beating *Oranje* heart, the bewitching Johan Cruyff. Revered by many as footballing gods of the seventies, how they missed Cruyff's, not just his ability, but all consuming presence. Now, to try and find a way through Passarella's creaking, but still brave and determined *compadres* to fight (quite literally to the death), Holland, for want of a better expression would lump it for Nanninga.

 Menotti reacted by bringing on the strong-running Omar Larossa, for a tiring and injured Ardiles, plus Rene House Houseman for his left-winger Oscar Ortiz, who had suffered a desperate night. Despite it being a contest of huge drama, the real quality had been lacking as both sides remained happy enough to kick each other in the air. A diabolical tackle by Passarella on Neeskens was ignored by Gonella, then, an even more outrageous lunge by Luis Galvan on the same Dutch player, yet still no booking? Gonella appeared shellshocked, unable to cope with the immense pressure now crashing down upon his shoulders. Shortly after, Alberto Tarantini joined in on the Neeskens, free for all. Still no card? To confound Dutch anger, Krol was then booked by Gonella for tripping Bertoni, amidst a chorus of howling Argentinian protests led by guess who? Passarella. Gonella, a bank manager by trade could not get the yellow card out of his top pocket fast enough.

 The *Monumental* was no longer a simple football ground, it had become a church, a mass congregation praying, clutching tight onto rosary beads, a roar of faith reaching high into the heavens, as Holland came forward once more with eight minutes left to play. The Dutch left-back from PSV Eindhoven, the tirelessly and hardworking Jan Poortvliet had moved forward to pick up a wild clearance form a tiring Tarantini. He found Haan, who from the centre of the field launched a pass out wide-right to René van de Kerkhof. His cross into the Argentina penalty was met with perfection by Nanninga, rising high to head beautifully past Fillol into the net. 1-1! A deathly, silence suddenly took hold and engulfed the *Monumental* terraces. The tall figure of twenty-nine-year old, Groningen born Nanninga disappeared under a mob of joyful orange. Menotti came off the bench to encourage his players, they appeared spent, exhausted, the crowd too stunned, their dream in shatters. High in the VIP box, the Generals applauded, but bore the look of being present at their own funerals. Lacoste especially, for it could well be his. Argentina restarted-as if in retaliation for the goal, once more the increasingly dangerous Neeskens was targeted, punched to the ground by Passarella. It was an astonishingly, brutal attack, worthy of a jail sentence, never mind a sending off. Yet, Gonella never acted, claiming instead he saw nothing? Far more worryingly, the two linesman refused to acknowledge Passarella's actions. As players of both sides squared up to each other and passions raged, it felt the best scenario was reach full-time without anyone actually being killed! The game continued with Holland going for Argentina's throats at the death and the deafening whistling from the *Monumental* terraces demanded Gonella ended their torment. A Ruud Krol free-kick from inside his own half, somehow found its way through to Robbie Rensenbrink inside the home penalty area. With 45-12, showing on the electronic scoreboard and defenders watching, as if hypnotised, Rensinbrink managed to get a shot off, only to see it roll agonisingly onto the post, then an Argentine shirt hack the ball away to safety. How it stayed out? Maybe the prayers of the many outweighed the best wishes of the *Oranje* few, but the Dutch had come so close to winning the trophy with almost the last kick of the game. Robbie Rensinbrink looked to the heavens, just an inch the other way? Even the

Argentinian woodwork appeared to be doing its national service. A last post.

Looking at his watch, a sweat-stained Sergio Gonella blew for full-time to try and separate the two football, warring, nations with an extra, thirty minutes. Everyone inside the stadium took a huge breath, for the eleventh World Cup was still alive.

…Ernst Happel walked amongst his team sat lying on the turf. He urged patience, for Argentina were rocking, more importantly stressing they kept calm. Easier said than done maybe, but Happel insisted it was theirs' to win now. The burning pain of losing to West Germany when the Dutch mentality had been all about revenge for World War two. How the Nazis even stole their bicycles when retreating. Of how they threw it away in all of cities, Munich, where the bastards plotted in bier-kellers. A first minute penalty, after the Dutch had toyed with the Germans from kick-off- a sudden acceleration form Cruyff into the penalty box, Berti Vogts brought him down and Neeskens smashed it with a historic relish past Sepp Maier. Holland's indulgence in possession, their over-confidence in just wanting to show off, punish the Germans ultimately cost them everything, Happel did not want history to repeat itself. Seven of the 1978 team had played in the 1974 final. Jongbloed, Suurbier, Haan, Krol, Neeskens, Rep and Rensinbrink. They had suffered terrible trauma through that loss, their coach pleaded for them to ensure not again. This time around to do their job proper and send the South Americans into mourning.

Cesar Menotti fought hard to raise his team's spirits. Eight minutes from victory, only then for the skies to so nearly fall on their heads, if not for the width of a goal post, it could easily have done so. *El Flaco* stayed upbeat, he talked again of the people, their families. That special bond Menotti had created between himself and players certainly shown itself, for when extra time began, they came out with an even greater desire to win.

With both sides seemingly still insistent on causing GHB upon the other, the substitute Omar Larossa went for Suurbier like a drunk in a bar room brawl and was actually 'miraculously' booked by Gonella, as the Dutch demanded he rightly be sent off. A minute later Larossa struck again, this time for a shocking, scything, tackle on Jan Poortvliet. Astonishingly, to the disbelief of Happel's men, Sergio Gonella refused to expel the Independiente man? Holland retaliated when Poortvliet tripped Kempes from behind and to no one's real surprise, especially those in orange, Gonella booked him. In between the mayhem, opportunities arose. Houseman ran though only to be bravely blocked at the last. Inspired by this, Argentina, with the crowd rising at their back took over, their football once more expansive. Luque and Kempes in particularly found a second wind-*El Matador* flew into the penalty area riding Dutch defenders almost on his back, before facing Jongbloed, who dived at the Argentinian's feet, the ball falling, as Poortvleit and Suurbier tried to block, it rolled in slow motion over the goal line. 2-1! All down to the fleet of foot and sheer determination of Mario Kempes. Argentina led once more, the *Monumental* bayed in ecstasy and sheer relief.

The first period of extra-time closed and Menotti was off the bench once more pushing, cajoling his shattered troops. Almost there. High in the VIP box, Videla and the Generals applauded. A long night under the Buenos Aires stars was building to a climax. As for Holland? Happel simply urged keep going. Nothing was settled yet, although they appeared out on their feet. Gonella restarted proceedings just in time for the wild Larossa to foul Arie Haan, who in turn went for Leopoldo Luque, sending him crashing! Luque stayed down, no rush, the electronic screen wasn't going to stop. After what felt an eternity, he got back up, dusted himself down, the game went on-Houseman went through once more, as the *Monumental* held a collective breath, the Huracan man fired into the side netting. The Dutch were reeling, almost spent, Luque also careered through, only to be stopped by Jongbloed. Five minutes remained as Holland still tried to pushed forward. The game was stretched now beyond all measure-more like basketball. Argentina won back possession, Mario Kempes raced as the wind once more into the Dutch penalty area. A one-two with Daniel Bertoni saw the ball run clear and as it fell loose, Bertoni was first on the rebound, making it 3-1! Total delirium exploded!-Argentinians danced, cried and screamed at the heavens above. The *Sun of May* in the centre of the Argentinian flag was blinding. The drums and songs rang out in salute. For the first time ever, the World Cup was most definitely theirs!

So, amidst scenes of crazed hysteria and madness, all that remained was to receive the coveted World Cup trophy off President Jorge Videla. That dubious honour fell to a young man born in Chacabuco, the run-down backwaters of a Buenos Aire province. He began his journey at third division Club Atlético Sarmiento, before leaving the hometown of former first lady Eva Perón, to join River Plate. Despite small in stature for a central defender, this boy had something special, off he soared up through the ranks. In time to Captain the first team. Argentina, with Cesar Menotti eventually called and with five River Plate players already in his squad, *El Falco* handed him the armband. A natural leader, Daniel Passarella took the trophy from Videla's bloodstained hands, he did so for the people who roared across the *Estadio Monumental*, as their *Capitan* held it high. 'Riotous, exuberant chants of 'ARGENTINA!'' filled the air across Buenos Aires and beyond, millions of people took to the streets in celebration. As for Videla? He bore the look of a conman who had just gotten away with the biggest scam of his life.

In the complex hidden behind the palm trees and classical statues on the Avenida del Libertador, it was indeed another story. The reality beyond the illusion existed a short walk away in *ESMA*. The revelry, the deafening, uplifting-sounds of joy and festivity, as the people let rip their emotions. The horns, out of tune bugles, drums, fireworks and the singing resonated loud through the prison walls and could all be heard clearly by the prisoners. Some, no doubt chained to the walls, waiting for the next cut. In what was a play on the word, debauched, a chosen few were allowed out of their cells to watch the match and the trophy presentation with the guards on a tiny, black and white television set. Many of these poor souls being tortured by the same men only hours before. Come the full time whistle, the chief torturer at ESMA, a brute of a human being by the name of Jorge Acosta embraced the selected prisoners one by one, repeatedly shouting, 'We won! We won!'

Some of these were taken by a drunken Acosta out in an unmarked car, driven amongst the thousands of vehicles around Buenos Aires, filled with flags and their countrymen honking horns, a traffic jam of pure joy. One of the prisoners was Graciela Daleo who survived to tell her tale. Graciela later testified about that unholy, ghastly experience. 'So close, and light years away from *ESMA*. If I had attempted to shout out that I was a *desaparcida*, nobody would have given a damn.'

Before returning to *ESMA*, the laughing Acosta stopped off at a restaurant with the prisoners and treated them to a pizza. Shortly after they were all returned to their cells, where the blood had been wiped clean off the walls and soon Acosta would start on them again. This, despite the confetti snowstorms, the public joy and wonder of the *Mundial,* was the true story of that heady, long, gone footballing fiesta. The people may have thanked God for their great victory, but, in reality, it was the Generals who won. That final evening on the 25th June 1978, as the screams of the tortured at *ESMA* were drowned out by the roaring of the crowd, the *Estadio Monumental*, like the entire tournament that had gone before it,

was nothing more than a tomb of angels.

For the victors, the culmination of a long-perceived plan that had a perfect ending. Later that evening, at the Ornate Ballroom in Buenos Aires, a triumphant President Videla declared in his speech to hundreds of drunken revellers. High ranking officers and officials, all with their wives, girlfriends, or prostitutes, 'I want to thank those who permitted Argentina to be the host of this event and gave the Argentine people a chance to show what it is capable of. This World Cup was the symbol of peace.'…

'I have nothing to regret, I was very loyal to my team and to the people.'
Cesar Luis Menotti

CHAPTER NINETEEN

In November 1978, just four months after *Mundial 78* finished, Sheffield United and Tottenham Hotspur manager's, Harry Haslam and Keith Burkinshaw, along with other club officials, flew out together to Argentina on scouting missions. The World Cup had electrified people back home, the chance of a bargain to be had was high. Times were changing, at least for a while. The once defining image of the Argentinians relating back to 1966, personified by the English media of the Captain Antonio Rattin, being sent off in that infamous quarter-final against England, was being severely tested. Back then, Rattin simply refused to go, swapping tasty insults with English supporters on the terraces, squatting down on the velvet-red carpet, before finally the long walk of shame, but not before wiping his hands on the Union Jack corner flag, as he went to a cacophony of boos.

Times were most definitely changing!

The emotional scenes of the ticker tape receptions for Cesar Menotti's team had become the new 'defining' image of the nation. It was to live long in the memory, an all engulfing veil, proving highly effective in hiding the reality really occurring. A hell on earth. Haslam had moved fast already provisionally sealing deals for two Argentinian players. River Plate forward Alex Sabella and Estudiantes midfielder Pedro Verde. Like a kid let loose in a toyshop, it was believed he also had first option on Osvaldo Ardiles and Ricardo Villa, but reneged, leaving Spurs free to take over the deal bringing both back to White Hart Lane. There was though one other who it appeared was up for grabs.

Already in Argentina, acting as an interpreter for the Sheffield United party was Oscar Arce, who played in England for Aston Villa, back in the late sixties. A tip off from his friend, the one and only Antonio Rattin, about a very special eighteen-year-old kid called Diego Maradona, who had already played for Argentina and was currently plying his remarkable talent for Argentinos Juniors. The word was from Rattin that for the right price Maradona could be available for a transfer to England. Harry Haslam was taken to see Diego play and he knew at first glance they had to act fast, turning to Arce saying, 'I'll take him now, how much!?' Haslam was introduced to Jorge Cyterszpiler, who explained Diego was willing to go, so long as the money was right and the deal included his close friend, who also played for Argentinos, Carlos Fren. Haslam instantly agreed, sums were discussed, a fee of around £400,000, including Fren was set. Cyterszpiler told Hallam he would deal with the troublesome Argentinos President Prospero Consoli, but told the Englishman make sure the money was available and 'rapido!' It all felt too good to be true for the Sheffield United manager, who was yet to even meet Diego face to face. This apart, all appeared the road was clear for a deal to be done and fast.

That same night Haslam went back to the hotel where he was staying and later received a knock on his door, an army officer in full uniform, claiming to speak for the Argentine Junta. It was explained to Haslam by this charming, young, smiling, military officer, that if the Maradona transfer was to be allowed to go through, then the Generals must also be compensated-taken cared of to the sum of another £150,000, otherwise, Maradona wouldn't be allowed near the plane, never mind on it. Although smiling, there was the air of a threat, the something of the night about him, this man, that deeply troubled Haslam.

The next morning he rang home and spoke to the Sheffield United chairman John Hassall. Haslam explained all that had occurred. Hassall listened and told his manager to ring back later that day after he had passed on the news to the director who was going to bankroll the deal, the multi-millionaire Albert Bramhall. Originally, the Bramhall family was more than willing to put up the money for the Maradona deal, for they trusted their manager's opinion implicitly, but the latest development with the army officer's visit sounded like nothing more than a bribery attempt. It most definitely spooked them. So, they pulled the plug. Although hugely, disappointed, Haslam was also a realist. They were used to back handers and the Mr ten per cent in English football transfer business, but this one? This one had real teeth. Haslam and the Sheffield board had no wish to dip their toes into the murky world of Argentinian politics. Especially with the likes of Videla and his Generals. They knew of the rumours. Instead, they contacted River Plate and Estudiantes and went ahead with the Alex Sabella and Pedro Verde deals. For a time, Sabella's wing play lit up Bramhall Lane, but he swiftly faded out of favour, into obscurity, before being shipped off to Leeds United in 1980. Verde sadly struggled from the off, playing only ten times in three years. As for Harry Haslam? He has to be congratulated for having the courage to try for Diego Maradona, if successful, who knows how history could have played out for Sheffield United, as they entered the eighties with Diego in their line-up? Sadly.

An angry, deeply frustrated Jorge Cyterszpiler tried a last gasp trick by claiming Arsenal had come in for Maradona to raise new interest, but nobody bit.

The sharks had already done their damage.

The deal was dead.

CHAPTER TWENTY
GLASGOW. EVER FALLEN IN LOVE WITH SOMEONE

The Buzzcocks sang gloriously in that period of the late seventies, *Ever fallen in love with someone.* On Saturday 2nd June 1979, an eighteen-year-old Diego Armando Maradona took the acclaim, along with the rest of his *compadres* from the Hampden Park centre-circle, after the 62,000 crowd rose as one after losing their hearts to the World Champions, one player in particularly. The Scots were spellbound. They had heard rumours, read newspaper stories of Argentina's army cropped, short-haired little playmaker. Tales abounded of a young sorcerer who could make the ball talk, maybe a little far-fetched, only then to witness Diego in action with their own eyes.

Not since 1960, when Real Madrid with Alfredo Di Stefano, Ferenc Puskas and Francisco Gento came to Glasgow to enthral and enrapture, taking apart Eintracht Frankfurt 7-3, to win a fifth European Cup on the row, had the famous old stadium seen such scenes. This was the final game of a European tour that saw a proud Cesar Menotti prove to the world after claims their triumph was only achieved because of being on home soil, that they could go anywhere and compete-also to showcase the outrageous talent of his new, magical, number ten.

Diego Armando Maradona.

After winning the World Cup, Argentina had basked in its glory for a long, maybe too long a period without playing any competitive matches. Her people still rejoicing in the memories of the *Mundial*. Helping them forget the everyday dangers of living in a Fascist dictatorship. The fear of saying the wrong thing, to be seen with the wrong person, becoming just another statistic in the ever growing number of the thousands of *Los Desaparecidos*. Their nation's triumph had for a short time hid many from the realism of their existence, but nothing lasted forever, they like their footballers had to face the cold, grim, day of reality that nothing had changed.

Come the start of 1979, Cesar Menotti, now a living God in Argentina and still a pointed thorn in the Junta's shoe that they daren't attempt to remove, went back to work. He successfully oversaw the Under-20's qualification matches for the upcoming World Youth Cup finals to held in Japan.

He also arranged a European tour for the senior team. The first stage of preparation for the next tournament to be held three years away in Spain. With being holders, they had no qualification matches to play, so these games would be integral for Menotti's future plans. Argentina would play Holland in an instant replay of the World Cup Final, Italy, the Republic of Ireland and Scotland. A tough schedule for the World Champions

Firstly though it came as no surprise that Menotti was being headhunted by many of the World's top clubs. Barcelona and Real Madrid at the top of a long and vaunted list. Flooded with offers *El Flaco* took a little time out to consider. A host of European entourages came knocking with promises of vast wealth, when in all reality he was not yet ready to leave for pastures new. It did though leave him with plenty of leverage to renegotiate his contract with the Argentinian FA. Initially, there was outrage, Menotti's demands were deemed outrageous, far too extravagant. So much that the AFA President Alfredo Cantilo, actually resigned for a time over the matter. In his place came a temporary President from Independiente, Julio Grondona, who succeeded in finally reaching a compromise with Menotti. A new four-year contract to 31st December 1982, a $120,000 signing on fee and a $10,000 monthly salary. Also, he would receive double any bonus handed out to the players. A lavish deal, an interesting side note to this drama, such was the fine job done by Grondona, he actually remained in position to become permanent President. Much to Alfredo Cantilo's shock! It also just so happened that Grondona had the backing of Vice-Admiral Carlos Lacoste. Not surprisingly, Cantilo went quietly.

Finally, on 25th April 1979, Argentina took the field once more. Before setting off for Europe, Menotti's team played Bulgaria in Buenos Aires winning 2-1, the goals from Daniel Passarella and Rene Houseman. The World Cup holders official tour began in Switzerland, against Holland on 22nd May 1979, at Berne's *Wankdorf* stadium. The venue for the 1954 World Cup final. A special friendly to mark the 75th anniversary of FIFA. In all truths, this was no friendly, Holland desired revenge. Before and during that final, some Dutch players feared they might not have been allowed to leave the country alive if having won in extra time. Or had Robbie Rensinbrink's last minute effort gone the other side of the post and into the net. To imagine such, the nightmare of falling at the last for a nation, a hysterical crowd, a Junta seething for revenge, who knew what could have been the result of such torment? These memories still resonated loud for the men in orange, they were angry. Also, the Dutch felt cheated as to the pre-match goings on, the rancid one-sided performance of the Italian referee Sergio Gonella. This would be no friendly. Argentina were equally keen to win the game to prove their own point. The players had heard of the strong rumours regarding the *Mundial*. How sweet to put Holland to the sword proving that whatever happened before the final, that evening in the *Estadio Monument*, on Sunday 25th June 1978, it was indeed a fair scrap to the finish. Not even the Junta could have bribed a goal-post..

They began the game with nine players who started the final, plus defender Hugo Villaverde in place of Luis Galvan and for the injured Mario Kempes, the new kid on the block, Diego Maradona. Although the actual match finished 0-0, this was by no means a dull contest, as both sides went hell for leather to win it. Captained as ever by their wonderful defender Ruud Krol earning his 65th cap, it was soon apparent just how desperate Holland were to beat the South Americans, as they dished out some horrendous challenges, mostly on Maradona. This occasion was Diego's major debut on the world scene and he was determined to impress. Despite being picked out by the Dutch defenders for special treatment, most of the time the orange shirts couldn't get near him. Come the second half, they appeared happy to settle for the penalty shoot-out to decide the result. Menotti shown his hand by withdrawing the attacking Bertoni and Luque and replacing with the defensive duo of Barbas and Trossero. Left fighting a lone battle up front, Maradona continued to tease and torment Krol's men. It was a performance of sufficient quality to suggest that the rumours were true-late on he soared through clear on goal before being brought to ground by

Jan Peters. A clear penalty not given. Appearing very much a political decision by the referee. The game finished scoreless-pride kept by both sides, the fact Argentina won the penalty competition 8-7, with Maradona amongst the scorers, to receive a meaningless FIFA Jubilee Crystal trophy, was something the Dutch players could just about live with. Another defeat to the South Americans, away from their tricks and sheer hostility they encountered back in the final, might have tipped some over the edge.

Four days later,
the tour moved onto Rome where Italy lay in wait at the *Olympic* Stadium. The previous afternoon saw both teams received an audience with Pope John 11, at the Vatican. For a highly, devoted Catholic like the teenage Maradona, this must have felt like touching the hand of God himself. The kid from Fiorito, the son of Diego senior and Dona Dalma Salvadora. His mother lighting candles for him as a small boy praying that their Diego would with his blessed talent find a way out of the ghetto. Her dreams it appeared in the shadow of Saint Peter's square were answered. The game against the Italian was a minor classic, as they fought out a 2-2 draw in front of 60,000. This again, no friendly as the tackles flew in thick and fast. On six minutes, Argentina took the lead when Passarella sent Tallares de Cordoba midfielder Jose Valencia clean through to beat Dino Zoff, despite AC Milan defender Fulvio Collovati's desperate attempts to clear off the goal-line. The Italians poured forward and grabbed a deserved equaliser just before the half hour, when winger Franco Causio smashed a superb volley past the keeper Ubaldo Fillol. Cesar Menotti's side had come to play and with Enzo Bearzot's team in in equally expansive mood, chances were aplenty. Ten minutes after half-time, the *azzurri* went in front when

their brilliant, young midfield playmaker from Florence, Giancarlo Antognoni set up Paolo Rossi.

2-1. A minute later, the World Champions hit right back when Gaetano Scirea brought down Maradona for a penalty and Passarella smashed past Zoff making it 2-2! These were the goals,

the true story of the game was a magnificent personal tussle between Diego and his man-marker, the twenty-five-year-old defensive-midfielder Marco Tardelli. The Juve man tried everything to curtail the threat of Maradona, but simply struggled to stay with him throughout The electric surges of sudden, blinding, pace as Diego received the ball, a drop of the shoulder and he was gone, with the Italian chasing in hot pursuit. The highly technical, clever, if needed to be brutal, Tardelli, did manage to catch Maradona at times, but it always appeared to be a desperate lunge, or an off the ball shove. Mostly, the Argentinian number ten ran him ragged to earn a well-deserved Man of the Match award. The next time the two sides came together, the *azzurri* would hand Diego Maradona over to someone who would enjoy taming 'El Diego' and more than blessed with the dark arts to do so. Claudio Gentile.

Three days later, Argentina played in Dublin at Lansdown Road against the Republic of Ireland. A charity match in aid of *UNICEF*. Cesar Menotti rested Diego Maradona on the bench, but come the second half with the game still

0-0, he unleashed him! Immediately, the South Americans went up a gear and the Irish crowd watched on in disbelief as Maradona tore past their terrified defenders, laying on chances for Barbas and Reinaldi, whom both hit the post.

Come the final whistle it finished scoreless, in amazing scenes, Lansdowne Road stood as one to applaud Diego Maradona's, short, but unforgettable cameo. The next day, the Irish newspapers went into overdrive about Diego. Headlines such as *'The Next Pele'*, typical of their reaction.

Finally,

It was off to Scotland for the final game of the tour. On a gloriously, hot Glasgow, summer's day, Cesar Menotti reverted to his strongest team that had played against Italy. Jock Stein's side opened well with half, decent opportunities for Arthur Graham and John Wark, but it wasn't long before Argentina took control and their number ten entered stage left. There were already murmurs of appreciation from the Hampden crowd when Maradona took possession, dragged the ball clear and hurtled at breakneck speed through six, dark blue, home shirts. It was electrifying to watch and on the terraces very much appreciated. On thirty-three minutes, Diego went once more accelerating down the middle of the park leaving two Scottish players gasping for breath, before passing for Leopoldo Luque to control, before hammering low past the keeper George Woods. Maradona had cut Scotland apart with alarming ease and it was a mere glimpse of what was to follow. The second half swiftly turned into a procession as the South Americans turned on the style looking every inch World Champions. Though still haunted by their nightmarish short stay at the *Mundial* twelve months previous, the Scots remained tough opposition with names such as Kenny Dalglish, John Wark and Asa Hartford on the team sheet, but all were made to look like stooges as Diego Maradona ran amok. On the hour, Luque dribbled around the substitute keeper for the injured George Wood,

Alan Rough, to make it 2-0, game over. All that was left to enjoy was a masterclass from a young kid swiftly becoming regarded as the finest young player in the world. George Wood recalled being in the tunnel before the game. 'Argentina were World Champions and had some big, tough men who looked like real footballers. There was this little fella who looked like the mascot-just a wee boy. I kind of acknowledged him as if to say, 'All the best, son, you'll need it!' Then, then the game began and he started beating our players as if they weren't there.' Twenty minutes from time the moment arrived on this late, June, Glasgow afternoon, with sun shadows sweeping over the pitch, that it felt like all in the stadium had been waiting for.

A breaking Jose Valencia played a cross-field pass into the Scottish penalty area, where a lurking Diego Maradona killed the ball dead, as Rough came charging out. Diego dummied him-the keeper dived the wrong way and the youngster rolled a nonchalant, cheeky shot in at the left hand post. Off he soared, screaming towards the heavens with arms raised. Maradona's first international goal and one that brought applause from all across Hampden Park. Astonishing scenes broke out as the home fans rose acclaiming Diego's moment of genius. It was the beginning of a beautiful affair between the two that seven years later in Mexico city reached a moment of pure rapture. Four minutes from time, the winger Arthur Graham ran through to pull a goal back that appeared yards offside, but it was scant consolation for the embarrassment they had been forced to endure. Come the final whistle, chants of 'ARGENTINA!' roared loud with Scottish accents. All eyes concentrated on one bare-chested youngster, with a swapped Scotland shirt draped over his shoulder. They could only dream! Diego Maradona was deeply touched by these scenes, they have always stayed with him. 'Afterwards, the crowd started to scream 'ARGENTINA!' I couldn't believe it! I took a good look at the stands to convince myself I was in Glasgow and not Buenos Aires!' As Argentina left the pitch, the Scottish players formed a guard of honour for them to walk through. A last standing ovation from the crowd, a final wave from Diego to his new adoring audience, he was gone, out of sight, but never to be forgotten. On what had been the hottest day in Glasgow for thirty years, a star was born and wrapped in a tartan scarf. Diego Maradona may have hailed from Villa Fiorito, not the Gorbals, but that mattered little, as the Scots from that day on regarded him as one of their own.

CHAPTER TWENTY ONE
ALL STARS

Once back on home soil from the European tour, Cesar Menotti's tired team had a last game to play before returning to their clubs, arguably the most prestigious match since actually winning the World Cup. Organised by the bestselling newspaper and highly influential *Clarin,* they would be up against a FIFA Rest of the World 11, to commemorate the first anniversary of Argentina winning the trophy on 25th June. It would take place on the same date, same venue, the *Estadio Monumental.* The World eleven would be managed by the Italian coach Enzo Bearzot, his players each on a £5000 appearing fee, although for one in the squad the money meant nothing. Twelve months previous Brazil had taken apart Poland 3-0 and had every reason to think it would be they in the World Cup final, not Argentina. The host nation to overtake them needed four goals, this they achieved as Peru all fell down to cause tears of rage and frustration on the Copacabana, the Favelas and beyond. One of those caught in the trap of the illusion, was the sublime forward Arthur Antunes Coimbra. More well known as Zico. He was heading to Buenos Aires as were his fellow countrymen goalkeeper Emmerson and midfielder Toninho Cerezo, with their own point to prove and it had nothing to do with celebrating Argentina's *Mundial*.

Bearzot was taking the match extremely seriously picking a side to show his intent to win it. A few days earlier, he lost through injury his own Roberto Bettaga and Hungary's Andras Torocsik, but it remained a powerful, starting line up.

FIFA Rest of the World.
Emerson Leão *(Brazil)*, Friedrich Koncilia *(Austria)*, Ruud Krol (Captain) *(Holland)*, Bruno Pezzey *(Austria)*, Antonio Cabrini *(Italy)*, Marco Tardelli *(Italy)*, Michel Platini *(France)*, Juan Manuel Asensi *(Spain)*, Franco Causio *(Italy)*, Paolo Rossi *(Italy)*, and Zbigniew Boniek *(Poland)*
Manfred Kaltz *(West Germany)* Toninho Cerezo *(Brazil)*, and Zico, *(Brazil)*, would come on at half time.

As for who would be handed the gauntlet of trying to man-mark Diego Maradona, the dubious honour would again go to Marco Tardelli, who this time around appeared hell-bent on not being given another run around. The referee in a warped time-frame was none other than the wonderful Abraham Klein. One wonders the result of the final, if Klein had been in charge, not the hapless Sergio Gonella? On the now familiar confetti scattered pitch, with

82,000 in the *Estadio Monumental,* once more evoking an atmosphere of utter euphoria, the two sides appeared into sight. A penny for the thoughts of Holland's Ruud Krol at that moment. Bearzot's ploy was to lure Argentina in, then hit on the break with his immensely, talented, midfielders such as Platini and Boniek, supporting a lone Rossi up front. For some reason, despite the air around them crackling once more with rabid, fervid, patriotism, Argentina were unable to fire. For long periods in the first-half, the Rest of the World controlled the game with the raiding, powerful, Pole, Boniek, causing the home defence endless problems. The Maradona-Tardelli duel began with the Italian receiving howls of abuse from the crowd, as he clung to Diego's heels, shirt, shorts, anything to curb the threat. Yet, on twenty-eight minutes, Maradona managed to break clear from the Juve man's clutches to curl a stunning left-foot shot past Leao from just inside the penalty area. A true moment to treasure for both player and the roaring, bouncing terraces of the *Monumental,* as they celebrated Diego's first goal for his country on home soil. It was a stunning effort-igniting the stadium. Despite Maradona's moment of sublime genius, the opening period had been disappointing for Argentina and come the interval, they were rather fortunate to be in front. Bearzot made changes bringing Kaltz, Cerezo and Zico on-their impact was dramatic, immediately pinning the Argentinians back. Finally, with Tardelli still chasing Maradona around like a lunatic reared on red meat, a mad glint in his eyes, the Rest of the World grabbed a deserved equaliser. Twenty-two minutes remained when the *azzurri* winger Franco Causio broke clear on the right and crossed into the penalty for his countryman Paolo Rossi. As he came racing on, the Argentinian defender Luis Galvan

collided with him-only to turn the ball past Ubaldo Fillol, for an own goal.1-1! As Argentina restarted, they swiftly lost the ball as the pressure continued from the All-Stars. Menotti's team had simply not performed, much to the chagrin of the crowd and the Junta General's all sat alongside President Videla with equally grim faces. Five minutes later, a darting Zico performing like a man on a mission won the ball on the edge of the penalty area, before laying it wide for Causio. He found Cerezo wide-left, whose precise cross into the six yard box, was met by the incoming Zico, finishing with relish into an empty net. 2-1! A tiny piece of justice for the Brazilian duo. Going behind roused Argentina and at last Menotti's team started to finally play. Led by Maradona, the World Champions roared forward with their number ten leading the charge, only for Marco Tardelli with a truly, brutal, lunge from behind bringing Diego to earth. It was beyond cynical by the Italian, rightly receiving a red card off Abraham Klein. After this the game petered out and ultimately ended with a much-deserved victory for the Rest Of The World. All be it, a little tainted after Tardelli's shocking tackle on Maradona. Unlike twelve months previous, up went a smiling Ruud Krol to collect the trophy watched by the Generals, offering polite, if forced applause. Afterwards, with a shrug of his slim shoulders, Menotti played down the defeat and was lush in praise of the opposition. 'It's no shame to lose to a team with such great players.' He also claimed all focus would now be on the forthcoming Under-20's World Youth Champions in Japan, with their new world superstar Diego Maradona set to captain the team.
 Diego's star was set to rise even further in the east.

CHAPTER TWENTY TWO

1979. *Estadio Tomas Adolfo Duco*. Huracan 1 Argentinos
Juniors 3. After six games played, Argentinos had gone top
of the league above River Plate. These were heady days.
Diego Maradona had been unplayable-immediately after
the game finished, an excited Jorge Cyterszpiler grabbed
Diego, telling him, 'Get your stuff together amigo, we're
off to Brazil!' For a long time Maradona held a burning
desire to meet the great Pele and had already told
Cyterszpiler to arrange it. 'Make it happen Jorge,' when
his agent heard these words, it just had to be done. Best
friends or not, Cyterszpiler needed to deliver. By this
period, Edson Arantes Do Nascimento, the beloved Pele
was retired, basking in the warm glow of a wonderful,
twenty-one-year career. The two season at New York
Cosmos from 1975-1977, the final chapter, after all those
years with his beloved Santos. The crowning glories, his
three World Cup winning medals from 1958, 1962 and
finally in 1970-the coronation bestowed on him in Mexico,
at the *Azteca*, by all who believed in the beautiful game, as
the finest player of all time.
Suddenly,
  along came Diego Maradona, a cocky Argentinian street
kid from the slums of Buenos Aires, to possibly challenge
his mantle.

El Grafico journalist, Guillermo Blanco, first came across
a thirteen-year-old Diego, when covering the 1973 *Evita
Youth Games*, where he excelled with *Los Cebollitas*, as
the Little Onions surprised all with their quality. In the
final they beat Banda Rojo, (later a youth side of River
Plate), 5-4, with a hat trick from Maradona. From that
moment after meeting the two bonded and struck up a

close friendship. Over the following years Blanco was one of the few journalists Maradona ever really truly trusted. He also became a trusted confidante of the family and Jorge Cyterszpiler, privileges only a rare few received. This was the man Jorge turned to regarding Diego's request to meet Pele, if anyone had the contacts in the industry to make it happen, the much respected Guillermo Blanco was that man. Blanco was only too happy to arrange this coming together between two footballing Gods of differing generations, he also knew it would make a stunning exclusive for *El Grafico.* Blanco was already well aware of Diego's wish, for when as a guest of the Maradona's at their beach holiday home of Atlántida, in Uruguay, the player actually told him, 'My dream is to meet Pele, Guillermo'. This conversation took place shortly before the 1979 World Youth Championships, when Blanco was there to do an interview about the forthcoming tournament with Diego, the Pele chat simply fell away, amongst other subjects they chatted about. So, it was when Cyterszpiler approached Blanco, it came as no surprise and he began to make calls.

 Another memory of that time for Blanco was watching Diego's dad, Chitoro, throwing himself into the sand and running towards the sea like a big kid. The years of sacrifice and pain, of having to hold his tongue as bosses used and abused, as he worked like a dog, all hours to put food on the table for his family were over. Chitoro had just turned fifty and his son had insisted that he was now the breadwinner, those torturous days were over for Don Diego.

 Guillermo Blanco contacted a Brazilian journalist close to Pele called Tarlis Batista, just to ensure the great man was open to seeing Maradona. Not all legends would be comfortable coming face to face with the one many were calling a heir apparent. Especially when this heir was Argentinian and he was Brazilian, but seemingly not Pele, for the word swiftly came back that he would be delighted to meet Diego. Several dates were set up, all totally coincidental, Mondays, but strangely when these were put to Maradona, he said no? This carried on for a while, until Blanco told him that he couldn't keep putting it off. Finally, it transpired there was a charity match Pele was taking part in with Zico's Flamengo against Athletico Miniero, for which he was flying in especially from the United States to play. This meant Pele would be in Rio de Janiero, on a definite date, again, unbelievably, a Monday! This time Blanco insisted, 'It's now or never Diego!' He agreed and the plans were put in place.

Following the Huracan game, Guillermo Blanco quite literally pulled Maradona out of a live television interview, the usual delirium, a hundred cameras clicking on and threw him in a waiting car! Everything had been arranged, *El Gráfico* had sorted out the flight to Copacabana, but it was a tight schedule. Jorge Cyterszpiler and Don Chitoro had already checked in at *Ezeiza* airport, all was being done in great secrecy, for the magazine wanted total exclusivity. Not even the Argentinos President, Propspero Consoli, had a clue what was occurring. Amidst scenes of lovely skulduggery at the airport to hide Maradona from unwanted fellow journalists and quizzical onlookers, he and Guillermo Blanco finally joined their other *compadres.* Early on Sunday evening, the airplane carrying the four Argentinians soared off the runway in Buenos Aires, heading south for Brazil. Once on board, Blanco was sat next to Maradona and when chatting he asked him

'Why did you keep refusing the earlier dates?' Diego's answer both surprised and charmed the journalist, when he declared, 'Because they are sacred. Mondays are for Claudia.'

Waiting to meet them was *El Grafico's* legendary photographer Ricardo Alfieri. He also a confidante of Pele and would be documenting the meeting for posterity. Alfieri drove his fellow Argentinians to an apartment for them to rest up and get some sleep before heading to meet the one all Brazilians had lovingly christened 'El Rey del Futbol',(The King of Football). With only two bedrooms, Blanco shared with Alfieri, whilst the unlikely trio of Diego, Don Chitoro and Jorge Cyterszpiler were in the other! Around midnight, the phone rang and Blanco picked it up. On the line was Jorge from the other room apologising for the interruption asking permission for himself, Diego and his dad to go and have some ice cream and cokes from the kitchen fridge? A smiling Guillermo obviously said 'No problem', but he couldn't get over them actually asking for permission? 'Such simpler times,' he once recalled.

Monday 9th April 1979. The Copacabana. On arriving at Pele's Rio home, the Argentinians were told he was out, but would return soon. At first they felt maybe the Brazilian was making them stand in line? After being given a short tour of a beautiful, palatial, apartment overlooking the wonders of Rio, a commotion was heard and suddenly a smiling Pele was stood before them. After a rush of embraces and handshakes, they all settled down to chat. About the meeting itself, Blanco recalled, 'It was an incredible hour, because with Ricardo, who already knew Pele, the ice was broken straight away.' Maradona was obviously thrilled, if a little overcome to meet one of his idols. A gracious Pele replied how humbled he felt that Diego in the midst of the football season, had taken the time from his very busy schedule to come and see him. Their exists an amazing photograph taken by Alfieri of the two men talking with Don Diego, Jorge Cyterszpiler and Guillermo Blanco sat watching on, seemingly unable to believe their own eyes. Three mere mortals in the company of footballing Gods to millions. Pele held Diego's hand as they talked, or more the Brazilian gave out advice how to survive on that rarefied pedestal both existed upon. Of all that Pele spoke about, what resonated most with Maradona, was to take perfect care of his body. Rather than keep any golden nuggets to himself, Pele offered up a treasure chest of goodwill to *El Pelusa.*

'Never listen when they tell you you're the best. The day you feel the best, you'll stop being serious forever. Accept the applause, but don't live with applause.' Contracts. 'Each player has their own problem. It's a very personal matter, but always keep in mind that you have to fight for what you're really worth.'

 Lastly,

  a few tunes on the guitar to serenade his guests and Pele had to leave. Whether it was do another commercial, record a song, sign off on a business deal, kiss another sick child on the head, or just smile at the opening of a food store. This had become his life now. A final round of embraces, a last word in the ear of his heir apparent, 'Look after yourself amigo,' he was gone. An enchanted Diego Maradona was left moved to tears and never forgot the generosity of Pele that day on the Copacabana. Sadly, in time the two became sworn enemies, but for a few hours only back in 1979, they were close amigos.

CHAPTER TWENTY THREE
TOY SOLDIERS
'I wanted a rematch of the World Cup and I got it.
This team was by far the best I've ever played in.'
Diego Maradona

A *supernova*-a star that suddenly increases greatly in brightness because of a catastrophic explosion that ejects most of its mass. In the season following Argentina's world cup win, an on-fire Diego Maradona lit up every stadium he played in, scoring twenty-two goals and taking Argentinos Juniors into the higher echelons of the table to a remarkable fifth place. Maradona was incredible, in full flight unstoppable. With the ball at his feet, accelerating, running at petrified defenders, a drop of a shoulder and away. All happening in the blink of an eye, he was gone.
  Finally, Cesar Menotti had come calling once more, the two made up and he was back in the international picture, starting with Maradona being recalled back into the first team squad for the summer European tour, but more importantly, what came after. This was by now a boy king. An entire life being played out in the media spotlight. Away from the public glare, the real Diego was a happy, go-lucky kid, busy looking after his family with newfound wealth. Before the selection eruption, he and Menotti had become close. More so, Diego senior trusted him, to young Diego that crossed all borders and knocked down many walls. Now, their relationship was as previous, the World Cup Winning coach took Maradona aside to tell him that together they would triumph at the 1979 World Youth Championships. Menotti was already planning for Spain in

1982 and retaining the trophy won so memorable on home soil. To achieve this he would need a Maradona fit in both body and mind ready to take on the world. Leading the country's youngsters in Japan would be a testing ground to see if he had the temperament to go with the God-given ability. As all this played out, it has to be remembered once more that Argentina remained in the grip of a Military Junta government, winning the World Cup changed nothing, still no one was safe. It was akin to a Cartel kidnapping an entire nation and God help anybody who spoke out against them. Except Cesar Menotti, for nobody hated them more, but such was his popularity after the *Mundial* they daren't, they just daren't, for fear of themselves being lynched. A left-wing, long-haired, chain-smoking 'hippy' (for want of a better world), a man who stood for everything they despised, had brought them the greatest prize of all. It was a paradox, one they simply had to put up with. National Service under Videla and his ice-cream Generals was obligatory and footballers were no exception. Indeed, six members of Menotti's youth squad were eligible to be called up. Including Diego Maradona. Just four months before the tournament began, Maradona and the others were inducted, their football careers temporarily postponed, alas for Diego, his famed scraggly, curly, hair cut short for army protocol. For Videla's mob had swiftly learned that the power of football was such, even their ungodly sins could be hidden away from prying world eyes-like the International court of Human Rights and Amnesty International, whom were forever all over them like a rash. This being so, footballers were spared the worst of hardships whilst in uniform, many never even saw a weapon, not least fire one. The six footballers were not surprisingly given permission by the Junta to go to Japan and represent Argentina, but under strict orders that once it was over, they returned to their National Service roles. In Videla and his henchmen's warped mindset, these young men were a mirror to show up to the world with Diego Maradona at the helm displaying his unique talents to all, they believed themselves would be reflected and so share in the glory of their toy soldiers.

Diego had led and starred from the front in Argentina's successful qualification campaign. None more so than a 4-0 victory over Peru, when he was literally on fire torturing the Peruvians from the first minute to the last. Astonishingly, despite the fierce rivalry between them, made even worse after the event of the *Mundial,* even Brazilian journalists present at the match claimed they had seen nothing like him since his amigo Pele. As a world waited with baited-breath, Cesar Menotti unleashed a frustrated Maradona upon it!

Argentina began their quest by hitting Indonesia for five, with Diego scoring twice and another prodigy Menotti held great hopes for, the centre forward Ramon Diaz smashing three. The South Americans 5-0 up at half-time. He and Maradona appeared to read each other's minds on the pitch. It was a wonderful understanding, with Diaz appearing to know just where to be as Maradona probed, ran and carved out opportunities for him. Next, a closely fought game against a tough, talented Yugoslavia side that was only decided by Velez Sarsfield's striker, Osvaldo Escudero's, second half goal. The first period had left Cesar Menotti fuming, he sensed a lack of desire, for him there was nothing worse. Menotti tore into his young players at the interval, telling them if any thought their performance was acceptable, then they should pack their bags right there and then and 'Fuck off home to Argentina!' His harsh words impacted, the second half saw the Argentinians go up a gear, even though there was just the one goal to show for the vast improvement.

The final group game saw Menotti's boys blow Poland away 4-1, by this time the Japanese crowd had fallen in love not just with Argentina's blistering, attacking football, but had adopted Diego Maradona as one of their own. A stunning free-kick by Diego began the rout, as Argentina took a strong Poland apart. Each passing game he was proving the hype was real, the frightening speed, dancing feet, magical tricks and explosive finishing had captured the home nation's heart-along with a big huge smile that could light up Tokyo. They were no longer neutrals, for as Maradona's name roared out from the terraces, it was like playing on home soil. Come the quarter-final, Argentina took apart a talented Algeria whom simply did not what hit them. Maradona again began proceedings, Ramon Diaz blasted another hat-trick, the final score of 5-0 saw the Algerians on the floor, after chasing Menotti's boy around for ninety minutes. Both Maradona and Diaz ended the match with shirts hanging off their backs.

The Semi-Final brought into sight, ferocious, near-neighbours, Uruguay, whom had performed equally impressive as their amigos from across the River Plate. They also had won every game so far including impressive showings against Hungary, the brilliant Soviet Union and a highly rated Portugal. The *National* stadium in Tokyo provided the venue and in a fiercely, fought encounter between the two aged old rivals, goals from Diaz and Maradona in the second half saw Argentina through. Diego's killer second, a fine header after a stunning counter-attack.

Only the Soviet Union now stood in the way of Cesar Menotti earning a second world title in as many years. A fantastic achievement, but one that would not be easy against the extremely powerful, highly technical, Russians whom had slowly improved as the tournament wore on. Menotti gave a passionate rousing speech to his boys beforehand. He told them the result didn't matter, for they had already shown Argentina was the best in the world. Menotti went on to tell the players just go out and entertain the Japanese crowd, whom had adopted them as their own. On Sunday 7th September 1979, in front of a hugely biased 52,000 Japanese crowd, again at the *National Stadium, Tokyo*, Argentina won the Youth Cup final, after an outstanding performance against their toughest opponents so far. In an even first-half where the Russians more than matched Argentina, it was they whom went in front through midfielder Igor Ponomaryo, seven minutes after the interval. For the first time in the tournament Menotti's team had gone behind, now would be the time to see what they were made of against a truly worthy opponent. *El Flaco* need not have worried as Argentina went up a gear blitzing the Soviet Union. Diego Maradona appeared electrified, the Russian red shirts tried desperately to stop him, but it was impossible as he tore through, past and over last gasp tackles and desperate lunges. A goal from Alves levelled, then, Ramon Diaz swooped moments later to put them deservedly in front. Ten minutes from time, The *National Stadium* held its collective breath as Maradona stepped up to fire a magnificent free-kick from the edge of the box to ignite the crowd, winning for his nation the World Youth Cup and for himself the player of the tournament. For one night only Tokyo became Buenos Aires, as celebrations continued long into the night.

Similar to 1978, this team was a light in the dark night for the people of Argentina, for their coach Cesar Luis Menotti, a candle held up to the world saying, this is my Argentina! *La Nuestra*, played by boys!

One thing was now becoming blatantly obvious, that after the masterclass against Scotland at *Hampden Park* and his more recent exploits in Japan, the whole world now knew the name of Diego Armando Maradona.

That very same day as the Argentinian kids were delighting the world with their footballing skills, an Organisation of American States committee arrived in Buenos Aires to investigate the Junta's vile record of abuse. Human rights protesters had gathered in the Plaza de Mayo in front of the *Casa Rosada*. Soon as the trophy was won in Japan, pro-government radio stations called on the people to go to the Plaza and celebrate their team's victory, thus in turn swamping the protesters in huge numbers, drowning them out with the triumphal cries of 'ARGENTINA!'

The Junta moved fast to exploit Argentina's victory for their own aims. This 'New triumph over communism!' blared out on the radio. Immediately, on the team arriving home, to Menotti's disgust, they had little choice but to take part in a public celebration alongside Videla and the Generals. The team was taken to the *Casa Rosada,* where Maradona and his teammates were paraded like Junta stooges before them. Hardly surprising, Diego was pushed into the dark heart of it by having his picture took with all the Generals. To capture this propaganda/publicity stunt, State controlled television were present to ensure they recorded every greeting and handshake for posterity. Smile for the camera, though mostly their cameras focused on one figure. Diego, still a teenager, these evil, murderous men of power in their pomp and braid uniforms, with bunches of medals on show, for some make-believe act of bravery, stood in line to be photographed with *El Pelusa,* the kid from Villa Fiorito across the *Alsina* Bridge. The players simply had no choice, it would only be many years later on opening up about that period, Maradona let it be known his true feelings regarding what was really going on. 'That bastard Videla used us.'

This sad episode apart, what must be remembered above all is the beautiful, football played by Diego Maradona and his young compadres in Japan, as they took on the world's best,

and beat them well.

CHAPTER TWENTY FOUR
A PRELUDE TO A RECKONING
ENGLAND V ARGENTINA (FRIENDLY)

Wembley Stadium. Tuesday 13th May 1980. Only eight days on from the end of the Iranian Embassy siege, a 92,000 home crowd still basking in the glory of their SAS heroes, God Save the Queen was sung with all the patriotic fervour of a nation off to war, not the prelude to a simple football match. The reaction to the Argentine anthem equally emphatic as it was drowned out in a torrent of undignified, patriotic, fervour. Theirs' was a bitter rivalry going back to 1966, Antonio Rattin upsetting all the Queen's men, followed by Sir Alf Ramsey labelling the Argentinians in a post-match rant as 'Animals'. Since, the two mad footballing nations had met twice. A bad tempered 2-2 draw at Wembley in 1978, an even more heated encounter three years later in Buenos Aires, that finished 1-1, with Daniel Bertoni and Trever Cherry sent off. This after Bertoni had punched Cherry and knocked out his two front teeth, taking exception to the Englishman's late tackle. Legend even has it that the Argentinian winger still bears the marks on his right knuckle from that particular right hook!

Cesar Menotti's World Champions were embarking on a short, European tour, that also consisted of matches against the Republic of Ireland and Austria. Menotti's preparation to defend their title at *Espana 82,* was hindered with no qualification required, so these games were deemed hugely important as he attempted to continue to build a side around Diego Maradona, the Captain Daniel Passarella and centre forward Mario Kempes, who would miss the game against England, due to playing for Valencia against Arsenal in the European Cup Winners Cup final. A full house at Wembley was mostly down to the excitement generated around Maradona, following his magical performance against Scotland, the previous summer. Due to industrial action there had been no television coverage of the *Hampden Park* game, so all was word of mouth, or through the radio and newspaper reporting of Diego's dismantling of the Scots. A powerful tool that only increases supporter's imagination to see the real thing with their own eyes, filling the national stadium for what was just a friendly.

Diegomania had truly arrived in the United Kingdom.

England, under Ron Greenwood, were preparing for their first major international tournament since the 1970 World Cup, a decade earlier. Greenwood had yet to settle on his strongest line up, but there had been some promising signs England were once more becoming a major threat. They were coming into the match against Argentina on the back of five consecutive wins, after topping their European qualifying group and a stunning performance in Barcelona, beating Spain 2-0 in a friendly.

The starting line-ups.
England: Ray Clemence, Phil Neal, Kenny Sansom, Phil Thompson, Dave Watson, Ray Wilkins, Kevin Keegan, Steve Coppell, David Johnson, Tony Woodcock and Ray Kennedy.
Argentina: Ubaldo Fillol, José Van Tuyne, Alberto Tarantini, Jorge Olguín, Américo Gallego, Daniel Passarella, Santiago Santamaría, Juan Barbas, Leopold Luque, Diego Maradona and José Daniel Valencia.

  It was a fantastic game of football that England finally won 3-1, but only one player grabbed all the headlines. Nineteen-year-old Diego Maradona caused gasps across the terraces every time he received the ball by dancing and twisting, soaring away from terrified, home defenders. The initial boos and jeers that greeted Maradona in possession swiftly turned to applause and delight, as this diminutive, but stocky figure in blue and white hoops dropped a shoulder many times, sending half the England team trying to thwart him back towards the direction of the tunnel. Playing in their striking new Admiral home kit, England started on fire pummelling the Argentine goalkeeper Ubaldo Fillol.
A Kenny Sansom throw in was headed back by the centre-half Dave Watson for the former Liverpool, by that time, SV Hamburg superstar, Kevin Keegan, who rifled a shot inches wide of a diving Fillol's, right-hand post. Shortly after, a Trevor Brooking free-kick found Keegan, whose flick back into the six yard box was met by David Jonson. What looked a certain goal as the Liverpool centre forward

met it perfectly was somehow tipped around the post by a cat-like Fillol! Wembley was a blaze of noise as the siege continued. From the following Brooking corner, Keegan again involved-his header found Watson. The Manchester City defender's point blank effort somehow, to the astonishment of all, was pushed around the opposite post by a leaping Fillol once more! Off the Argentinian bench came a furious Cesar Menotti remonstrating with his defenders.

Slowly the South Americans opened half an eye. In typically, no-nonsense-brutal, manner, with Apache-like defending, Daniel Passarella went through the back of Tony Woodcock, leaving him writing in pain on the turf. No foul was called, as Passarella found Jose Valencia on the half-way line. A swift one-two with Maradona, saw Valencia away, flying clear of the English defence with just the goalkeeper Ray Clemence to beat. The winger fired past Clemence, only for a sprinting Sansom to race back and clear. In the following melee, the ball fell once more at Valencia's feet, who this time shot low against the post! A warning, the World champions had come to play and there was more to come.

A prelude to a reckoning.

Maradona picked the ball up thirty yards out. A sleight of foot to drag it clear from a befuddled Phil Thompson, before accelerating at blistering speed through a host of bewildered, white shirts, clear into the penalty area. Across the Wembley terraces, there was a sense of utter disbelief as Diego slipped a last, gasp, tackle from Sansom, before a flick of his left foot sent the ball mere inches wide of Clemence's right-hand post. Across this grand old stadium, applause broke out for a youngster, whom they had heard and read so much about and were now witnessing with

their own eyes. The way Maradona with the ball at his feet cut through like a bolt of lightning, making international class defenders appear as if stuck in slow-motion mode, trying to catch him was a sight to behold. With head in hands, Diego looked up to the London skies, it would have been a goal talked about so long as Wembley Stadium stood. That time in 1980 he missed, six years later in Mexico City,
it was to be a much different reckoning.

Chances came and went at both ends, then, four minutes before half time, David Johnson finally beat Ubaldo Fillol. A brilliant, diving header after Steve Coppell ran past two Argentinian defenders, before putting in a fine cross for the Liverpool forward to bury. Straight after, Johnson flashed a long range effort that sizzled inches over Fillol's crossbar. England were on the up. Come early in the second half, Maradona was almost cut in half by Dave Watson, as he attempted to spring free. Though no booking for Watson, it was clear the English felt they had suffered enough already at the hands of the little magician! Moments after he was tormenting them again, Diego took on, dummied Watson, roared past three more England players, before finding Newell Old Boys winger Santiago Santamaria, wide right. His cross was met and mishit horribly by Valencia at the far post, after Phil Neal let the ball pass him by. It was to prove fatal for Argentina, as England swiftly went 2-0 up. Johnson again on the scoresheet bundling a cross from Liverpool teammate Ray Kennedy into the net, leaving Fillol stranded and frustrated, after the ball had dipped agonisingly over his head. The World Champions hit right back, it was Maradona who received the ball, beating Watson and Thompson leaving them like spinning tops, before bursting clear into the penalty, only to be sent crashing to earth by the trailing leg of Kenny Sansom, after leaving him also in his blistering wake. A penalty. Up came Passarella to smash into the top corner past Clemence, who never moved. 2-1, game on! Again, Maradona causing a buzz of incredulity to fall over the Wembley crowd as he had gone into overdrive. By this time Diego had been joined off the bench by his amigo, partner in crowd from the World Youth Cup, Ramon Diaz, as Argentina went all out for the equaliser. It was though England's Kevin Keegan who decided the match with twenty minutes remaining, when he flashed home a fierce low-drive from the edge of the penalty area, after being set up by Coppell, who killed the ball dead for him. Wembley exploded at Keegan's thrilling finish that looked to have finally saw off Argentina. Twenty minutes remained and despite the score line Menotti's men kept going. Maradona almost grabbed one back when he beat Watson, cut inside the penalty and let fly a screaming left-foot effort that Clemence stopped, but almost got knocked off his feet, such was the power of the shot. Still, Argentina would not give up. Diego again cutting through a crowded midfield, before putting Ramon Diaz clear. Running through Diaz rounded Clemence, who had come flying out of his area, shot goalwards, only for Kenny Sansom to again appear like a speeding train to clear miraculously off the line! The Arsenal full-back had endured a busy evening in North London, keeping the Argentinians at bay! The final whistle, the crowd roared, England were back, again! 'This is the standard that we must try to maintain now,' said a highly satisfied Ron Greenwood post-match. The Union Jacks waved, the crowd sang 'You'll never walk alone'. A sign of the times. Five days later, Greenwood's team were hammered 4-1 away to Wales in the Home Internationals, later crashing out in the first round of the European championships, played that summer in Italy.

Diego Maradona left the field wearing an England shirt with Kevin Keegan's arm around his shoulders. The two smiling wide. As he came closer towards the terraces, the Wembley crowd stood to applaud Diego. A standing ovation broke out, for they surely realised, as had the neighbouring Scots before them, that it was nothing short of a privilege to watch this young boy play football. Their attitude to Diego would change in time, but on that long gone evening, Wembley belonged to Diego Armando Maradona.

Four days later Argentina played the Republic of Ireland at Lansdowne Road, in front of 31,000 Irish supporters, all desperate to witness Cesar Menotti's World Cup holders, but most off all, *El Pelusa.* Maradona had a quiet afternoon, but still did enough to enthral those who had come along to see him play live. This being his first game as manager, Eoin Hand's Ireland had no intention of treating this game as a friendly and they tore into Diego, whenever they managed to get near him. One time in the twenty-eighth minute, the midfielder Tony Grealish took out the youngster in a manner resembling more a street mugging than a tackle. As Maradona lay on the turf nursing his leg, the English referee George Courtney appeared totally bemused by the ferocity of Grealish's assault, so much he never even bothered to book the Luton Town man. Diego dusted himself down, stared daggers at a still, growling, bearded, bushy-haired Grealish, who made up a two man wall along with Gerry Daly, before planting in a lovely cross for Jose Valencia, to head beautifully past the Republic's goalkeeper Gerry Peyton. Payback in the finest way!

On Wednesday 21st May 1980, Argentina wrapped up their mini European tour in Austria, at the *Praterstadion*, Vienna. On a night when the World Champions, in front of 67,500, cut loose in breath-taking style, Diego Maradona scored his first and what was to be only hat trick in Argentinian colours. It began in the opening moments with Maradona's astute pass slicing apart the Austrian defence, slipping in Jose Santamaria, to make it 1-0 past Austrian keeper Friedl Koncilia. Luque swiftly added a second on ten minutes, when he chipped wonderfully over Koncilia, after that it was a Maradona parade. His first a rapier one-two with Valencia, then back once more to Diego, who held off both a defender and Koncilia, dribbling around them, before squeezing the ball into the net. It was an electric move between the two finished in style by Maradona. Austria pulled a stunning goal back through midfielder Kurt Jara, when he smashed an unstoppable shot past Fillol, from an almost impossible angle, but this apart, the South Americans ran the home team ragged. Diego Maradona scored his second fifteen minutes from time, when Luque played him in through the middle of the Austrian defence. After an electric burst of pace Diego fired past Koncilia making it 4-1. As the clock ticked down, the hat-trick was completed when from six yards, Maradona slid in to poke the ball past Koncilia-to be embraced by jubilant teammates.
A perfect way to end the tour.

Diego Maradona was no longer a prince of one continent, he was now being widely regarded as the finest player on the planet. Not yet twenty years old, in Argentina, the battle for his footballing soul was on. Diego was no longer a simple human being, he was a young god to millions, for others, a money cow to be milked, the likes which had never happened before to any sportsman. They even invented a name for it.

The *Maradollar*.

CHAPTER TWENTY FIVE
THE MUNDIALITO: 1980

The 1980 *Mundialito* (Copa de Oro), hosted by Uruguay was a competition commemorating the fiftieth anniversary of the inaugural, World Cup played back in 1930, when the Uruguayan beat their great rivals Argentina 4-2 in the Final. This Mini-Tournament was to involve all the previous World Cup Winners, for Cesar Menotti, as ever vital preparation for *Espana 82*. All past winners agreed to participate, except England, who claimed as defence, a crowded, heavily, congested, fixture list. Into their place stepped Holland. However, Dutch attendance was put into jeopardy as the *Mundialito* drew close, the government ordered the Dutch FA that the team shouldn't play in Uruguay, due to their opposition to the regime. The parliament verdict that the tournament would be used by the Uruguayan dictatorship as a propaganda tool was seemingly shared by others, when it emerged that forty one Italians footballers,(including two international players), had also signed a document condemning the military rule in Uruguay. Officials tried to cover up the embarrassment, indicating that not all players had signed, those who did were unaware of what they were signing. Hardly an auspicious start to the *Copa de Oro*. Ultimately, Holland took part and all the matches would be played in the stadium that was the original venue for the 1930 Final. Montevideo's *Estadio Centenario*. The six teams would play in two groups of three, both were mouth-watering. Group A, consisted of Netherlands, Italy and Uruguay. Whilst Group B, current holders Argentina, Brazil and West Germany. The winners of each group facing off to decide the tournament winner.

Since 1973, Uruguay, like Argentina had lived under the jackboot of an unelected, military government, suffering the cruelty and bloodshed that naturally came with such a brutal regime. They, like the Argentina Junta counterparts in 1978, aimed to use this tournament for their own needs. A show of Uruguayan nationalism that would present itself to the entire world as the football team strove for glory in the *Estadio Centenario*. The people of Uruguay had suffered silently through the previous eight years, for like in Argentina, it didn't do to raise your head above the pulpit for fear of it blown to pieces. There was though hope in the air that the nightmarish era was drawing to some kind of closure. A month before the tournament began the government organised a referendum, in which a new constitution was going to be voted upon. If approved, the already, established, dictatorship would have strengthened and been able to play around with the Uruguayan constitution to its own ends. Remarkably, despite all efforts to fix the ballot, the propaganda for a YES vote dominating the television, newspapers and billboards, Uruguayans rejected it, with a fifty-seven per cent of the voters, basically telling their military oppressors to fuck off! Obviously, democracy for the military Generals was for them just a fad, a means to an end that unexpectedly blew up in their faces. However, a spark had been lit that would see them ousted just five years later, for the belief amongst some in power at least that they needed to legitimize their proposed constitution, by holding an actual referendum, as opposed to simply falsifying the voting results and killing anyone who attempted to stop them, was itself an indication that democracy was lighting fires in Uruguay.

Welcome to the *Mundialito*!

After being confined to just friendlies for the last two years, tournament football for defending Champions Argentina was crucial, as the weeks and months ran down to the real business in Spain. Under Cesar Menotti, they had toured Europe twice with great success in 1979 and 80, introducing Diego Maradona to disbelieving European and British eyes. Maradona was by this time being proclaimed as the greatest player in the world, *Espana 82* was to be the stage to confirm his inauguration as such. In Menotti's squad for the Mundialito, there still existed may of the 1978 heroes. Captain Daniel Passarella, Ubaldo Fillol, Luis Galvan, Alberto Tarantini, Jorge Olguin, Americo Gallego, Leopoldo Luque, Osvaldo Ardiles, Daniel Bertoni and Mario Kempes. Add Maradona and River Plate hot shot Ramon Diaz, Argentina remained a serious threat.

Their first game of the tournament took place on New Year's Day, Thursday 1st January 1981, against the-then current European champions, Jupp Derwall's West Germany. Diego Maradona found himself targeted by the huge man-mountain from FC Kaiserlautern, Hans-Peter Briegel, who did so in a hard, but fair manner, that even drew compliments from Diego afterwards. In a first-half in which the German appeared by far the most composed side, they took the lead on forty-one minutes, when a Hansi Muller corner was headed past Ubaldo Fillol, by another large, brute of a figure, the centre-forward Horst Hrubesh. Following the interval, it was Derwall's impressive team continuing to control the game, only to be ambushed in the last six minutes as Argentina finally awoke from slumber, after a sloppy, at times, deeply, worrying, display for Menotti. With Maradona under lock and key, his every move shadowed by Briegel, who loomed over him like a giant, his side appeared tired, old, even. Then, all hell broke loose in the *Estadio Centenario*! Firstly, it was Daniel Passarella causing havoc in the German penalty area that led to the Hamburg defender Manny Kaltz putting the ball past his own keeper Harold Schumacher, to be followed moments later by Jose Valencia racing down the pitch, before finding Ramon Diaz to chip beautifully over Schumacher, stealing the game for the World Champions! A first defeat for West Germany in twenty-three matches, as for Cesar Menotti's men, a surprising two points, but a huge uplift in performance was urgently required, for next up was a team bearing not so much gifts, but grudges and bags of potatoes on both shoulders, when it came to playing the World Champions.

Something had turned rotten in the soul of Brazilian football. Not since 1970, when Pele, Jairzinho, Carlos Alberto, Rivelino, Garrincha, Tostao, that team of hearts, whom charmed and exhilarated a world-wide audience in the Mexican sun, had they truly performed to the beating heart of their *Samba* drum. In West Germany 1974, Brazil showed a talisman devil version of themselves when up against a Dutch team simply a class above, whilst in Argentina 1978, again, the spark was missing, despite the dark circumstances of their ultimate exit. In 1980, came a new coach Telê Santana, a true believer that Brazil must return to their footballing roots. No more attempts to duplicate the last coach Claudio Coutinho's European style-concentrating more on the destructive/negative aspects of the game. Such tactics were simply unnatural for a kid born in the Favelas, or learning his trade on some dustbowl, ramshackle piece of dirt ground, beyond eyesight of the beautiful, Copacabana beaches. Santana was building a side to restore former glories, once more attack to the resonating, beat of the Samba. Players were picked for their attacking flair first and the coach was blessed to have inherited a fabulous generation, easily their best for ten years since Mexico. Zico, Junior, Cerezo, Eder, Reinaldo, Falcao, maybe above all, from Corinthians, the Captain, twenty-six-year-old Sócrates Brasileiro Sampaio de Souza Vieira de Oliveira. The wonderfully, long-legged, bearded, midfielder-forward, known more widely as simply Socrates. So much more than a footballer, back in Brazil, he was a left-wing activist, even forming his own movement against the Brazilian military dictatorship. Socrates was an intellectual, a heavy drinker, a smoker, a physician holding a bachelor's degree in medicine from the *Faculdade de Medicina de Ribeirao Preto*. Led by such a man, Brazil arrived in Uruguay looking to lay down a marker that they were back.

Just three days on from beating West Germany, Argentina took on the Brazilians in what was a pulsating, if typically, bruising encounter, verging at times towards carnage, it eventually finished 1-1, honours shared. Only to be settled in a free-for-all at the full-time whistle. Earlier, any thoughts that Tele Santana may have held about attempting to take on their great South American rival by playing beautiful football, swiftly disappeared amidst an early hurricane of wild tackles by both sides and off the ball, near-assassination attempts. When the game finally calmed down Brazil pushed Argentina back, only as the Germans discovered, Menotti's team despite on the retreat, always remained deadly on the break. A piece of Diego Maradona magic on thirty minutes, saw the World Champions go in front, as he cut inside the penalty area, before firing low past the keeper Carlos Gallo at the near post. It was one of the few moments Diego had managed to escape a Brazilian blockade, as the many attempts previous to set up attacks, ended with yellow shirts doubling up to see off his threat.

Two minutes after the interval, Brazil levelled when a scramble in the six yard box ended with the ball finally falling to the unmarked defender Edevaldo de Freitas, who crashed his shot past Fillol. From that moment Brazil dominated, with Maradona becoming increasingly frustrated at being mugged every time he received possession, come full-time, tempers finally exploded as a full blown riot exploded on the pitch between the two teams. What began with a small ruckus when the Brazilian forward Paulo Isidoro kicked Valencia, escalated within moments into chaos! Immediately, an already head-fried Diego Maradona had raced to his amigo's aid with fists flying. Soon, every player was involved to different levels, whether it was trying to act as peace-makers, or pushing and shoving. Officials of both sides careered onto the field to join in with a relish-armed Uruguayan soldiers rushed from the side-lines trying and failing to separate the warring parties. With almost half the pitch full of fist fights breaking out, it appeared the murky events of Rosario were finally being expunged out of the Brazilian's system. Finally, the situation calmed as Cesar Menotti and Tele

Santana entered proceedings, themselves pushing their own players away from the madness. Led by Socrates, Brazil marched off towards the tunnel, whilst the Argentinian players from the centre-circle, mocked and waved ironically to the Uruguayan crowd, who hated their guts. It was a gruesome post-match aftermath, as the media of both nations sought explanation for such shameful scenes. One could only imagine what would occur if their paths were to cross in *Espana* 82?

To remain in the tournament Argentina had to hope West Germany did them a huge favour holding Brazil to a draw, or beating them. As it turned out, after a tense first-half, the Germans took the lead against the run of play on fifty-four minutes, when Bayern Munich's Karl-Heinz Rummenigge cross was finished at close range by Fortuna Dusseldorf striker Klaus Allofs. Suddenly, the World Cup holders looked set to make the final after all, only for two minutes later Brazil to strike back through a beautifully hit free-kick by Junior. It was like the switching on of a light after years of darkness. The moment for Santana's Brazil to rouse themselves as they set about Derwall's men in intoxicating style. The shackles were gone-the samba beat was back. On the half-hour Edevaldo fully recovered from his histrionics against Argentina, crossed brilliantly for Cerezo to finish with a stunning volley past Schumacher. Now, Brazil had drawn level with the Argentinians on goal difference, a toss of a coin would decide who went through if the score stayed the same, but they had far from finished. Fourteen minutes from time, the masterful Socrates tore into the penalty area, before crossing for his centre-forward Serginho to tap into an empty net! As the Brazilian supporters drenched yellow on the Centenario terraces danced with joy, their team finally buried

Argentine hopes when Ze Sergio, watched by a clutter of seemingly, uninterested, German defenders, went around Schumacher to make it 4-1. 'I suspected I could build a good Brazilian team, but tonight's performance went higher than I had thought possible,' said a beaming Santana, at the post-match press conference.

Adios Argentina!

Cesar Menotti was far from happy at the application of some the German players second-half, as Brazil came on strong. This had been their worst defeat since losing 6-3 to France during the 1958 World Cup. 'I don't accuse them of anything. This is a problem of conscience. Argentina has a clear conscience. I don't know if the Germans can say the same.' He also remarked, 'The Germans were excellent at man to man-marking against us, but somehow left a lot of space against Brazil.' On being informed of Menotti's comments, Jupp Derwall hit back saying they were at full strength, but did admit that maybe some of his team were not fully motivated. If there was one nation that hated Argentina more than the Brazilians, it was Uruguay. These feeling summed up nicely by a Uruguayan supporter basking in Argentinian misery, 'The Argentines are such pigs, we are sick and tired of hearing them boast about being the World Champions and the best in everything.'

As Cesar Menotti's side returned home the final was to be a repeat of the 1950 contest that decided the tournament. Uruguay were managed by their legendary, World Cup winning goalkeeper Roque Maspoli, the man who broke Brazil hearts in that defining game, ultimately causing them to change their kit from white to yellow. Missing out on the *Mundial* in Argentina was a huge blow for the Uruguayans, whom took huge pride in the national team. The home side's preparation for the *Mundialito,* was by far of all teams partaking, the most intense, as they held a *concentracion* for two and a half months. Their best player, the midfield maestro from Penarol, the delightful twenty-one-year-old Ruben Paz, who had been tagged the 'Uruguayan Maradona!' Uruguay had missed the two great South American rivals in the draw, meaning hopes were high that Holland and Italy might prove easier to overcome on home soil. Ultimately, Maspoli's team did so. After an impressive opening 2-0 victory over a poor Holland, where Paz shone like a diamond in an attacking line up, they played against an Italian side determined to ruin Uruguay's party. In what was a snarling, vicious, encounter, the home side eventually won 2-0, but in a contest with five bookings and three sending's off, there was little football on show. That litttle came from Ruben Paz, who despite some typically, brutal, attention from the *azzurri,* Marco Tardelli foremost, he never flinched, continuing to probe and play. Goalless at half-time, the deadlock was finally broken on sixty-seven minutes. The Italian defender Gabriele Oriali was deemed to have fouled Martinez in the box, the Spanish referee Emilio Guruceta pointed to the spot. It was dubious at best. Enzo Bearzot's men were outraged, but to no avail as Julio César Morales shot past Ivano Bordon. Moments after, tempers flared up again, as José Moreira and Antonio Cabrini clashed and were both sent off. Ten minutes remained when the game was finally settled. The Penarol winger Venancio Ramos crossed for Nacional centre-forward Waldemar Victorino, to trap and control, before firing home. 2-0, game over. With seconds remaining, a fed up-agitated Tardelli was sent off after having enough of Ruben Paz's artistry, hacking him down one too many times! Post-match, Enzo Bearzot directed his anger towards Senor Guruceta, who in the aftermath of the penalty incident had insulted using profanities towards two of his players Bruno Conti and Francesco Graziani. A fuming Bearzot went on to say he was going to report Guruceta's actions to FIFA. Might be worth remembering, this the same referee Emilio Guruceta, who years later was alleged to have taken bribes off Anderlecht, before the UEFA Cup semi-final against Nottingham Forest in 1984... Guruceta was killed in a traffic accident on 25th February 1987.

The last act,
 a final between Uruguay and Brazil. On Saturday 10th January 1981, in front of a carnival-coloured, 71,250, Blue, white and yellow crowd at the *Estadio Centenario,* Maspoli's team delivered the trophy in a hard, fought game against Santana's reborn Brazilians. After a rather cautious first period, the match erupted into life five minutes into the second-half, when Ramos sent the wonderful Ruben Paz clear on the wing. The boy born in the Uruguayan border city of Artigas, separated only from Brazil by a bridge, cut inside to lash in a shot the Keeper Joao Leite could only parry to midfielder Jorge Barrios, who poked his leg out through a gaggle of yellow shirts, sending the *Estadio Centenario* into meltdown! As if fused by the shock of going one down, the Brazilians suddenly started to play. With Socrates dropping back pulling every string from centre-midfield, they instantly went up a gear pinning back the Uruguayans. Just after the hour, Socrates went over the leg of full-back Walter Olivera in the box and a penalty was awarded, much to Uruguay's huge chagrín. None more so than the fuming goalkeeper, Captain Rodolfo Rodríguez, who had a close up view of Olivera's challenge on Socrates. He attempted everything

to try and put off his opposing Captain, who simply waited patiently to take the spot-kick, as Rodriguez was in his face, kicking the ball away, shouting and screaming. Finally, the Peruvian referee Enrique Labo lost patience threatening his expulsion, the keeper gave up and went to ready himself on his goal line. Up Socrates stepped to beat Rodrigues with ease levelling the final.1-1. A dark depression dropped over the vast majority of those at the *Centenario*, as it appeared their team was about to blow it at the last to a rejuvenated Brazil. Maspoli's men though possessed *Garra*, they were full of ferocious, Uruguayan fighting spirit and came roaring back. Ten minutes remained when a Ramos free kick wasn't cleared by panicking Brazilian defenders and Victorino once more struck from close range to electrify the stadium! With that goal so went the trophy, a happy ending for the Uruguyan people, but, sadly also for their Generals and Fascist state.

The *Mundialito* may have been a success for Uruguay, yet it counted for very little when just seven months later Peru won in Montevideo, ending the Uruguayans World Cup qualification hopes for *Espana 82*. A desperate shock after expectations had been raised so high from winning their own tournament. Nothing though could take away the memories of their Captain Rodolfo Rodriguez raising high that small, beautiful trophy in the *Estadio Centenario*. The *Mundialito* may have become lost in footballing history, but for a very short time, three million Uruguayans danced in the sun and shadows of their extremely, proud nation.

CHAPTER TWENTY SIX
THE GAME WAS AFOOT!

Guillermo Suárez Mason was born in Buenos Aires. He enrolled at the National Military Academy in 1944 and graduated in 1948, along with future Junta leaders Jorge Rafael Videla and Roberto Viola. A handsome, charismatic figure, A Bon Viveur, shall we say, he loved the ladies, fine wine and a good party. Suarez Mason was also a murderous, fanatical, Argentinian nationalist, who took part in the failed 1951 uprising against General Juan Domingo Perón, (husband of Eva Peron), as a result he was forced into exile in neighbouring Uruguay. There, Suarez Mason continued to conspire with fellow like-minded individuals to bring down Perón, until the latter's overthrow in 1955. Argentine Generals loved a good coup, in 1966, during the dictatorship of President Juan Carlos Onganía, (another meglomaniac), Suárez Mason was made military attaché to Ecuador. There he stayed for six years, until 1972, when promoted to General and handed a prominent role in state intelligence. Come the 1976 military coup, Suarez Mason's close friendship with Videla and other powerful, top ranking figures saw him appointed Commander of the First Army Corps, whose principal duty was to garrison the capital, keep order. In reality, Suarez Mason was like his overseers, a murdering jackal obsessed by power and building himself a huge nest egg for the inevitable, early retirement abroad.

Suarez Mason also held power over the ever increasing number of detention centres popping up over Buenos Aires, (in time there would be sixty in all), where unspeakable acts of cruelty/bestiality were carried out against prisoners declared to be subversives, agitators, Communist, anybody who dared whisper a wrong word against the Junta. Indeed, anybody the Generals took a dislike to at a whim ended up at one of these unholy places. Suarez Mason made it personal business to take a close interest in the dark deeds done on his orders by Army

Intelligence 601,who specialised in extortions and kidnapping for ransom. Most of the dollars being siphoned off in the General's direction. Far ghastlier, Suarez Mason was highly involved in the lucrative stealing of babies that were taken from their Mother's at birth in detention centres, notably *ESMA*. This was a monster in human clothing and it was he who ensured Diego Armando Maradona stayed at Argentinos Juniors for an astonishing five seasons.

As a young man, Suarez Mason was believed to have been an enthusiastic goalkeeper and amongst his many titles after the 1976 coup, he was made honorary chairman of Argentinos Juniors, by the club's President Prospero Consoli. A former Army college of the General, Consoli handed over all financial responsibilities to Suarez Mason, whether he had an option remained open to debate, but it was akin to letting a fox loose in a chicken coup. Suarez Mason had already placed himself on the boards of highly, profitable state companies and one major airline, Austral. He had a fascination with Diego Maradona, thinking nothing of arriving at Argentinos' training ground in a private helicopter, to keep an eye on his most precious asset. There had been attempts by the giants of Boca Juniors and River Plate to sign the wonder kid, but these advances were met with a simple 'Fuck off' by the General. On River's board was Vice-Admiral Carlos Lacoste, who had been a huge supporters of River since childhood. Between the Junta hierarchy, it sometimes became a game of sorts to try and get one over the other. The rivalry between army and navy forever poisonous. Only President Videla's ability to bang heads together and the promise of soothing egos with more stolen dollars prevented it ever, really, exploding out of control. Football for the Generals, Admirals, and Vice-Admirals became simply just another battlefield, but Suarez Mason always remained adamant that on his watch, over his dead body would Maradona be going anywhere, especially to Lacoste's River Plate. A dangerous phrase to live by, back then in Argentina.

 After the 1979 World Youth Championships, when Diego's star was irreversibly rising, Suarez Mason was forced to act into tieing down *El Pelusa* even further, for from foreign fields, the European vultures were starting to circle. None more than Barcelona and Juventus whispering pearls and diamonds into Jorge Cyterszpiler's ear. Knowing they would come offering absolute fortunes, Suarez Mason 'diverted' funds of $250,000 from Austral to Argentinos Juniors, covering Diego's upcoming contractual negotiations. Who was ever going to complain? The player himself had only to wear a baseball cap and tee shirt emblazoned with the airline's logo at various photo opportunities and of course the press conference for the signing of the new contract. Diego remained calm as the world around him trembled. He was content, in no mad rush to move elsewhere. Cysterszpiler was proving true to his word providing the cash for both the player and his family. Maradona was already the face of the giants Puma and Coca Cola and many more lucrative, brands were queuing up to use him. Boca Juniors had always been Diego's boyhood club, they were the team of every young *Porteno* from Villa Fiortito and were not going away. Still, only nineteen-years-old, Diego Maradona's dream of running out at the *La Bombonera* would happen soon enough.

1981. Two years passed before Diego Maradona finally pulled on the legendary blue and gold colours of Boca, as everything involving this remarkable character, it was to be a transfer saga of epic proportions. Ultimately, it came down to a loan deal for one season, although that doesn't come near to telling the full tale. In his final two seasons for Argentinos Juniors, Diego signed off in explosive style scoring twenty-two, then twenty-five goals, before he finally said a truly emotional, if long drawn out adios! Mostly due to Maradona, Argentinos Juniors came a magnificent second in 1980, he had quite simply, mostly still as a teenager over those five years, turned their fortunes around to drag them by their lapels up the table. By this time the murky, cesspit of Argentine politics had done for Suarez Mason. A falling out with his boss President Videla occurred after a disagreement over a proposed invasion of Chile. Operation *Soberania*. Suarez Mason was side-lined, time to watch his back and check under the car every morning. There suddenly became far more important things to worry about than Maradona.
 Always in the background were Barcelona officials whom spoke at great lengths to Jorge Cyerszpiler-with a provisional deal in place to take him after the 1982 World Cup, but this remained shrouded in mystery and could not be cast in stone. Indeed, all hell let loose when it became known Argentinos Juniors, Vice-President Settimio Aloisio had travelled to Catalonia and agreed a transfer in principal to sell Maradona. On his return to the airport, Aloisio was met by a seething mob of supporters intent on a lynching, club President Prospero Consoli was forced to publicly tear up any agreement denying the alleged Barca talks were his doing. This, just in case outraged Argentinos supporters burnt down their stadium with him in it! Poor

Aloisio survived the airport mugging, but received a mass of death threats due to what was deemed treacherous behaviour. Such was the venom aimed towards him, Aloisio duly resigned his position as Vice-President. This done with much public encouragement from Consoli, backed by the Junta regime. Their boy was not leaving for foreign shores just yet, if ever. These were the passion evoked at any thought of taking Diego Maradona out of the country, but in time FC Barcelona would return. With this known to River Plate, who knew Diego had outgrown Argentinos Juniors, also the fact nobody else in the country could afford him, an approach was finally made to Jorge Cysterszpiler by their President Aragon Cabrera. He informed him that if Maradona signed for *Los Millonarias,* Cabrera would make him their joint, top-paid player, alongside World Cup winning goalkeeper Ubaldo Fillol. Hardly a grandstanding offer, but Cysterszpiler went digging to check out Fillol's contract and found he was earning a tidy sum, one that was actually worth sitting down talking with Cabrera over.

An interesting take on Fillol's contract. Back in 1979, Ubaldo's Father received a phone call telling him that if his son didn't sign an extension to his contract at River Plate, both of them would disappear. Then, just to ensure the message was clear enough, let Fillol take up the story. 'One day Lacoste called me in and put a revolver on top of the table. He told me, 'If I wanted to, I make you disappear and nobody, no one will find out.' I was a kid, I didn´t understand a thing, so, I signed.'

Diego's mind drifted back to a conversation with his Father years before. Diego senior was never one to push his son on anything, but he did disclose a dream to him of how great it would be to see Diego in a Boca strip one day and all the family cheering him on at the *La Bombonera.* This for young Maradona meant the world, for so rare did Chitoro open up with his feelings. There remained one huge problem for this to happen, for in all truth Boca Juniors were at that time truly broke, with hardly a peso to spare and a pauper's bank balance.

Meanwhile,

over at River Plate's *El Monumental*, Cabrera, after receiving little or no interest from his opening offer, came up with an outlandish plan. This started to form in the River President's mind after Sunday 5th May 1980, when Maradona had scored twice in a 2-0 win for Argentinos Juniors and electrified the *Monumental* in a stunning performance. Diego ran a River team ragged that was led by Daniel Passarella, who couldn't even get near enough to kick him. He was indeed showing off! *El Pelusa,* the street kid with the scraggly hair from the shanty towns over the *Alsina* bridge, taking the piss at the home of the aristocracy. After witnessing this Cabrera held an emergency meeting with his Board of Directors to put forward an idea to ensure they got Maradona in a River Plate shirt. The Barca rumours had never completely gone away, regarding a deal to take him after *Espana 82.* Indeed, the Catalans were doubling their offer every year to Cyterszpiler. It could only be a matter of time. So, it was River needed to raise a fee to match, or even beat what Barca had agreed. They would be helped by the fact a debt-ridden Argentinos Juniors were desperate for cash straight away, for their coffins had run bare. Maradona incorporated was an expensive animal to feed and had left them close to financial ruin. A $400,000 subsidy off the Argentina Football Association was needed to keep them in business. At one point the AFA appeared set to renege on the money, but Diego Maradona himself went to press threatening that he would quit the national team if they did so. This proved sufficient to change their minds and the deal went ahead. An empty threat? Maybe so, but it worked! It had become clear the time had finally arrived that Argentinos' jewel in the crown could be had for the right price, but there would be many palms needing to be crossed with silver. Mostly those in uniform and not forgetting the player's cut.

 A sum of $10 million dollars was mentioned by Cabrera to his shocked directors. The masterplan was for a thousand members to contribute $10,000 apiece to reach the golden target for the golden boy. It was an enormous fee and outlay, but Cabrera stressed if they signed Diego Maradona, such a figure astronomical as it was would prove a bargain. Sadly for the President it was felt by the board members simply too much of a gamble, his grand scheme was turned down and it was back to the drawing board for Cabrera to come up with something else to prise Diego away from Argentinos. He offered an opening $600,000, plus a choice of two from six top players. Leopoldo Luque, Pablo Comelles, Héctor López, Luis Landaburu, Pedro González and Alfredo De Los Santos. A laughing Consoli immediately turned this down and demanded $13 million dollars!

 Cabrera's reply isn't known.

The game was afoot!

A story was leaked to a newspaper by the Maradona camp that turned into a steady flow, then a Tsunami! A headline appeared on the front page of *Cronica, MARADONA TO BOCA!* This was news even to the Boca directors, Carlos Bello and Domingo Corigliano, whom contacted Cyterszpiler to ask, 'What the Fuck is going on Jorge?'

Diego was asked by them if he really wanted to come, or was it all just a game to bleed more money out of River Plate? The reply was succinct and clear enough. Maradona wanted Boca, if they came up with the right numbers, sensible-not what was being demanded off River, then he would sign for them. A loan sum paid in instalments of $4million, plus assuming a further $1.1 million dollars of Argentinos debt for one season was finally agreed upon and two Boca players. A suitcase of cash Boca had to beg and borrow by going to the banks with cap in hand to raise it. This in the midst of yet another, financial crisis engulfing Argentina, but ultimately, by the skin of their teeth, every last peso was found and they succeeded. On Friday 13th February 1981, in front of Channel 13 cameras, whom had exclusive rights, Diego Armando Maradona officially became a Boca Junior player, and River Plate could go to hell!

CHAPTER TWENTY SEVEN
BOCA: SEASON IN THE SUN (PART ONE)

Boca Juniors. Formed 3rd April 1905, by football mad Italian, Greek and Irish immigrants, Boca Juniors prided themselves in being the team of the working classes. The vast majority of their followers hailed from the poor, downtrodden, neighbourhoods of the Buenos Aires' sea ports. The city's other major club, River Plate, were every Boca Juniors supporter's sworn enemy from birth. When the two clashed either at the home of Boca's *La Bombonera*, or River's *El Monumental* stadium, all of Argentina anticipated fireworks. The *Superclasico* rarely disappointed, as these giants went for each other's throat with a blazing ferocity dipped in the dangerous waters of tradition and class.

The origins of both clubs emerged from the working class docklands and port areas of Buenos Aires. River are the older, hated brother, formed in 1901, Boca,1905. However, in 1925, River moved to the north of the city, the affluent district of Nunez, ever since Boca have remained the club of Argentina's working class, the heart and soul. The people's club. Boca fans became known as the *Xeneizes, (Genoese)*. Whilst, by sharp contrast, River Plate took on the title of *Los Millonarios*, backed by a much, more, upper class support base, though come the early eighties, that no longer applied, with River fans coming from all social classes. The hatred between the two resembled a blood feud. From the cradle to the grave. Boca fans refer to River supporters as *Gallinas, (Chickens),* claiming the River players lacked courage and guts, whilst River's called them *Los Chanchitos,* (Little Pigs), because they mocked that their stadium, located in the less affluent La Boca area, stunk to high hell. Theirs' has both been such a bigoted, twisted history, tinged with hatred and violence. More so, tragedy.

On Sunday 23rd June 1968, in the *El Monumental*, River Plate and Boca Juniors played out a scoreless draw. It was to be a season where neither were victorious in the championship, but that date still remains the most infamous, the darkest day in the history of both clubs. Before kick-off, the Boca hordes had made the journey, trampling, singing and dancing with their flags and banners across Buenos Aires to the detested home of River Plate. The game itself was dreadful, each in the end content not to be beaten. The headline writers struggling with what to lead with when suddenly all hell let loose at the final whistle. As the visiting Boca fans headed down from their terraces in the upper *Tribuna Centenario*, where the ill-fated gate 12 stood, disaster struck. In spite of the gate being blocked, people continued to rain down in droves down the badly, lit stairwell, crushing those below whom had nowhere to go. Of the seventy-one supporters crushed to death, most were teenagers. The accounts of what happened in the aftermath of the tragedy varied, even today matters are no clearer. Some accounts suggest that Boca fans had thrown burning River flags from the upper tier which caused a stampede in the tier below, whilst others claim that River fans had entered the Boca section, prompting a rush down the stairs to the exit. Both of these accounts place the responsibility with the supporters, but there are other versions of events suggesting gate 12 was either locked, or at least blocked making it impossible for those caught to escape. The River president William Kent, placed the blame bluntly at the feet of the police force. He claimed that police outside the stadium refused to allow Boca supporters through the gate, after being annoyed at having urine thrown on them from the stands. As they forced the exiting supporters back in to gate 12 they were met with hundreds still coming down the stairs to leave, and thus in a horrific turn of event trapping those in the middle down at the gate. None of the differing accounts were ever truly proved. Later, when the two sides clashed once more, both sets of supporters sang out in unison, 'No habia puerta, no habia molinete, era la cana que pegaba con machete.' ('There was no gate, there were no barriers, it was the police hitting with knives'). A rare moment of solidarity.

In 1971, after three years of exhaustive investigation, a government inquiry found nobody guilty, much to the despair of the families, whom had lost loved ones. A whitewash they claimed. The official stance appeared to blame too many people leaving at once creating a bottle-neck at the gate. A River Plate lawyer at the time said, 'What happened was an accident caused by the misconduct of the crowd rushing out.' All threw up more questions and answers, as the families howled in tears at what they had been told by the authorities. In the following months more investigations followed, ultimately two River Plate directors, Americo Di Vietro and Marcelino Cabrera, were both sentenced to jail for negligence. Just five months into their sentences both men were released and on appeal cleared. The following year the case was permanently dropped-Archived. Argentina was a hard place to find justice when you came from the other end of the *Alsina* Bridge. Since the tragedy, the gates at *El Monumental* have been changed to letters instead of numbers.

A side-note to these horrific events, at the end of the 1968 season, all the clubs in the Argentine Football Association came together and collected one hundred thousand pesos for the families. However, only two of them accepted the money raised, for if they did so it meant having to sign papers meaning they would be unable to take any further action against the AFA, or River Plate. Shameful.

At the *Monumental,* River Plate replaced the numbered gates and gate 12 became gate L. Though forever drenched in blood.

To such a world arrived Diego Armando Maradona.

After five years performing footballing miracles to drag Argentinos Junior from the lower clutches of the league to a side challenging for honours, their talisman, Maradona finally joined the club of his boyhood dreams. It all began with a little embarrassment for Diego, on the first day of arriving at Boca's *La Candela*, in Jorge Cyterszpiler's Mercedes Benz 450. He suddenly realised that all the Boca players were sponsored by Adidas. Diego noticed them pulling up in their fancy sports cars and Porsches, stepping out dressed in fantastic, smart, sponsor's clothing and trainers. All having over their shoulders the classy three-striped, sports bags adorned in the colours of the club's traditional blue and gold. Whereas he was sponsored by Puma and had only a normal tracksuit plus a scruffy little bag containing his gear. A horrified Diego refused to leave Cyterszpiler's car until he went inside and brought him back some new Adidas training kit! Off went his agent into *La Candela*, where finally he was able to track some down and return with it to get his client out of the car to join in training with the rest of the Boca players!

Diego's last time wearing an Argentinos Juniors shirt, came in a match that was part of the transfer agreement, where he was to play the first half for Argentinos, then change to Boca colours after the interval. Maradona handed the shirt he worn in the first half over to Francisco Cornejo. Their journey to the stars together now over, Cornejo had finally lost out to the bigger dogs, the magic boy was gone. Unbeknown to most, Diego was suffering from a muscle strain in his left leg, but had taken a painkiller injection earlier to mask it. However, after just fifteen minutes, to huge groans on the terraces, he was forced to leave the pitch, such was the torment of the injury. Diego did return in the second half, following another painkiller, a stronger one this time around, all to finally wear the Boca blue and gold, but he was still clearly far from fit. The pressure already overwhelming to play from others, but more so himself. The curse of the witch doctor-Cacho Paladino. For Maradona this was normal, the way of things in the professional game. Somehow, he managed to struggle through to the final whistle, but appeared in agony at the end. Diego later admitted he had not slept for three days because of the pain beforehand. This was the reality behind the glory, the blue and the gold.

It had been four, long, years since Boca last won the Metropolitan Championship, a statistic made infinitely worse by it becoming almost the personal property of their deadly rivals across the city. All Maradona heard was deliver us from the curse of River. Rip the trophy back from *Los Millonarios* grasps and bring joy on earth once more upon the rarified air of those legendary, steeped, terraces of Boca's home, that reached high into the Buenos Aires heavens. It was no simple job description handed to Diego Maradona, more a religious crusade that began on Sunday 22nd February 1981. Just two days after signing, a nervous, looking Maradona crossed himself before stepping out into an emotionally, torrid, atmosphere that even this fanatical church of football, *La Bombonera*, had hardly experienced. Huge showers of ticker tape engulfed a stadium bathed blue and gold. Maradona claimed he thought the ground moved, as 65,000 spectators hailed their new hero. Amongst these the Maradona clan, his Mother and Father with tears streaming down cheeks watching their boy achieving his dream, Chitoros' also. The roaring crowd screaming his name, 'MARADONA!' He was one of their own, a kid like them in looks and background, but that was where it ended, for when on the football pitch they had never witnessed anyone like him. Still, and maddeningly frustrated for Diego, the injury from the Argentinos friendly hadn't shifted, he had spent the entire afternoon with an icepack on his damaged left leg. Diego had also been given another course of painkillers by Boca doctor Luis Pinto and even sleeping pills to calm him down. It was only through dogged determination and gritted teeth that Maradona made it onto the pitch. To the extent when the muscle in the leg sprained backwards, aided by what he'd taken, Diego pressed it forward through a sheer force of will. Again, there was never a chance he would not play against Talleres de Cordoba. Outside pressures like Boca officials and sponsors insisted, but more importantly, the voices inside his own head meant there wasn't a chance in hell of him missing the match. That he managed to score twice in a 4-1 win, two penalties was miraculous itself. A song broke out on the terraces, 'They wanted him at Barcelona, they wanted him at River Plate. Maradona is of Boca, because he is not a hen!'

Off the pitch, Maradona initially had a frosty relationship with the new coach Silvio Marzolini, the son of a carpenter who emigrated from Udinese and the charismatic goalkeeper Hugo Gatti. Marzolini was a Boca legend as a player, twelve years at the club, widely regarded as one of Argentina's finest defenders. He also bled blue and gold. Marzolini worked huge on the values of teamwork, he worried whether such a free spirit as Diego would be able to show the discipline required, reminding him at Boca there would be no privileges like those enjoyed at Argentinos. All players travelled to the matches together, not with families. Maradona would be subjected to the same rules as everyone else. It was a measured attack, done with a smile, but it immediately put the player on the back foot with his boss. Although no longer the humble, quiet, kid from Villa Fiorito, far too much had passed for him to be so-an arrogance now existed that wasn't there before. There was also the fierce pride burning inside that would never fade, it had been hurt, for Maradona had always been a team player. To even suggests he wasn't, pricked at this young king's crown of thorns.

Then, there was Hugo Gatti.

The Previous season, on Sunday 9th November 1980, Argentinos Juniors played Boca Juniors in the National Championship and during the build-up the Boca goalkeeper was quoted in a newspaper article claiming, 'Maradona was a good player, but overhyped.' He went on to say, 'Diego should take care of himself, as he tended to be chubby!' As expected, to no one's real surprise Maradona hit back with a smile on his face, 'I had proposed to score just two goals against Gatti, now, I'm going to score four!

The final score-Argentinos Juniors 5 Boca Juniors 3 and Diego scored four! There was a penalty and two exquisite finishes making Hugo Gatti appear like a wriggling fish caught on a hook. A fourth, a remarkable free kick of insane precision planted like a guided missile over a stranded Gatti into his top far-left corner-simply sublime. Diego's every touch that day came with a whisk of revenge for the lack of respect shown. It became a trait throughout his career that when armed with a point to prove Maradona was virtually unplayable. Watching such sheer, unadulterated magic play out before their eyes caused even the most fanatical, Boca supporters to ultimately start singing his name. This had a profound effect on Diego hearing such acclaim. If there had been any doubts where Diego Armanda Maradona's next port of call in life would be, it ended that day. As for a red-faced Gatti?

He claimed to have been misquoted!

During the opening stages of his Boca career, the injury Diego Maradona sustained from day one to his left leg haunted and after playing the opening four game in searing agony, even though Diego had endured many painkilling injections, the decision was taken finally to rest him. Even then the sponsors and some on the Boca board disagreed. They had gambled the club's entire future on this wonder kid, some demanded he still played on one leg. Luckily, Silvio Marzolini insisted his best player was taken out of the firing line and Maradona was given a much-needed break. During his four game absence Boca won all the games without truly impressing, their dressing room, a mixture of youngsters and veterans, new faces and old that had not yet truly clicked. It remained volatile and spiteful-money always an issue, especially when it came to *El Pelusa.*

On Sunday 29th March 1981, Diego Maradona returned to the line-up in a home match against Newell Old Boys, but events did not go as wished. A lousy first-half performance from Boca, after their other new signing, the thirty-one-year old veteran forward from Huracan, centre-forward Miguel Brindisi headed them in front, only to be cancelled out by a penalty scored by Old Boy's striker Hector Yazalde. Maradona was hardly in the game and come half time all hell erupted in the Boca dressing room. On entering, a ranting, swearing Diego took off his shirt and threw it to the floor complaining, 'What's the point of me playing, if nobody is passing the ball?' Suddenly, he was surrounded by fuming teammates. Notably, long-time veteran defenders Jose Maria Suarez and Vicente Pernia, who each told him to pick the shirt up, otherwise he would be in big trouble and if Diego insulted them by showing such a lack of respect again for the blue and gold colours in the Boca dressing room, they would hit him! A shocked Diego did as told and asked for explanations as to why nobody appeared willing to pass? Their answer not what he expected, as it was explained because of Maradona being so heavily marked and clearly still not yet fully fit, they didn't want to keep giving him the ball, just in case he became under pressure from the crowd by keeping losing it. A few more games with match fitness under his belt, then the players would look to find him.

'It is to protect you Diego,' Suarez told Maradona, who was said to have been moved to tears by the incident. Come the second-half, Maradona slowly started to find form, it was his penalty fifteen minutes from time, after Newell Old Boys had taken a 2-1 lead, that saved a point for Boca. The *La Bombonera* sang his name once more, as Diego swiftly snatched back the ball, desperate to try and win the game in the time left. That it ended in a draw was swiftly forgotten, for next up a team that every Boca supporter had been taught to despise from the moment they left their Mother's womb.

On Sunday 10th April 1982, Buenos Aires awoke from a fitful sleep, if any, for it was the day of *Superclasico*. Boca Juniors v River Plate. The hatred between the two sets of supporters had always been immeasurable. The terraces bloodstained when they clashed-it was tribal warfare driven by history, tradition and racism. The signing of Diego Maradona by Boca inflaming passions no end. When playing for Argentinos Juniors, Diego had experienced chants regarding his family's Indian heritage, the childhood of pitiful poverty spent in Villa Fiorito, but never to the extent of what he was set to endure against River. A game Maradona had dreamed about playing in all his life, ever since he clutched the ball tight given to him on his third birthday by cousin Bete Zarate had arrived. It would be worth the wait!

In a stunning performance by Boca on a rain-lashed, spattered, swamp of a pitch, to the utter joy of the mass dancing, blue and gold painted, fervid terraces, they put River Plate to the sword 3-0. No goals at the interval, two wonderfully taken finishes from the deadly Brindisi, a third to put the topping on the *La Bombonera* chocolate box from Maradona, that left the stadium close to emotional turmoil, toppling, collapsing on itself. From the opening whistle, Diego appeared determined to tease and torment River on a treacherous surface, that for him proved effortless to overcome, dancing, drifting over puddles, soaring through the mud. *La Banda* tackles flew high, wild and savage from the River defenders in desperate efforts to curtail this little magician, who showing tremendous courage, repeatedly cut them apart whilst attempting to set up opportunities for his *compadres,* or trying to score himself. There was even a moment when Diego flicked the ball with his hand over Fillol into the net from a free kick, only for the eagle-eyed referee to blow up. There would though be plenty of time to perfect this trick, first tried on Villa Fiorito's dust bowls. The goal when it came was a fitting finale to an unforgettable night, for all those with Boca in their hearts.

With just over twenty minutes remaining, Maradona found himself six yards out faced by international goalkeeper Ubaldo Fillol-he gave Fillol the eye, before dancing around him, as another World Cup winner Alberto Tarantini, went flying onto the goal line, Diego waited, put

Tarantini on the floor with a dummy, then slid his shot past him into the net. It was a glorious moment and as Maradona raced away disappearing amidst the euphoria and sheer fucking madness of a *La Bombonera* on fire, a legend was born. *El Pelusa* knew high in the stadium his family were watching and would be crying with joy. He blew kisses in their direction thinking of his dad. Both their dreams had come true.

A side-note-Shortly after the final whistle Silvio Marzolini fell ill with a suspected heart-attack and was rushed to the hospital and placed in intensive care. All this initially brought about after Maradona's goal. Happily, he recovered, but Marzolini struggled from that moment onwards. Boca Juniors were officially bad for your health, as for Diego? It would not be the first heart attack he would hand out over the coming years…

After the magnificent victory over their rivals, Boca were brought crashing down to earth five days later at the *Jose Amalfitani* stadium, home of Velez Sarsfield, who deservedly won 1-0. Velez midfielder Jorge Sanabria hitting the winner on the half-hour. This Boca side was a new creation taking time to gell. Maradona himself remained reliant on painkillers as the injury to his left leg was proving terribly slow to heal. Boca's form remained inconsistent, but they always managed to stay top of the table, or within breathing distance of it. Their closest rivals for the title were not as expected River Plate or Independiente, but the small and ferocious Ferro Carril Oeste. Formed 28th July 1904, by a hundred employees of the Buenos Aires, Western Railway, Ferro were coached by the wily, dogmatic, Carlos Griguol. An old seadog whose tactics divided opinion. He did have a fan in Diego Maradona, who referred to him as the 'Old Master.' A man whose last act before his players took to the pitch was to slap their faces! Ferro under Griguol's leadership would take Boca Juniors all the way to the last day of the Metropolitan Championship and when the two sides met on Sunday 3rd May 1981, they quite literally kicked holes out of Boca, one player in particular, to claim a 0-0 draw on home turf at the *Ricardo Etchevveri* stadium, in Cabillito, Buenos Aires. A full house of 24,000 screaming them on against the big city boys from *La Bombonera*. Maradona was hacked down, punched, elbowed, kicked, all but beaten up by Griguol's fired up green shirts to the point of madmen! Finally, running out of patience, he snapped second half, retaliating by swinging out a leg and was duly shown a yellow card by the referee. It was a booking akin to a man being attacked by a pack of snarling wolves, then being punished for kicking one back! That Maradona made it out of Caballito in one piece was itself a minor miracle. Following the battle with Ferro, a thrilling 3-2 victory over Rosario Central on home soil, with Diego grabbing a last minute winner from the penalty spot. The next three matches saw Boca slip badly by drawing twice against Racing Club and Instituto, then losing at Talleres. Despite the bad run, come the mid-way point of the championship, they remained five points clear of a chasing pack led by Ferro, but fooling few of blue and gold persuasion. Silvio Marzolini's team were catchable, they wasn't planning any party celebrations just yet.

CHAPTER TWENTY EIGHT
BOCA: SEASON IN THE SUN (PART TWO)
The rollercoaster continued for Boca Juniors with another exciting 3-2 win, this time over Huracan at *La Bombonera*, swiftly followed by a 4-0 away thrashing of Platense, with

Diego Maradona scoring twice, including a penalty. A 2-1 victory against Sarmiento at home came next and Boca Juniors were flying once more, their belief started to rise as did the supporters', only all to go wrong horribly again away at lowly Union Santa Fe, where in a terrible display, they went down 2-0. Reminiscent of earlier in the season when the wheels came flying off, the coach Silvio Marzolini watching despondently on the touchline of the *Estadio 15 de Abril*, in Santa Fe Province. Something just wasn't ticking, but so far Boca were getting away with it, as no other side could find the form to power past them. It was no lack of effort from Marzolini's players, it just appeared at times the ball was square and they wasn't clicking as a team. Frustrations were running high, meeting were called, tempers frayed. Diego Maradona was already a leader in the dressing room, but the relationship with Marzolini remained cold at best. There had been an instance back in April before a game away to Independiente. Maradona had felt the ferocious defender Oscar Ruggeri should play because the defence was struggling and Ruggeri was always good for a goal or two when rampaging forward from corners and free kicks. Marzolini dismissed him immediately, not wanting his authority to be usurped. Instead, Diego gathered all the more experienced players who believed as he did, together they made their case to the coach. Angered by his superstar's continued stance, but not wanting to lose the dressing room, Marzolini gave in, come the day, Boca won well 2-0 with Maradona scoring a fantastic goal from outside the box in the first half and who else but Ruggeri grabbing a second with a header ten minutes into the second half! A peso that day for the thoughts of Silvio Marzolini

Sunday 28th June 1981. Boca Juniors 4 San Lorenzo 0, the rollercoaster continued to fly wildly out control as the *La Bombonera* rocked and swayed to a stunning performance by Diego Maradona. Appearing back to his beguiling best and the injury finally settling down, Maradona finished off a wonderfully, majestic display with a stunning free kick around the outside of the Lorenzo wall. Hit with such sumptuous ease. The stadium roared out his name, the blue and gold giving thanks to their young saviour. Three days later a hard fought 2-0 away win at Newell Old Boys meant with just nine games to go, the Championship was Boca's to lose.

To lose…

What followed was four straight draws that caused eruptions amongst all connected with Boca Juniors, as it appeared the players had lost their nerve at the worst possible time of the title run in. Firstly, home to Independiente, only a late Maradona goal salvaged a 1-1 draw, but it was a beautiful one at that. A chipped half-volley on the turn from the edge of the penalty area, beating the goalkeeper and a defender on the goal-line. Off Diego soared with both arms raised as he had done when scoring back on the *Siete Conchita* all those years ago back in Villa Fiorito. The difference being then Maradona kicked up dust, now it was confetti thrown from his adoring fans. Racing through a sea of white on the turf towards a dancing sea of blue and gold madness. Still only twenty-one-years-old, Diego Armando Maradona had already lived a life and it had not yet really begun.

The following week was the second *Superclasico* of the season away to River Plate, at the *El Monumental,* with revenge in the air. In a typically, warlike-breath-taking, atmosphere-the air thick with insults and chants. The 3-0 defeat at *La Bombonera* had cut deep, but with the game scoreless shortly after the interval, it was Boca who struck first. Diego Maradona twisting and turning before chipping from a wide angle over Ubaldo Fillol and two defender's heads into the top far corner! Magic again from Diego-the Boca fans going crazy in this place, their idea of living hell. Maradona raced to celebrate with them as the River hordes fumed. Known as the *Los Millonarios*, here was something even their club's treasure chest could never buy. Ten minutes later an equaliser for River Plate, when their beloved Captain Daniel Passarella smashed in a thirty yard free kick that Hugo Gatti failed to hold and Mario Kempes struck from close range, to ignite the *El Monumental*. The two World Cup heroes combining to save the day for *La Banda*.

   The next game for Boca at home to Velez Sarsfield couldn't have had a better start, when after just five minutes Diego Maradona chested the ball down in the penalty area, turned and fired low past the goalkeeper Luis Landaburo. As Diego raced to the corner flag, jumped on by jubilant team mates, as the stadium exploded in a cascade of utter delirium, a footballing massacre appeared on the cards, only for everything to fade once more from blue and gold to grey. Nerves engulfed the *La Bombonera*, whistles and jeers even, what the fuck were their boys playing at? It came as literally no surprise to anyone present when Velez's legendary, forward Carlos Bianchi smashed home just before the interval, to ultimately gain a point, causing worrying rumblings amongst the Boca heartbeat. With Diego missing through injury, more points were dropped three days later away at relegation threatened Argentinos Juniors, (how they had missed *El*

Pelusa), where a Brindisi penalty saw Boca escape with a 2-2 draw. Just four games remained to play, Griguol's Ferro stood ready to pounce as Boca wracked by nerves, players seemingly incapable of being able to handle the pressure, an unfit Diego trying everything to stay on the pitch but failing, a support suffering a collective breakdown. Something extraordinary was required to reignite the passion, or indeed the will to get over the winning line. it duly occurred.

Barra Brava, (Fierce Gang). Thirty-year-old José Barrita was known as

El Abuelo, (The Grandfather), because of his unusually early head of silver grey hair. He was the leader of the infamous *La12*, the most infamous of *Barra Brava* groups whom followed Boca Juniors. Barrita grew up in the sea port area of Buenos Aires, a tough street kid few messed with. A passionate follower of Boca, he became a member of La12, which at that time was led by another notorious character, Quiche, *El Carnicero,* (The Butcher). In the summer of 1981, as Boca appeared set to blow the title, Barrita took over the group in his own way by pointing a gun at Quique making it apparently clear there was a new boss in town. Quique was never heard of again.

An incident at *La Candela.* Boca's *concentracion*. It was the eve of the must-win Estudiantes home game. All the players including Diego Maradona were resting, lounging around. Diego himself was arguing with his *compadre* Hugo Perroti to come off the phone, so he could call Claudia. A smiling Perotti was ignoring him sat with his legs up, when suddenly they were kicked from beneath him!

The *Barra Bravas* had come to *La Candela.*

In they trampled, the self-styled protectors and voice of the Boca terraces. Hundreds had swarmed the *concentracion* to take it over, some armed with pistols, the rest, knives, chains, iron bars…It was a small army on a mission.

The one who knocked Perotti on the floor was harangued by an angry Maradona, who in turn was told to keep out of it, for he was the only player they didn't have a problem with. Meanwhile, the rest were being rounded up. In the *Barra's* midst was the unmistakeable figure of the silver-grey haired, *El Abuelo.* He approached Maradona who was fuming as he watched his team mates being screamed at. Threats made that they knew where families lived and warned to up their game against Estudiantes. As for, *El Abuelo,* he spoke with great respect in explaining the reasons they had to come was because the newspapers were claiming some of the others didn't want to run or pass to him and this couldn't be tolerated. Maradona was told if they didn't change the *Barra Bravas* would make 'mincemeat' of them! Silvio Marzolini was also brought before Barrita, he too was given a mouthful. 'Buck the fuck up or else!' Still, Diego argued back, much to the shock of all present, both footballers and hooligans, because nobody did such with *El Abuelo.* A twenty-one-year-old kid from Villa Fiorito taking on the *Barra Bravas* single-handedly? Not only was Diego Maradona the best footballer on the planet, but he had huge cojones. Diego told Barrita that he wouldn't play against Estudiantes, unless his boys stopped threatening the Boca players. Barrita agreed, but added that if the Championship wasn't won, the *Barra bravas* would return to 'Sort them out.' Although, once more Barrita went to great lengths explaining none of this was aimed towards Maradona, for they viewed him as a Captain and leader. One of their own. Thinking the point had been clearly made with many Boca players crying and scared to death, Jorge Barrita gave the signal and the *Barra Bravas* vanished, swift as they arrived. Leaving in their wake a shell-shocked Boca Juniors *concentracion*.

If one good thing came of the incident at *La Candela*, it was to bring the players closer together and for them to realise that in Diego Maradona they had in their line-up, not only a special talent on the field, but also a young lad willing to stand up for them off it in frightening circumstances. Undoubtedly, there had been clashes on and off the field with Maradona, certain players, whether it was jealousy, or those whom believed this kid was simply too big for his boots. Such thoughts ended on Saturday 19th July 1981, when the fearful *El Abuelo* came to *La Candela,*
and met his match in *El Pelusa.*

The following day at a highly charged, emotional *La Bombonera*, a 1-0 victory was earned with an astonishing goal from the darting, left-winger Hugo Perotti, who only the day previously had seen his legs swept away from him by one of the *Barra Bravas*. Though wonderfully finished by Perotti, huge credit deservedly was given to the keeper Hugo Gatti who set off on an incredible run charging into the Estudiantes half, with the home crowd roaring him forward! On went Gatti before releasing Perotti who dribbled through five Estudiantes players, before shooting low past the opposing keeper Enrique Vidale, into the bottom corner of the net. A stunning, individual goal that electrified the *La Bombonera!* Only four games remained, all Boca had to do was keep their nerve and they would win the Metropolitan Championship.

Easier said than done.

On Sunday 26th July 1981, Boca Juniors travelled to Santa Fe where in a brutal encounter with two sent off against lowly Colon, they won 2-0. Boca were forced to dig deep and inspired by Maradona who was besieged from the opening whistle by the fiery *Los Sabaleros'* defenders, seemingly intent on crippling him, it was a fight on the pitch at the *Estadio Brigadier General Estanislao Lopez*, but, finally, battered and bruised-one won by Boca. A venue christened the 'Elephants graveyard' due to the amount of top sides beaten there over the decades. None more so than the wonderful Brazilian side Santos, that included the great Pele back in 1963. Two more points secured, Silvio Marzolini's boys returned to Buenos Aires preparing for a match that if won, all but guaranteed the title. Carlos Griguol's Ferro who remained like a stray dog with a blue and gold bone between their teeth were coming to the *La Bombonera* with a last chance to drag Boca back.

A week on from the battle of Santa Fe, Ferro turned up and scared the living daylights out of the 65,000 supporters thinking the path to the championship had become nothing more than a carnival parade. For eighty minutes, Ferro were by far the better of the two sides, as Marzolini's team went into frozen mode once more. Diego Maradona found himself crowded out in a midfield area resembling a free-for-all, his every move stalked. Guignol's tactic to strangle the match and Boca's best player, then sneak a goal appeared to be coming to fruition, as the *La Bombonera* shrieked and whistled sensing a goal for the visitors-enter Maradona. With ten minutes remaining Diego finally found half an inch and with a beautiful slice of a pass put Hugo Perotti away to sprint between two green-shirted defenders, before slipping the ball past the keeper Carlos

Jose Barisio, to ignite the Boca terraces! Madness reigned as Perotti disappeared beneath a pile of bodies. One name resonated as it thundered loud from the terraces, like a war cry to the heavens, 'MARADONA!'

Tears of Rosario. Like a trampling army of old, Boca Juniors and their huge travelling army of blue and gold followers draped in flags, drunk on dreams of glory and wine travelled three hundred miles to Rosario and the *Estadio Gigante de Arroyito.* Home of Rosario Central and where Argentina fought out their second group matches during the *Mundial.* Every Boca fan was desperate to be present for they needed only a point to clinch the Metropolitan Championship. It would be something to tell their children and grandchildren. Sunday 9th August 1981. I was there in Rosario when *El Pelusa* made all our dreams come true. On the banks of the great *Parana* River that flowed through Brazil and Paraguay, then Argentina, before finally emptying into the Atlantic Ocean. Here would surely be where the torment ended for Boca Juniors?

So, unfolded the story of Boca's season as they again struggled to find any semblance of real form when the pressure was truly upon them. All appeared to be going to plan when despite having struggled to put a decent move together, they went into the interval at 0-0. However, the *Canalla,* (The Rabble), sensed blood and on fifty-four-minutes took a deserved lead when the Rosario born twenty-five-year-old defender Jorge Alberto Garcia smashed home a twenty-five-yard free-kick hit low that surprised Hugo Gatti! Garcia raced to his supporters near the corner and dropped to his knees with arms raised. Suddenly, Boca were in desperately trouble, a loss and the title remained uncertain and would go to the last game.

Maradona came alive, urging his *compadres* forward, but the yellow shirts of Rosario appeared determined to ruin the party for the big city amigos. Not on their fucking turf. The visitors poured forward in search of salvation. The songs from their supporters on the Rosario terraces now sung with sheer desperation, sticking in their throats. It was all happening again, then, with fourteen minutes remaining a penalty for Boca!

Diego Maradona went to accept the ball.

A chance gifted to finally end the pain of what had been a torturous, at times season for Diego, but now it came down to a one-on-one duel with thirty-five-year old veteran, Rosario goalkeeper Daniel Alberto Carnevali. A former Argentinian number one, Carnevali was the keeper in the 1974 World Cup, until replaced by Ubaldo Fillol. He stood ready to face Maradona's spot kick, as behind him stood the vast majority of the praying Boca support. Thousands of prayers drifting high into the Rosario sky. Up came Diego and with a delicate flick of his left foot he hit the ball against the crossbar. The game finished 1-0 to Rosario Central, meaning the title would go down to the final game of the season at the *La Bombonera* against Racing Club. No foregone conclusion. A devastated Maradona wept afterwards at seeing the faces of forlorn Boca supporters through the team bus window, as they returned to Buenos Aires. Flags were at half mask, a sense of despondency engulfed the blue and gold draped convoy of cars, lorries and buses heading home, frustrated beyond belief. This club for whom they would die for, their whole lives, their every waking moment now rested on a final ninety minutes. Making matters infinitely worse, the one they trusted more than any other had just failed from twelve yards to grant their rainbows end, maybe it simply wasn't written?

Seven days later, on a beautiful, Sunday 15th August 1981, in a heaving, boiling pot of emotion, on a white-littered snowstorm of a confetti surface at the *La Bombonera,* Diego Maradona scored the goal that secured for Boca Juniors the long awaited Metropolitan Championship. Albeit, amongst five sending offs, three for Boca, two for Racing. A bloodbath! It was a breath-taking encounter against Racing Club, who came to attack and a 1-1 draw meant heaven on earth was forthcoming to the blue and gold swamped terraces at the full time whistle. Diego's moment to put the pain of Rosario behind him arrived shortly before half-time, when he was sent sprawling in the penalty area by Racing's charismatic goalkeeper, Alberto Pedro Vivalda. This time he made no mistake placing the spot kick into the middle of the goal, as Vivalda dived to the right. As if possessed by demons, Maradona sprinted towards the terraces, fell to his knees screaming at the heavens. Redemption for Rosario. Diego crossed himself in front of an adoring mass of roaring humanity. All across the stadium was on fire! The noise incredible as the fans bounced and bounced, roaring out the name of their saviour. It appeared impossible for them to love him more.

The clock ticked, more trickled down, two minutes remained, the nerves exhausting, the whistling, grown men crying, end it, just fucking end it-Racing equalise! 1-1! The substitute forward Omar Roldan flashes a header past Hugo Gatti at the far post. Despite a small pocket of Racing fans going crazy high in the second tier, the *La Bombonera* fell silent as the grave. On the touchline Silvio Marzolini screamed for his team to keep their heads. Already playing only with nine men, as were Racing, after

Hugo Perotti and the left-back Carlos Cordoba were dismissed first half, to Marzolini's horror, they went down to eight, when midfielder Roberto Passuci was shown a red also by the card happy referee Abel Gnecco. Seconds remained, the eight men of Boca against the nine men of Racing. Another goal for Racing meant a play-off with Ferro for the title was more or less on the cards, as they could do no more leading 3-0 away at Platense. An astonishing finale and then Gnecco's whistle resonated, lost amidst the noise and furore, it felt like Buenos Aires had been struck by an earthquake!

For the first time since 1976,

Boca Juniors were champions!

On the pitch they poured from all angles heading for *El Pelusa.* Including a man going hell for leather in his wheelchair! The first to reach him was kid brother Lalo, who dived on Diego's back telling him Argentinos Juniors were safe after a relegation battle! A double celebration for the Maradona's, Cornejo and his little onions forever in Diego's heart, Soon, they were joined by a mad rush of players, officials and fans simply desperate to just touch Maradona. High in the stands, parents Tota and Chitoro hugged and wept tears of joy for their boy. Embarrassed, but touched by Boca fans falling at their feet giving thanks for bringing Diego into this world! 'Without suffering it is not Boca,' said one afterwards being interviewed on the radio. A last word for the brave Ferro, whom fought to the last, they would go on to triumph magnificently in the league the following year and then again in 1984. Carlos Griguol's tough hombres, born from a Buenos Aires Western railway company, many generations previous, had given their all and were to be saluted.

Across the *La Bombonera*, the terraces bounced, rumbled and played host to a party not witnessed in Buenos Aires since the *Mundial*. At its very heart, surrounded by a huge posse of photographers, cameramen and worshippers, Diego Armando Maradona leapt high in the air blowing kisses to an adoring crowd all singing his name. The kid from Villa Fiorito had achieved the dream, and as to what happened next, well, this was Maradona.

Welcome to Diegoland!

Interviewed afterwards Diego opened his heart on what he had been going through. 'I feel very happy. Boca are champions and in the end Argentinos stayed up. I already had everything calculated in case Argentinos had to play a tiebreaker on Monday, because I wanted to go with my red flag to support the boys. But, I can't complain about anything now. Boca are champions! I felt guilty about what happened in Rosario, Yes, the dollars that were paid have weighed heavily on me, but never on the pitch. Never. There, I forgot everything. Thank God at the time of the penalty today I was calm, after blocking out the memory of the previous one. I knew it would be okay though, because this morning I prayed a lot. I asked God for Boca and I asked for Argentinos. I had blind faith, because he was with me.'

Later that evening Diego turned up with his entourage at Argentinos Juniors, *La Cantina,* where he continued his partying from winning the title. At the request of some fans and old amigos, Maradona put on an Argentinos Juniors baseball cap to give a short speech, 'To all the people of Argentinos, I want to let you know that my team now is Boca, where I have just lived one of the greatest days of my life. But, one day, I don't know when, I will wear my first shirt again.'

CHAPTER TWENTY NINE
THE PRICE YOU PAY

From the moment the final whistle blew on the Metropolitan Championship, all that filled the headlines was what next for Diego Armando Maradona? Just three weeks on from winning the title, Boca found itself unable to make up the latest instalment to Argentinos Juniors for Maradona. It was a swift fall from grace as Argentinos took them to court for breach of contract. If this wasn't bad enough, the central bank of Argentina froze Boca's account when a number of cheques bounced. These actually included one to *Maradona production*s, a company set up by Jorge Cyterszpiler to look after all of Diego's business interest. Now, Cyterszpiler got edgy. As ever, Barcelona continued to whisper into his ear, they were never going away. Left with no option Boca Juniors went on a world tour like a rock group in order to stay afloat. It would be Diego Maradona and a supporting cast.

Not since PT Barnum partook on his own incredulous world-wide tour had there been such an extensive, exhaustive schedule! Diego Maradona's debut for Boca came on 22nd February 1981, his last game, 6th February 1982. Below the list of games (friendlies) played and countries visited during that period. All designed to keep Boca financially afloat, paying Diego's wages and keeping the Argentinos Juniors cash instalments flowing.

20/02/1981 Boca Juniors v Argentinos Juniors (Friendly) 2-3
24/02/1981 Independiente Rivadavia v Boca Juniors (Friendly) 1-2
05/03/1981 San Lorenzo v Boca Juniors (Friendly) 2-4

01/04/1981 Belgrano (Cordoba) Boca Juniors (Friendly) 1-2

12/04/1981 Gimnasia y Escrima v Boca Juniors (Friendly) 1-1

17/04/1981 Alianza Paranaense v Boca Juniors (Friendly) 1-3

22/04/1981 Combinado de Tucuman v Boca Juniors (Friendly) 1-1

20/05/1981 Espanol de Barcelona (Spain) v Boca Juniors (Friendly) 0-0

25/05/1981 Deportivo Guaymallen v Boca Juniors (Friendly) 0-2

17/08/1981 Boca Juniors v Racing Club (Atlantic Cup: Friendly) 1-0

27/08/1981 Nexa (Mexico) v Boca Juniors (Friendly) 1-1

03/09/1981 Real Zaragoza (Spain) v Boca Juniors (Friendly) 2-0

05/09/1981 Paris Saint Germain (France) v Boca Juniors (Friendly 1-3

08/09/1981 Milan v Boca Juniors (Italy) v Boca Juniors (Friendly) 1-2

15/09/1981 Flamengo v Boca Juniors (Brazil) v Boca Juniors (Friendly) 2-2

06/10/1981 Stade Abidjan (Ivory Coast) v Boca Juniors (Friendly) 2-5

08/10/1981 Asec (Ivory Coast) v Boca Juniors (Friendly) 2-3

18/12/1981 Universitario (Peru) v Boca Juniors (Friendly) 1-0

20/12/1981 Barcelona (Ecuador) v Boca Juniors (Friendly) 3-2

22/12/1981 Alianza Lima 9(Peru) v Boca Juniors (Friendly) 1-2

06/01/1982 El Salvador v Boca Juniors (Los Angeles) (Friendly) 0-2

10/01/1982 Seiko (Hong Kong) v Boca Juniors (Challenge Cup)(Friendly) 0-0 and Boca Juniors won 7-5 penalties

12/01/1982 Selangor (Malaysia) v Boca Juniors (Friendly) 1-2

16/01/1982 Japan national team (Tokyo) v Boca Juniors (Friendly) 1-1

20/01/1982 Japan B v Boca Juniors (Kobe) (Friendly) 2-3

24/01/1982 Japan national team (Tokyo) v Boca Juniors (Friendly 0-1

26/01/1982 America (Mexico) v Boca Juniors (Friendly) 1-2

27/01/1982 Comunicaciones (Guatemala) v Boca Juniors (Friendly) 0-1

30/01/1982 Boca Juniors v Racing Club (Gold Cup) (Friendly) 4-1

03/02/1982 Boca Juniors v Independiente (Gold Cup) (Friendly) 1-0

06/02/1982 Boca Juniors v River Plate (Gold Cup)(Friendly) 0-1

An endless journey, seemingly, forever on the road. Of the 349 days Diego was at Boca, they played an astonishing eighty games with Metropolitan and National championship ties, plus friendlies across the globe. All took an enormous toll on the players when trying to win the Metropolitan championship and may explain some of their many lethargic showings throughout the season, despite managing to crawl over the winning line by the skin of their teeth. Interesting, that when the *Barra Bravas* came calling at *La Candela*, some players blamed the number of friendlies they were being forced to partake in as the reason for their inconsistency. The same applied when the National championships began. This, a second major tournament that followed the Metropolitan which saw Boca knocked out at the quarter-final stage to Velez Sarsfield.

On Wednesday 2nd December 1981, the first leg took place at the *La Bombonera* and turned into an absolute madhouse! A shattered Boca Juniors team in both legs and mind more than played their part in a footballing bloodbath, with three sending's off on both sides, including Maradona's. All came in a manic second-half, with the under-fire referee Carlos Esposito requiring eyes in the back of his head, as personal duels were being settled all over the pitch. Ten minutes remained with the game still scoreless and both sides down to nine men, Velez Sarsfield took the lead when midfielder Juan Bujedo smashed a header into the net past Boca keeper Rodriguez Alberto, who had replaced Hugo Gatti. This was the moment for Diego Maradona to finally snap, when after being hacked, slashed and chopped down by his Velez man-marker Abel Moralejo, from the opening moments, he retaliated by lashing back and was duly dismissed, along with Moralejo by the referee Esposito. As a fuming Diego watched on from the touchlines, surrounded by cameramen and photographers, his Boca *compadres* staged a remarkable comeback in the dying moments. Firstly, when defender Oscar Ruggeri surged forward to thunder a right-footed equalizer past the Velez keeper Jorge Bartero into the top corner, causing mayhem on the terraces. As the fans were still celebrating Ruggeri's goal, Hugo Perotti danced past two Velez tackles, before letting fly a low shot from twenty-five-yards, leaving Bartero well beaten at his near post! 2-1! The stadium exploded as if hit by thunder! It was a comeback to remember for the Boca Junior supporters, but one tinged with sadness, as this was to be the last time they would see Diego Maradona play in a Boca shirt in a Championship capacity.

Four days later at the second-leg, in the crammed *Jose Amalfitani* stadium, with Diego suspended and the Boca players understandably out on their feet due to the crazy schedule, Velez blew them away with a three-goal blast to delight *El Fortín! (The Small Fort).* After just five minutes, the centre-forward Carlos Bianchi ran through to keep his nerves and beat the keeper Rodriguez Alberto with a calm finish into the bottom corner. As Boca toiled, Velez went two up seven minutes before half-time. Their midfielder, the twenty-eight year old, Sante Fe born, Ricardo Roldan hit a wickedly, curving shot from fully thirty-yards out that soared into Alberto's top corner like a rocket! Shortly after the interval, it was three when Velez winger Jorge Comas sped into the Boca penalty area and flashed a shot past a diving Alberto into his far corner-again a fantastic goal! To the utter joy of their home supporters, Velez Sarsfield were hammering nails into a dreadfully fading Boca Juniors. Though they hit back one last time, another great effort from Oscar Ruggeri surging forward to finish off a superb break, it was all too much. Boca were out of the National Championships.

It was the price you pay.

Mar del Plata is a city located on the Argentinian, Atlantic coast and on Saturday 6th February 1982, although unknown at the time would prove to be the place where Diego Armando Maradona played his final game for Boca Juniors against River Plate, whom won 1-0 with a goal

scored by Diego's amigo Ramon Diaz. By this time Silvio
Marzolini's heart problems had caused him to step down.
His assistant Horacio Bongiovanni had run things for a
while, now, the new boss was forty-eight-year-old former
Platense coach Vladislao Cap. It was Cap who finally gave
an exhausted Diego permission to return to Buenos Aires
for a break with girlfriend Claudia and his family. The
1982 World Cup where Argentina would defend their
crown on European soil was swiftly hurtling into sight. A
four month *concentracion* with the national team
upcoming and Maradona needed to rest both his shattered
body and mind for that. National coach Cesar Menotti had
gone public that his team was to be, 'Diego Maradona and
ten others.' The madness around Diego never ceased. The
one question constantly being asked of him whether by
Boca supporters or journalists who followed his every step,
'Are you going to Barcelona Diego?' The player himself
was being pulled both ways. He so wished to play for Boca
in the *Copa Libertadores,* (South American Champions
League), but financially and the searing pressure of feeling
like he was burning alive in the spotlight, meant Barcelona
was indeed a welcome escape route-a lucrative one at that.

Even his parents, living, now settled in a one-million
dollars apartment in Villa Devoto, of north-west, Buenos
Aires, were hounded. Diego had also bought adjoining
apartments for all other family members. It was designed
to be a place of peace and calm away from the spotlight.
This, a quiet, residential neighbourhood, so far removed
from Villa Fiorito, the Maradona's were still finding
themselves harassed every time they stepped out of their
front door by encamped television crews and snapping
paparazzi, inquiring about Diego's future. It became a

siege, to the extent Tota started to suffer badly with her nerves. A furious Maradona went public threatening to move to Europe if they were not left in peace. Diego's private life with Claudia also came under constant scrutiny, even going for a pizza turned into utter chaos. The gossip pages talked of other women and wild nights out without Claudia. Kiss and tell-run and take the fucking money. It was like living in a fishbowl.

The year previous Diego had departed along with his entire family and Claudia to Esquina. There alongside the *Corrientes* River, he and his Dad would fish for hours on end. Diego spoke of all that was going on and over a beer with a few guiding words, Don Chitoro would listened and calm his son down, giving him the strength to go again. However, on that visit word got around of the Maradona's visit and the usual peace and serenity Diego found at Esquina wasn't forthcoming. The photographers came to snap their pictures, autograph hunters forever in his face. Family meals interrupted in local restaurants, People singing his name-others though demanding to know, 'What next Diego?

'What the fuck next?' He was no longer invisible in a place for him that was a last bastion of a hiding place in Argentina. So, with his little time for rest and recuperation before the incarceration of the *concentracion,* Diego Maradona headed over the ocean to Las Vegas. Yet, even there they found him. Photographs of Diego sunbathing and enjoying a beer or two and three with *compadres* by the pool were circulated amongst the Argentinian newspapers, saw Maradona hammered once more. A World Cup to play for and here was their best player on another continent getting drunk! Ultimately, a pissed off

Diego returned home and as *Espana 82* loomed large, informed Jorge Cyterszpiler to contact Barcelona.

It was time to go…

CHAPTER THIRTY
FEEDING THE WOLVES

The beating of the drum roll. In the end it took nearly a decade, but this is how it all began. A message from an old Catalan friend residing in Buenos Aires, begging sixty-seven-year-old Argentine born, FC Barcelona vice-President Nicolau Casaus, to come and view for himself, a little waif of a genius causing an almost like religious consternation in Argentina's football circles. Casaus was well used to receiving such messages, for he was head of Barca's world-wide *Penas* system. *(Fan clubs)*. Normally, Casaus dismissed these calls for him to act, supporters just got so carried away, or had a financial angle, but such was the passion and enthusiasm, in his old friend's voice simply begging him to come, Casaus packed his suitcase and headed to Buenos Aires.

To stir the soul of the cynical, hard-bitten Casaus took some undertaking, but that one summer's day in the district of La Paternal, at Argentinos Juniors training ground, it duly occurred, as he watched this young boy with magical dancing feet. The locals told him his nickname was *El Pelusa* and as he dribbled across the pitch leaving in his wake a trail of chasing, bedraggled defenders, Nicolau Casaus was spellbound. Never had he witnessed anything like him. For the grand old man of Barcelona, it was indeed akin to a spiritual awakening. Forever, always insistent in the belief that his good friend the legendary Barca midfielder of the twenties and thirties, Josep Samiter, was the finest player he had ever seen, now, where before there had been certainty, Casaus truly believed he had come across someone who in no time at all would leave Samiter and the rest in the shadows. For the more Casaus watched this raggedy, mop-haired phenomenon from the back of beyond, raised in some shanty town called Villa Fiorito, the more he sent shivers down his spine. Occasionally, just, the boy passed the ball, but only ever a loan. Soon it returned with a grateful smile, then, a dummy, a burst of speed around the stranded keeper, before being walked into the net. There were times he would charge with the ball into a pile of bigger opponents ready to kick him-all would disappear in the dust off the surface, then, emerging into view came *El Pelusa,* racing away to score! The speechless opponents would smile and shake his hand as he headed back to the restart. It wouldn't be a long goodbye, for the youngster soon returned tormenting, before they had chance to draw breath. Such rare talent and beauty in one so young could not stay silent for long and no surprise Boca Juniors and River Plate watched him like a hawk, just waiting for the moment to make a move. Far more worryingly for Casaus was the fact Italy's Juventus had people in place ready in Buenos Aires, if the opportunity ever arose to snatch him away. Such a thought mortified Casaus, for this was a boy born to play for Barcelona, their standards were beyond excellence and *El Pelusa* as they called him was beyond the stars.

So, it was for Nicolau Casaus, already a life of dedication to the Barca cause, there remained one last task to fulfill. Whatever it cost, for here was a rare breed of player that came along only once every other generation. At the time Barca still had Johan Cruyff at the peak of his awesome powers. The Dutch Prince of the *Camp Nou,* undoubtedly the world's best footballer. Yet, despite the prayers of millions, Barca Gods didn't go on forever. A heir to the throne would in time be required and Casaus was convinced the Argentinian boy could take on Cruyff's mantle and become not just a prince, but a God for Barcelona.

His name was Diego Armando Maradona.

Nicolau Casaus was a man whose love for Barca went much further than matters on a football pitch. His was a real blood on the ball. In 1939, Casaus was tried, found guilty-sentenced to death by Spain's Nationalist regime. His most heinous crime charged with treason for writing articles criticising General Franco. For seventy-two days he was left to rot on death row. Waiting for the keys turning in his cell door, then to be led handcuffed and blindfolded, like so many of his friends into a prison courtyard. Casaus heard often from the cell, the sound of dead men walking, their last footsteps, then the order to fire, followed by an awful silence. Yet, the order for his execution never came. Why? This remains shrouded in doubt. A mystery that even Casaus never really spoke of. Catalan legend claims it was a relative priest who pleaded with the war council for leniency to save his cousin's life. Not being able to refuse a man of the cloth, Casaus's sentence was instead reduced to five years in prison.

On returning home from Argentina, Nicolau Casaus headed straight from the airport to the *Camp Nou*, seeking out fellow board members to express his wonder at this precocious youngster, who he was convinced would one day rule the world. He raved endlessly of the boy Maradona born to perform in a Barca Shirt. At first the charismatic Casaus was deemed a little over dramatic by the other directors and club President Juan Luis Nunez. 'Nobody can be that good,' they claimed. 'The old man has had too much Argentine wine.'

Others, gently mocked, but such was Casaus' sheer enthusiasm for his subject and determination to ensure something happened, Barca arranged to have this wonder boy properly scouted. What happened next caused shockwaves through the *Camp Nou,* as trusted scouts reported back to confirm Casaus had indeed unearthed a gem. Diego Maradona had to be signed.

However, the Argentina of the seventies was not an easy place to do business.

Signing *El Pelusa* meant they would be forced into feeding the wolves. In doing deals with a whole cast of players interesting only in lining their pockets. The player's agent said already to be a hard negotiator, if nothing more than a street shyster demanding stupid numbers. Others, Argentinos Juniors and Boca Juniors officials, lawyers, solicitors and sponsors demanding their cut. There would be long, maddingly, frustrating years of bargaining before it finally happened. Others, characters few had ever heard of claiming to speak for Diego, that emerged from the woodwork to dip their beaks in the Maradona free-for all. Including several high-ranking military officials representing Videla, Massera, Agosti and Lacoste…All demanding their palms be crossed with suitcases of Barca dollars, or else? Threats, vile and obscene were made. For years they used him as a puppet performing in packed stadiums to take people's mind off what was occurring in their daily lives. 'The opium of the masses' went the saying is 'football.' Whilst the Junta were throwing innocent people blindfolded off helicopters into the River Plate, they paraded this kid from the gutter as a gift from God on people's television. He was viewed as a 'Natural Resource.' A perfect example of Argentine youth. A governing Junta poisoned blood red with those it murdered, interested only in milking the Maradona cash cow bare, before letting it slip their grasps into Catalan hands. The *Maradollar* had the power to bring all lowlife to the surface with the smell of making a killing.

Above all though,

Step forward to the roll of a drum beat Jorge Cyterszpiler determined to wring the Catalans for every dollar possible. Come the early eighties in Argentina, petty jealousies had overtaken the love and joy that Maradona brought to people on the football pitch. The pressure had become unbearable for the player. Still only twenty-one-years old, Diego failed to understand how people on the terraces and in the streets despised him for moving his family out of the slums into a new and better home. A lavish lifestyle for the Maradona clan compared to where they had come from. Photographs taken inside Villa Devoto were greeted with public disgust. A dining room decorated with marble, a swimming pool, maid's quarters. 'Fucking maid's quarters!' How dare they? The outrage simmered and erupted. The raggedy kid had got too big for his boots and could happily fuck off for the masses, yet, whenever the stories of Barca emerged, instead of wanting him gone, they hated him also for wanting to leave?

Maradona's sponsorship deals set up by Jorge Cyterszpiler were also a reason for people to slam Diego. Cyterszpiler was incredibly good at his job, like his client, all Jorge touched at that time appeared to turn into dollars. *Maradona Production*s was a money making business that only an idiot could fail at.

Jorge Cyterszpiler, despite the criticism always hurled in his direction. None more insulting than the Barca President Jose Luis Nunez, who when dealing with Cyterszpiler regarded him as 'Uncouth and unqualified. A fucking Argentinian upstart.' Even the International Herald Tribune joined in and took a swipe claiming he was nothing more than 'Maradona's fat, inseparable companion.' They also wrote with more than a hint of snobbery that his negotiating style was just, 'Bespeaking naïveté and greed.' In reality, nobody, saw Jorge coming! He was amongst the first to see what treasures could be had if you did business the street way and Cyterszpiler did so transforming a footballer into something that not just transcended the game, but in time, globally becoming bigger than any sportsman of the past. Including Pele and Muhammad Ali, for when it came to the amount of dollars *Maradona Production*s were cleaning up, Diego Armando Maradona, at still just a skip of a kid was globally becoming already the biggest sporting asset on the planet.

As for Barca,

Senor Nunez were going to pay through their arrogant, aristocratic noses for him. Jorge Cyterszpiler played hardball, he had a price in his head for Maradona's contract, not a peso less. For five years since they first shown up Jorge had been making plans for this moment. He played Boca and Argentinos officials off against each other, telling them just what they wanted to hear. He dealt with Catalan lawyers whom thought they were lowering themselves in dealing with such as him, when in reality Jorge had them twisted around his little finger. He even broke bread with military and navy officers looking to get their noses in the trough. Telling them to step carefully, there were always other higher up whom may also have an interest. It was a gamble, but played by this young streetwise hustler to perfection. It was all a game-a money game. Whilst Diego performed magic on the football pitch, Jorge Cyterszpiler produced his own by using the ways of the street. He planted fake news stories to keep fires burning, he whispered into favoured journalist's ears a little sweetener to put others out. A five-year-plan, all designed to ensure his amigo and family left Argentina for Barcelona with the best deal possible. Oh, they could call him names behind his back, Jorge had heard it all before. They could smirk and underestimate him, they could mock, but ultimately, it would be Jorge Cyterszpiler and Diego Maradona laughing last.

The transfer talks themselves when all parties were together in the same room were constantly fiery, tempers flaying, hands banging on the table! One of the main problems was that both Boca Juniors and Argentinos Juniors believed Maradona's was theirs' showing contracts bindings. The Club President's Martin Noel and Domingo Tesone steadfastly stood their ground. It was a spiders web for Barca's lawyers to overcome. Finally, excruciatingly, slowly, progress was made. A round figure of six million dollars was being spoken about between the three clubs. This was something the Catalans could accept, only for more arguments to break out when Jorge Cysterszpiler claimed it wasn't enough. The figure required remained steadfastly in his head. He was going to screw Barcelona for a few dollars more yet. 7.6 was the number Jorge demanded, another 1.6 or no deal. They would fuck off to Juventus already offering such a sum.

Argentina stood on the brink of conflict with Great Britain over the Falkland Islands, or the Malvinas, depending on your take and the nation was in a state of constant flux and near hysteria. The Generals were ramping up national furore over what was set to occur in the South Atlantic, yet, still all people spoke of was a mere football transfer that appeared far more important than the gathering war clouds. Amid an atmosphere of both terror and patriotic fervour engulfing Buenos Aires, the Barca deal to sign Diego Maradona collapsed like a pack of cards. The livid Catalans were breathing fire with Cyterszpiler, but were powerless to change his mind. A call home was made and a man from Catalonia arrived at Buenos Aires airport. He was dressed soberly in a dark suit, perfectly groomed and manicured, oily slick, black hair and wearing a pair of cufflinks, half the price of Argentina's monster, financial deficit. Fifty-two-year-old FC Barcelona President Jose Luis Nunez had travelled personally to bang heads together and meet with this peasant footballer's agent Jorge Cyterszpiler and officials of the two clubs. Nunez explained in no uncertain terms there was no more money. He insisted that the player be allowed to leave for Barcelona. They had all come too far, it absolutely made no sense for everyone to walk away without a single dollar in their pockets. None of them could afford this to fail. The Barca bid remained Six million dollars. Take or leave it, to which Cyterszpiler decided to leave. He was walking away from the table, because as he informed Nunez, Juventus were offering more. For both men, Jorge and an exasperated Nunez, it was mutual loathing at first sight. A first of many catfights. The lack of respect shown to Cyterszpiler by the President was not forgiven, or ever forgotten, as the Argentinian later claimed Nunez behaved like, 'Some kind of a fucking dictator in the talks, with a self-imposed sense of superiority.' With neither side willing to bend a time-out was called. Reinforcements arrived for Nunez in the shape of Nicolau Casaus.

He met privately with the youngster and agent extolling the virtues of his great club, their grand history and how with *El Pelusa,* the future promised glory and riches beyond Diego's wildest dreams. Yet, despite being won over by the old man, impressed by his honesty and integrity. So vastly different from their Napoleonic, arrogant clown of a president, word reached Cyterszpiler that officials of Juventus were actually keen to talk business. Somebody had leaked the required fee to them. I wonder who?

La Vecchia Signora, the Old Lady of Italian football was ready to cast her charms over the Argentinians. Nicolau Casaus reported the bad news back to Nunez. Knowing they had him over a barrel after already promising the player to the world-wide, expectant Barca support, Nunez had little choice but to cave in and pay the added sum before Cysterszpiler fell into bed with the Italians. To return to Catalonia without the deal done, he would have been lynched.

Then,

more drama as the youngster himself suddenly got cold feet about leaving Argentina. To help calm nerves President Nunez invited the national manager Cesar Menotti to speak with him. As added encouragement, Nunez promised Menotti that he never forgot friends who did good deeds. If he succeeded in changing Diego's mind, then, one day soon Cesar Menotti would be given the chance to coach FC Barcelona. Nunez's incentive scheme worked wonders, for after only a brief conversation with Menotti, who listened to worries of Maradona missing his family. Of how moving abroad may affect him being selected for Argentina, Menotti soothed the boy's troubled mind by advising to take the family with him. As for his national place? Menotti said even if he played in 'Alaska' Cesar Menotti would ensure Diego Maradona remained the first name on Argentina's team sheet. Finally, word was sent to Nunez from the player's camp that all had been agreed and they were ready to sign. Overnight, poor men became rich, rich men became kings. It was over. After years of bitter, acrimonious negotiations, FC Barcelona finally landed a young footballer destined to become the greatest of all time and Jorge Cyterszpiler, a streetwise hustler in the greatest of terms had squeezed them for the numbers required.

In all, a record 7.6 million dollars would be paid in six installments. Of that Argentinos receiving 5.1 million and Boca 2.2. Noel and Tesone were two of the happiest men in South America, when come the end of May 1982, all parties shook hands on the deal. Diego was set to earn fifty thousand dollars a season, a total sum of three million dollars over a six-year contract. Where Cyterszpiler proved really astute was in persuading the Catalans into letting the player forego certain bonuses, but in return the Argentinians kept hold of all legitimate, exclusive, advertising and merchandise rights relating to the name 'Maradona.' Both sides appeared delighted with this added small print to the contract and far as Jorge was concerned, they had struck gold. *Maradona Productions* was set to be a licence to print dollars.

All that remained for Diego Maradona to do before setting off for FC Barcelona and a new life, was the small matter of having to win the World Cup for Argentina.

CHAPTER THIRTY ONE
A JOKERS'S CALL

On Thursday 3rd January 1833, Captain James Onslow, of Her Majesty's Ship Clio, arrived in Vernet's settlement at Port Louis (The Falkland Islands), to request that the flag of the United Provinces of the River Plate, be replaced with the British one and for the administration to leave the islands. While Major José María Pinedo, commander of the schooner Sarandi wished strongly to resist, he simply didn't have enough forces. Also, amongst the crew was a large number of British mercenaries unwilling to fight their own countrymen. In such dire circumstances, Pinedo had little choice but to make known his protest, then, ultimately sail away two days later without having fired a shot, or a sword being drawn. Move forward a little, 149 years and finally Jose Maria's Pinedo's modern day generation returned to the islands they called the *Malvinas*.

Four hundred miles, south-west of Argentina, war clouds were gathering in the South Atlantic. In the April of 1982, the latest off the assembly line of Generals pronouncing himself President, Leopoldo Fortunato Galtieri, gave the order for the Argentine forces to invade the British territory of the Falkland Islands. In office for only four months and the nation in the midst of yes, yet another devastating economic crisis, seething civil unrest and anti-Junta demonstrations, becoming increasingly loud and volatile, Galtieri played his joker, the patriotic card. The people were finally sick to the stomach of these bellhop Generals masquerading as politicians/leaders, looting and murdering their way to personal fortunes before disappearing from their roles, like Jorge Videla, to enjoy the joys of their ill-gotten, sordid gains. Seeing no other way out Galtieri went for broke and did what many in his position before him had threatened to do, but ultimately didn't.

'If they want a fight, we'll give them a fight!' he raged to the baying crowd from the *Casa Rosada* balcony. Such was the deep feelings evoked by the *Malvinas* to all Argentinians, children were taught at school how the English pirates back in 1833 came and robbed the islands from them. It had always been a scar on the Argentine soul and a constant thorn in the relationship between the United Kingdom and Argentina. Suddenly, the protests against the Junta disappeared and in their place came huge outpours of public pride on the streets supporting Galtieri's actions. The Argentina Football authorities renamed the 1982 Metropolitan championship, *'Soberanía argentina en las Islas Malvinas!'* ('Sovereignty over the Malvinas!'). In the stadiums the supporters were burning English flags and singing, *'El que no salta es un inglés!'* ('Whoever doesn't jump is English!). Argentina was burning over with patriotic fervour. It appeared Galtieri's monumental gamble had worked. Britain was eight thousand miles over the horizon, they were simply too far away to do anything remotely militarily about the situation, or so went the thinking at *Casa Rosada*, but in London, matters were already in hand to take back what they claimed was their property.

The British Prime Minister Margaret Thatcher immediately ordered a seaborne task force to sail south and drive out the Argentine forces from the Falkland islands. It's WAR! and GOTCHA! declared the English newspaper tabloids. Galtieri had badly misjudged, for his timing couldn't have been worse-the people of Britain were in a foul mood. The country was in the midst of a dark recession, with unemployment passing the three million mark. Riots were exploding across the land, northern cities like Liverpool and Manchester on fire. Thatcher and her right wing Tories, similar to Galtieri, realised a way to ease the pressure on the home front and help win back votes in the forthcoming election. Cry havoc and Harry for England, let loose the seadogs of war and if the Argentinians wanted a war, then by God that fucking woman who claimed she wasn't for turning, would give them one by unleashing the might of the British forces against them.

After horrific suffering on both sides, for what was nothing more than a God forsaken, small, band of windswept, barren islands, with a population of barely 3,000-a climate battered forever by South Atlantic winds, a white flag was finally raised over the capital Port Stanley to end the carnage. It was on Monday 14th June 1982, that Argentina surrendered. From the sinking of the General Belgrano, to HMS Sheffield, being hit by a cruise missile. The battles of Goose Green and Mount Tumbledown, until finally a Union Jack hoisted high once more over the islands. 746 Argentinians and 255 British soldiers killed, without counting the hundreds of suicides that came in later life. Ten weeks of young men dying, being blown apart, maimed, all for the sake of a joker's call by Galtieri, that saw him removed from office within days of the war ending. In late 1983, he was charged in a military court with human rights violations during the Dirty War, also with mismanaging the Falklands War. It took time, but justice was served finally when in 1986, Leopoldo Fortunato Galtieri was sentenced to twelve years in prison.

In the opening, early, summer of 1982, As the battle raged on in the South Atlantic, Cesar Menotti's team were shepherded away in a *concentracion* and due to the heavily-censored, state television, had absolutely no idea the true situation occurring south-west in the Atlantic. A picture of great victory was being painted, with the truth being the Argentine conscripts were no match for the ultra-professional, British soldiers who yomped and fought with huge courage and a sheer ruthlessness that routed their badly, led, horribly, outclassed enemy. It was only when the footballers arrived in Spain for their final preparation, in the beautiful, seaside resort of Alicante, that the truth became known to them watching the news bulletins on Spanish television. Diego Maradona like all his *compadres* couldn't believe his eyes, 'We were convinced we were winning the war, but when we got to Spain, it was a huge blow for everyone.' The effect could only have been devastating watching these freezing, exhausted, Argentine soldiers, mostly conscripts, teenage kids with disbelieving eyes and scared expressions being rounded up, hands held high. British paratroopers looming large over them. Bloodied toy soldiers and so many dead.

As for Diego Maradona, he appeared not in a good place. In a host of friendlies played at the *Estadio Monumental,* leading up to the World Cup, against Czechoslovakia (0-0), West Germany 1-1) and the Soviet Union 1-1, Diego even found himself whistled on the terraces. Supporters not happy with his performances, when in fact Maradona had gone straight from Boca Junior's crazy, world-wide schedule, to a ferocious Argentinian *concentracion,* where the players were being physically driven to their limits for the tournament preparation, by Cesar Menotti's assistant, Doctor Ricardo Pizzarotti. The spark in Diego's game, if not out was most definitely flickering. To the angry hordes on the terraces, the move to Barcelona, selling his footballing soul to their Spanish old-world, colonial rulers for a pirate's fortune. Fuck him. They had read also of Maradona's so-called adventures in Las Vegas. The stories of himself and Claudia booking an entire cinema in downtown Buenos Aires, so they could watch a movie in peace. The posh cars, the big houses, *Maradona Productions* in overdrive, Diego's face in print and on huge billboards advertising, hawking everything from Puma to Coca-Cola, toothbrushes, soap... Jorge Cyterszpiler had even negotiated for Maradona, a line of football dolls! One of the few products he refused to market were cigarettes and wine, because he-Diego Maradona, was totally against all manners of drug taking. Such irony with hindsight, a truly wonderful thing. Deep down, Maradona missed a world long gone for him now and his family. Villa Fiorito may have never been anyone's notion of paradise, in any shape or form, but it was a time when he was surrounded by family, people he could trust-whom never leached or wanted nothing off him, but love. Not hangers on, fixers, sponsors, *hijos de puta* (Sons of bitches), whose name he didn't even know, but was told by Jorge they were on the payroll and worked for him. A part of Diego Maradona longed to remain a kid from the slums, who never forgot his roots, wanting only to play football, but there was also another Maradona, the one who desired the finer things in life. Why should he drive around in a battered, old, fucking Skoda, when there was a Lamborghini at home in the garage? It was a beautiful paradox for Diego, one that ultimately he could never win.

Against West Germany, it was claimed Maradona truly met his match in the brilliant, twenty-one-year-old Borussia Monchengladbach midfielder, Lothar Matthaus. When the two went up against each other, the fast, manipulative and explosive Matthaus put Diego in the shade and post-match, many doubts were raised that maybe Maradona's star was burnt out? Too much, far too young. Many happy to forget that just seven days previously at the *Maracana*, in front of 170,000 screaming Brazilians, Lothar Matthaus had performed a similar task on Zico, to earn generous plaudits off their journalists. The great Scottish journalist Hugh Mcllvanney of the Observer also wrote about something just not being right with the little genius. 'All the working parts were in place, just not clicking. As ever, Mcllvanney nailed it, for Matthaus had injured Diego's left foot early on in the match leaving him in agony and he was only able to continue on from half-time pumped full of painkillers. Again, in the next match versus the Soviets, the injury had not healed, but Maradona played anyway with the help of a doctor's needle. This bravery not known to those 80,000, at the home of River Plate, whom continued to whistle and jeer him. Two did stand up to defend, Jorge Cyterszpiler saying, 'It wasn't a good night for Diego, but all great players have such matches. He will forget it.' Cesar Menotti was even more unequivocally supportive for his young superstar, 'Maradona does things no other footballers would attempt. At twenty one he is a miracle.'

The pressure for Diego Maradona to deliver at *Espana 82* grew by the day-a secret, short, respite with Claudia to Esquina occurred, where with just the two of them for a few days, he managed to clear his head relaxing on the banks of the *Corrientes* River. Diego would fish with Claudia alongside him. They would go for long walks amongst the trees, no television, radio or newspapers. They stayed hidden. The two talked for hours of the future. Diego was reliving with his own girlfriend, the romance of

Chitoro and Tota many years previous. Finally, with Maradona feeling a little calmer, the couple returned to civilisation. Claudia back to Buenos Aires, whilst before he could concentrate fully on the forthcoming World Cup, Diego had some business needing settling in Barcelona.

CHAPTER THIRTY TWO
WELCOME TO BARCELONA

'When Diego slipped through my fingers, I felt I was losing the best thing in my life. He had given me so much happiness. From the touchline, I watched him grow up and his ability gave me so much pleasure. I looked after him, as if he was my treasure and then…he was gone.' In 2008, Francesco Cornejo died of leukaemia, his was a pauper's end, but Cornejo was insistent that he never turned to Maradona, even towards the end. 'I won't ask Diego for anything, I felt in my heart, I had already been paid a fortune just for watching him play.'

It was thirteen days before *Espana 82*.

Around midday, on Friday 4th June 1982, a plane in the dying embers of its flight from Buenos Aires, touched down upon the runaway at Barcelona and screeched to a halt. On board was an excited, but equally, nervous Diego Maradona, sat alongside his *compadre* and agent Jorge Cyterszpiler. Diego appeared fit to burst. Dressed casually in tracksuit bottoms, tee shirt, seemingly, on the outside, totally unaffected at the unfolding madness that surrounded his every move. A life lived in the blaze of the public since he was ten-years old, nowhere to hide, just the relative safety of a football pitch to perform his magic, trying to avoid opponents desperate to stop him by any means necessary. Over the years the pressure grew intensely worse at the realisation in Argentina, that through the clouds of dust kicked up off the crumbling Villa Fiorito, dirt and stone football pitches, had emerged a prodigy unlike nobody had ever witnessed. Treated with a religious reverence, Diego Maradona learned fast to survive, to live in such an environment, but it was never normal. Far from it, his world and the interest and exposure in it grew to such an extent that there became an inexhaustible thirst for all things *El Pelusa*. The record transfer to Barcelona, all its controversy was simply another step on the journey to God knew where?

There was relief for a smiling Maradona though as he appeared at the plane door with new found intentions to conquer the world once more, after the short retreat to Esquina with Claudia. Now, finally free in a new continent and country to show his true worth. A staggering fee of $7.6 million worth of pure Argentinian footballing gold. Welcome to Catalonia, FC Barcelona, Diego Armando Maradona!

There was another that day, Diego apart, who thought he had died and arrived not in Catalonia, but heaven on earth. In the beginning, the snobbish, racist Catalans had laughed at this lame, fucking, bullshitting, joker claiming to speak for the great Maradona. Whose only resemblance to his master was the bushy hair. A cripple, badly overweight, too quick with a bad joke. Not an opponent worthy of respect, more pity. Give him a handful of pesos and wave adios. Speaking to him in mocking tones, how he should kiss their feet that the great Barcelona had decided to come and do business. Yet, little did they know for although Jorge Cyterszpiler may have lacked their social airs and graces, when it came to grabbing a buck for Diego's services he was prepared to hammer them into the ground. As Jorge truly did and amongst the Catalans there appeared a new grudging respect for this streetwise, Argentinian boy, whom they had so underestimated. Suddenly, the laughing had stopped, Jorge Cyterszpiler's years of bartering, brinksmanship and underhand dealings would have done credit to the Borgias. It had to be admired.

Ravaged by polio since he was a child, Jorge lived out football fantasies watching his best amigo on a football pitch. He put away childish dreams, his job now was to ensure Diego and family, whose early years were blighted by poverty and hardship, never again had to worry where the next dollar was coming from. Apart from close family, Cyterszpiler was Maradona's most trusted confidante. Together, as dreaming youths they plotted to conquer the world, both on the pitch and off it. An unlikely friendship, but for one such as Diego who could count true friends on one hand, Jorge was a brother in all but blood. Sadly, now that their plans were finally coming to fruition, the innocence of youth so treasured in the past would suddenly in time become worthless. Business above friendship-the bottom line. They had reached a promised land, but it was one littered with pitfalls. For the moment though, the two young men remained attached at the hip and as for Jorge Cyterszpiler?

Nobody was laughing at him anymore.

Inside the airport, a reception committee numbering thousands of *cules* had gathered in an excited mass to catch an opening glimpse of the latest superstar to try his luck in the *Blaugrana,* (The red and blue). President Nunez promised them a latest savior and in Diego Maradona had delivered. FC Barcelona expected the best money could buy and demanded instant results. For Maradona, the pressure would begin instantly the moment he pulled on the Barca shirt that first time. The *cules* had been spoilt by a rich tapestry of great players, none more so than Johan Cruyff. Diego was under no illusions that he had to come out firing, creating magic, but for him this was nothing new, for Diego Maradona had been performing miracles on a football pitch ever since he could remember.

A media frenzy lay in wait, as a gaggle of manic, over-enthusiastic photographers and newspapermen cameramen flashed and placed their notepads and microphones within inches of Maradona's face. For one almighty worrying second, it appeared he would stumble as they hustled, pushed and blocked his way. The Catalan media pack seemingly intent more on a lynching than welcoming to their club the finest footballer on the planet. Finally, sense prevailed as security officials cleared a path to safety. All easily avoided if somebody had just thrown Maradona a ball, for then he could have just simply dropped a shoulder, leaving the lot in an embarrassing heap.

To ferry both Diego and Jorge the ten-mile journey to the *Camp Nou,* a VIP Limousine courtesy of FC Barcelona lay in wait. On board champagne, caviar and two young men struggling to believe what was happening to them. Cyterszpiler remained a little on edge at the thought of once again having to meet President Nunez. A man he hated, who had patronised and tried to make him feel lower than a snake's belly during the lengthy, explosive negotiations. Well, Jorge had made them pay top dollar for his *compadre*, he, Jorge Cyterszpiller. Now he felt worthy enough to look all the Catalans in the eye, especially Nunez,

'Remember me amigos, not fucking laughing now are you?'

Awaiting impatiently for the Argentinians at the *Camp Nou,* was the new masters. So little did the Catalans know or understand what was coming their way! The great and the good of the Barcelona hierarchy. Would be Presidents forever plotting. kingmakers waiting for one single moment of weakness to push forward their man. To strike and claim the grandeur of the title, not so much to open doors, more move mountains. The ultimate prize. For if you became President, you were in all but name be the King of Catalonia. All stood in keen anticipation, so curious to meet Diego Maradona, this slum prince whose blessed ability with a football had given him a raw natural power. Loved by millions, adored, idolised and bought for a king ransom. Barca money. Their money. Now in their eyes he belong to them heart and soul. Finally, with Maradona at the helm they could silence the mockers and win back the Spanish championship after a horrific drought. The wonderful Cruyff era, 1974-78, though magnificent, now a distant dream. Eight painful seasons endured watching mostly the dreaded Madrilenos, the white ghouls of Real Madrid from the *Estadio Bernabeu* sweeping all before them. By Barca's heady standards, an utter disgrace. They believed with Maradona touching down, the time was ripe to take back their rightful place at the helm of Spanish football. The legendary club motto, depending whether you resided in Barcelona or Madrid, either soul stirring, or pretentious diatribe, *Mes que un club,*(More than a club), appeared slightly hollow set against such a miserable, recent, record.

First amongst unequals, in his own high, mighty opinion was the current FC Barcelona President, Jose Luis Nunez. He had been in power for four years since 1st July 1978. A vain man, emotional, ruthless and impatient. Nunez was obsessed with power to the point he would cut a throat to win a vote. His was a dedication and adoration of Barca matched only by a greater love of himself. Though not of Catalan birthright, but Basque, Nunez became equally fanatical as any Barca *cule* in pursuit of glory. He wanted to leave a glorious legacy. So, much that in his time as President, managers and coaches were hired and dispatched without mercy at regular periods. It was like there was an ejector seat at the *Camp Nou*. Four had been shown the door without even given time to learn the names of their squads, proving patience clearly was not a virtue possessed by Nunez. The Frenchman Lucien Muller, former Barca Captain Joaquim Rife, the great club stalwart of old, Helenio Herrera, (twice) and yet another *Camp Nou* legend, Ladislao Kubala. All got rid of without mercy or sentiment by Nunez, when events went astray For this was a man in a hurry chasing his own destiny. The signing of Diego Maradona was a monumental, financial gamble, even for a club of Barca's size and it simply couldn't afford to fail. A hard face businessman like Nunez never bought into the fairytale of the little wizard from the poverty-stricken slums of Buenos Aires, being brought to Barcelona to rekindle and sprinkle gold-dust over the *Camp Nou.* Maradona was an investment, nothing more or less, one that had to work-would be made to work. Nunez had already spent millions in preparation for hosting the 1982 World Cup finals. He oversaw the expansion of the *Camp Nou* to a colossal 115,000 capacity, with 22,000 seats added. The building of new private and VIP boxes and an ultra-modern press-centre, all at an extortionate cost and to help pay, Nunez came up with the extraordinary notion of allowing supporters for a small fee to have their name inscribed on a brick. Thus, forever being part of FC Barcelona's history. Once completed, the President then had to conceive ways of filling the stadium. He needed the best of the best.

A true A-list star. Previously, when Barca still had the great Johan Cruyff at his peak, a 200,000 capacity wouldn't have been sufficient enough, but those times were over. In 1982, the great player's names still rolled off the tongue, Platini, Zico, Socrates…All crowd pullers, but what Nunez required was that little extra. A new Cruyff, impossible of course, for how do you replace genius? The well had seemingly run dry, but there remained one whom many were predicting worth a punt. They said Pele was the king, but this kid, definitely next in line for his throne. Words from the great man's mouth himself.

Then to claim the ultimate prize-the European cup. A dream of the Catalans since the dawn of time, one that if achieved under his stewardship guaranteed immortality. Jose Luis Nunez's personal golden ticket. For a club Barca's size never to have won this most prestigious trophy hurt beyond words, especially since their great rivals in Madrid had won it a remarkable six times. An undeniable fact that was thrown towards the Catalans at every, opportunity possibility. There was also a fourth reason for the signing of Diego Maradona. One that caught Nunez and all Barcelona by total surprise.

The danger in the north.

Never had the Catalans needed more a catalyst to propel them forward, for the power base in Spanish football had been shifted on its axis. The Basques had arrived conquering all before them. A formidable enemy. Twice recent champions, Real Sociedad, had been joined by their neighbours Athletic Bilbao, whom were also threatening a coming storm. There was a war brewing on two fronts, Barca needed a spark to fire them back to the top-this threat from the northern mountains. There was no love lost between Catalonia and the Basques, needed neither invitation, nor encouragement to make life hell for FC Barcelona. 1982-83 saw the Catalans coming off the back of an unbelievably rancid, disappointing season, in which a 3-1 defeat at Real Madrid in their penultimate game cost them that much yearned after title. Leaving the door open for the Basques of Real Sociedad to power through and deservedly take the crown. After appearing champions elect for almost the entire campaign, the last six games saw heaven turn to hell for Barca, whom ultimately finished second. Being in contention was never enough for FC Barcelona. It was first or nothing. Seeking redemption-a little was found with success in the European Cup Winners Cup. A final staged at the *Camp Nou,* saw Barca triumph 2-1 over the Belgians of Standard Liege, with goals from their Danish superstar Alan Simonsen and Spanish centre-forward Quini. Though celebrated and appreciated, it hardly satisfied the appetite for this monster of a club. Barca's rainbow's end remained far away as ever. A transfusion of new blood, special blood, Argentinian blood was desperately required.

Maradona and Barcelona.

It wasn't so much a coming together, more a collision of two worlds, that if not handled carefully would threaten to leave in a devastating wake, a heap of trouble. A perfect storm. The chic, aristocratic, stiff-backed, Barca overlords, the kid from the slums. One who may have struggled to survive in the high pressure, back-stabbing world of boardrooms and big business, but put him on a football pitch facing insurmountable odds, then you had a player unequalled since the retirement of Pele. Blessed with the ability to create havoc, to cause bewilderment, leave defenders shattered of both spirit and breath. To make the ball fall in love with him, to the extent it refuses to leave, forever tied by magic dust to his feet. A footballing miracle, the finest Van Gough. $7.6 million dollars, not a bad price for a masterpiece. FC Barcelona had acquired a talent that if treated correctly bore the potential to not just conquer Spain, but the world. This was what Nunez prayed they had bought.

Only time would tell just what lay in store?

The signing of Diego Maradona took place in Barca's main boardroom. Elegant, but respectful. A magnificent, dark, oak floor, the chairs upholstered with the finest black leather. The strong smell of history forever present. The epitome of power, big business. Portraits with knowing eyes hung on walls of great Barca patriots. The time over, but their spirits still present. Proud men of honour, forever looking down on Nunez. Watching, judging. By blood he wasn't Catalan, this mattered, all possessed worries at the latest chosen one to carry the FC Barcelona torch forward. Despite all, the grand speeches, back slapping, the toasts and raising of champagne glasses, an uneasy atmosphere remained throughout the meeting, as Diego Maradona finally put his name to a contract, long now agreed by both sides. A nervous cough, an awkward silence. Mutual discomfort. A slight ripple of spontaneous applause broke out that caused giggles amongst the Argentinian duo and Nunez cast an angry glare towards them. A laughing

Maradona caught his eye. A world apart, neither blinking. All of a sudden in that moment they knew tempestuous times lay ahead. For here was a loose cannon, albeit, one powerful enough to blow away any opposition, yet equally so, to misfire, self-explode taking all with him.

Naïve in some ways of the world maybe, the smell of the streets destined to follow him always, but talented beyond the heavens. Diego cared little for the authoritarian atmosphere that stifled the air around him. There he stood alongside Jorge Cyterszpiler, in the midst of old men drunk on power. Blind to the beauty of a game which for them exists only as a gateway to make money. Demanding obedience from those deemed beneath them. To bow in their presence. A toast was made, but the tension between President and player remained risible. Others though relaxed a little. Now Barca had secured the greatest player in the world, many in that boardroom felt content soon they would be back on their rightful perch. Not knowing if all went wrong, importing Diego Maradona was akin to blowing your head off with a shotgun, whilst trying to cure a headache.

CHAPTER THIRTY THREE
SAVING PRIVATE ESTEBAN
ARGENTINA V BELGIUM (1982 WORDL CUP OPENING ROUND)

'State television kept telling us how our armed forces had shot down three harriers and other British planes. They were all lies, we couldn't shoot down a little bird. Before the world cup in Spain we thought we were winning the war. Even if we don't approve of war, we all love our country. I think it's everyone's duty to be a patriot. But when we arrived in Spain, we realised the truth about the

war. It was a shattering blow for all of us.' Diego
Maradona

On Sunday 9th May 1982, with the entire country being
swept along on a militaristic patriotic wave and the war
drums resonating so loud they could be heard four hundred
miles south west, the Argentine state channel ATC aired a
special programme to support and raise money for the
Malvinas cause. The war had begun and both sides had
already suffered terribly. Argentinian air force MiG jets
screamed across the Falkland skies attacking the British
task force, whilst British Harriers mounted attacks on Port
Stanley airfield. Casualties were mounting steady, the
cruiser *General Belgrano* was torpedoed and sunk by the
submarine *HMS Conqueror*, killing more than 320
Argentinian sailors-the single biggest loss of life in the
war, suddenly, all hell exploded as Argentina went looking
for revenge. It came shortly after, as the Destroyer *HMS
Sheffield* had to be abandoned after being hit and set on
fire by a cruise missile, killing twenty of the crew…It went
on.

Jorge Cyterszpiler appeared on the television show to
represent Diego Maradona, who had gifted a cheque of
five thousand dollars. The show was a twenty-four hour
marathon of events ordered by General Galtieri's Junta to
raise the spirit of the nation, rouse the patriotic spirit, most
importantly raise some hard, needed cash. The highlight by
far of the fund-raiser came when towards its finale, the
Argentine national team took a break from preparation for
the 1982 World Cup, to show up and make their own
donation. The Captain Daniel Passarella, Osvaldo Ardiles
and Maradona himself armed with yet another cheque and
also to announce a special benefit match to be held in La

Plata, with the money raised going to the cause. There were tears and cheers, everybody chanted 'ARGENTINA!' All ending with a rousing version of the national anthem, dedicated to the lads fighting in the *Malvinas*. 'Don't cry for me Argentina,' so went the song, as her people were led to believe by the Junta, they were on the verge of a magnificent victory in the South Atlantic.

In friendlies leading up to the World Cup, the national team had took the field in several friendlies holding a banner reading 'Las Malvinas son Argentinas.' Football and war have since the first ball was kicked been inseparable. This was no different. A teenage Diego Maradona shortly after *Mundial 78,* claimed that 'The ball is always clean.' Diego was always a dreamer, such an opinion has to be applauded, even, if sadly looking back now, nothing more than a young boy's naive comment. There had been far too much blood on the ball.

On Thursday 1st May 1982, during the first Argentine air raid on the Falkland Islands, twenty-seven-year-old First Lieutenant José Ardiles was shot down. He was the first pilot to be killed in the conflict. His mirage jet, according to the official records of the Argentinian Air Force was, 'Was shot down by an English Sea Harrier.' Jose was the cousin of Tottenham Hotspur's, World Cup winning midfielder Osvaldo Ardiles, who was at his footballing peak, on the shortlist for PFA Player of the Year in England, when war broke out. Jose's Father, Ossie's Uncle spent a long time seeking out more details, for he believed his son might have still been alive. That was until the British pilot responsible was authorised by the Minster for Defence to inform him of grave news. The Sea Harrier pilot who shot Jose's mirage down over the Atlantic was adamant, 'Lieutenant Ardiles could not have survived' and Jose's crestfallen Father finally gave up hope of ever finding his son alive.

'When it actually started my entire world collapsed,' recalled Osvaldo Ardiles. The day after the war began, Spurs played Leicester City in an FA Cup semi-final at Villa Park, their supporter booed Ardiles every time he touched the ball. The response from his own fans was remarkable as they chanted back in defence their player's name. 'I will never forget what happened that afternoon,' said Ardiles, shortly afterwards. 'While the Argentines and the English killed each other, the Tottenham fans gave us a lesson.' It would be Ossie's final game for Spurs. 'I just can't play in a country that is at war with mine,' he sadly concluded and went off to join his nation in preparation for the 1982 World Cup.

Cesar Menotti hardly sounded like a man looking to win friends and influence the host nation when speaking on the eve of the tournament. 'The football in Spain is all about the pain. The Spaniards are the only team whose tactics worry me from the point of view of the safety of my players. Over there it has too much in common with bullfighting.' *El Flaco*'s team to try and retain their title would be in all essence, those that won it four years earlier, plus newcomers Diego Maradona, Ramón Díaz and Real Zaragoza's exciting twenty-two-year old forward Jorge Valdano. The champions opening game to begin the tournament would be held in of all stadiums-from Maradona's point of view, Barcelona's *Camp Nou*. An early opportunity no doubt for the Catalans, whom would be present in large numbers to see with their own eyes just how good this Argentinian kid being hailed as the greatest player in the world coming their way actually was. Four days before the game disaster struck in training when Diego pulled up clutching his left hamstring. The thought of lining up against Belgium in the *Camp Nou* without their star man filled Cesar Menotti with dread.

So, he summoned an old *compadre,* sixty-two-year-old Doctor Ruben Dario Oliva. Based in Italy since emigrating there in 1966, he had set up a highly, successful clinic in Milan. This was no ordinary Doctor, more of a traditional healer, or what Maradona would regard a medicine man not to be mocked at. The type his parents used when living back in Esquina as youngsters. Oliva had a passion for his work, he believed many injuries could be cured by simple powers of persuasion, Recovery was deemed by him a simple state of mind. Hardly surprising that such unorthodox methods made him highly mistrusted by others in his profession, but those sportsmen who worked with Oliva spoke extremely highly of his methods. In no time at all on being introduced to the doctor, Diego Maradona was charmed listening to the wise, old man's stories, but far more so on how he made the pain in his leg simple vanish, leaving him seemingly fit to face the Belgians. Maradona never forget what Oliva did for him, from that moment on he became part of his inner circle. Diego nicknamed him the 'Magician,' for putting him back on his feet for the World Cup, the doctor from that moment onwards would be by Maradona's side throughout all that was set to follow. An epic journey of unimaginable highs and unspeakable lows...

The Falklands/Malvinas. British forces had yomped from their drop-off site in San Carlos and were pinned down at the base of Darwin Hill-under heavy fire from troops dug in along the ridge, a mile away from their objective of

Goose Green. The settlement had Argentinian regiments garrisoned due to its strategic importance. Fourteen hours into the battle, the British suffered heavy casualties and were utterly exhausted. Paratrooper (2 Para), Major Chris Keeble had taken command after his superior Colonel H James was killed. Keeble made the decision of calling for air support in the form of two Harrier jets sweeping down over the battle-dropping cluster bombs on Argentine artillery positions. In the aftermath of the blitz, Keeble picked the opportune moment to bluff the enemy into an early surrender. He sent a strongly worded message to their commander demanding they surrender, warning him that he'll continue to bomb heavily, and hold them responsible for any civilian casualties if the fighting went on. Amazingly, the gamble worked and the Argentinian forces agreed to surrender! The next dawn, to 2 Para's disbelief and joy, over nine hundred Argentinian troops laid down their arms-twice their number and three times what they expected to face had the battle gone on. This loss set the precedent for the rest of the war and the surrender of Goose Green was a body blow to the confidence of Argentina and with the battle,
  only a matter of time would go the war.

Barcelona. The *Camp Nou.* Sunday 13th June 1982. Flowers were thrown into the crowd, thousands of blue balloons drifted off in the sunny Catalan skies and Andalusian Roma gypsies from Southern Spain with their Flamenco dancing captivated the 95,000 crowd on the pitch. So, began the fourteenth World Cup finals. British television had refused to show the game live due to Argentina's presence and all wasn't pleasant in the stadium. England mascot John Bailey dressed up as John

Bull tried to spread a little peace and happiness with the Argentinians supporters on the terraces, but was more or less told to fuck off and in a scuffle lost his hat and had to be rescued by Spanish police! On that same day, the final Argentine positions around Port Stanley, Mount William, Wireless Ridge and Mount Tumbledown were taken by the British forces, the war was almost over.

…But, not just yet for eighteen-year-old conscript soldier Private Edgardo Esteban from Cordoba, who remained in his foxhole, hungry and freezing, waiting for the final attack. Only a year previously, Edgardo watched Queen play in Vélez Sarsfield's stadium and saw Diego Maradona share the stage with Freddy Mercury. He so wanted to listen Argentina's first game against Belgium. 'The champions are making their debut. Today is a historic day,' sang El Gordo Muñoz on Radio *Rivadavia*. 'We were getting murdered in the Malvinas, and he was saying it was a historic day for the country,' recalled Edgardo's amigo, Rodolfo Carrizo, who watched in sheer terror as the British came at them and a shock wave blew Edgardo six feet in the air, but luckily he survived...

In front of a world-wide television audience, holders Argentina and Belgium kicked off *Espana 82* and the Belgians lined up to kick Diego Maradona off the pitch. Under their wily, old coach sixty-two-year-old Guy Thys, they were huge underdogs, but just two year previous had made the European Championships Final, only to lose a last minute goal to West Germany. Belgium were a tough, uncompromising, but talented side. Thys' plan to tame Maradona was not to man-mark him, but indeed pass Diego around, share the pain, more importantly the bookings! The South Americans began the match with nine players who had played four year previous in their own *Mundial,* plus two new faces, Maradona and Ramon Diaz.

Their full team Fillol, Olguin, Tarantini, Gallego, Passarella,(Captain), Bertoni, Ardiles, Kempes, Maradona and Diaz.

Cesar Menotti watched on from the touchlines in familiar, languid style, the archetypal cigarette in hand, more thinning, long hair, weary eyes that were clearly not happy at what he was witnessing. His team looked drained of energy and all inspiration. Sloppy, misfiring, whilst a bright, snappy Belgium were lock tight at the back and swept forward in the first half with some real style. The silky midfielder Jan Ceulemans and left winger Franky Vercauteren both going close to causing heart attacks in Buenos Aires and beyond.

Come the second half, Argentina started to dominate, only on sixty-three minutes to be caught on the break, when Belgian forward Erwin Vandenburgh found himself with Ubaldo Fillol, one on one and after what felt a lifetime to bring the ball under control, he finally shot low past Fillol, into the far corner of the net…

Again, far away in the South Atlantic, nineteen-year-old Private Marcelo Rosasco heard about Belgium's goal, whilst engaged in hand to hand combat on Mount Longdon. He was just thirty-three days away from completing compulsory service, just stay alive, was the thought in his head and fuck Belgium…

The next day Private Esteban and other soldiers, totally fed up with their officers, stole and ate some chickens and had a kickabout with helmets for goalposts, before surrendering. Several former combatants after the war were adamant that 'The main enemy was not the English, but the Argentine officers themselves.' There were many mistreating their own troops who would have committed atrocities already against their own people back home. Leopards never change their spots, especially Fascist ones.

Now something to defend the Belgians dug in and with Maradona seemingly under lock and key, by being spread around to be stopped by any manner possible, they appeared almost comfortable against the disappointing, under-achieving South Americans. Foremost amongst Diego's tormentors was the brilliant, giant, twenty-eight-year-old right back from Standard Liege, Eric Gerets, who was immense against Maradona. The closest Diego came to making his mark was a thirty yard free-kick late on that smashed violently against Jean-Marie's Pfaff's crossbar, bounced down-in a mad scramble Mario Kempes just failed to turn the ball over the line. The game ended deservedly 1-0 to Belgium, as for the World Champions? It had been a downbeat, listless performance by Cesar Menotti's team, when considering their crown was at stake. This had been the first time the holders had been beaten in an opening match since 1950. Diego finished the game limping, cutting a distraught, angry figure. The many Catalans on the *Camp Nou* terraces couldn't fail to be unimpressed with their new boy, so ineffectual had he been. The treatment meted out to him by Eric Gerets and his team as they hacked, slashed, bumped and dragged him back throughout was not forgotten, or forgiven by a sore, furious, petulant Maradona, who refused to shake hands or accept Geret's shirt. Also, post-match, he reacted badly by storming past waiting journalist and television crews, ignoring all questions, clearly sulking. The boos that rang around the *Camp Nou* at the final whistle were not just from Argentinians, but Catalans also. The locals, soon to be paying this upstart's wages sat drinking in the bars around their city that night wondering what all the fuss was about? As opening acts go, Diego Armando Maradona had clearly fluffed his lines and could only get better. Stage fright?

In Argentina they prayed so, but for many people their thoughts had already shifted from the football back to the South Atlantic, where the British had just retaken their *Malvinas*. At a fearful cost to both sides, the fighting was finally over.

Time line

April 2, 1982: Argentine forces invaded the Falkland Islands, and entered capital Port Stanley, forcing Governor Rex Hunt to surrender.

April 3, 1982: Invasion condemned by UN Security Council.

April 5, 1982: British task force of more than 100 ships set sail for Falklands, including aircraft carriers HMS Hermes and HMS Invincible. Lord Carrington, the Foreign Secretary, resigned over the invasion, and was replaced by Francis Pym.

April 25, 1982: South Georgia was retaken by Royal Marines. Prime Minister Margaret Thatcher refused to answer questions from the press on the operation, she just said, 'Rejoice at that news and congratulate our forces and the marines.'

April 30, 1982: Task force arrived in the 200-mile exclusion zone that surrounded the Falklands.

May 1, 1982: Argentine aircraft attacked the task force while British planes mounted their first air raids on Port Stanley airfield.

May 2, 1982: Argentine cruiser General Belgrano torpedoed and sunk by British submarine HMS Conqueror, killing more than 320 Argentine sailors – the single biggest loss of life in the war. Margaret Thatcher faced criticism over the sinking because the vessel was outside the 200-mile exclusion zone around the Falklands.

May 4, 1982: Destroyer HMS Sheffield abandoned after being hit by missile, killing twenty of the crew. The Sun published its infamous 'Gotcha' front page headline about the sinking of the Belgrano.

May 19, 1982: Twenty-two British servicemen killed when a helicopter transporting SAS soldiers crashed into the sea.

May 21, 1982: British landings began at San Carlos. Frigate HMS Ardent sunk by Argentine aircraft, killing twenty-two sailors. Fifteen Argentine aircraft were shot down.

May 24, 1982: Frigate HMS Antelope abandoned after bomb detonated while being defused by disposal officer.

May 25, 1982: HMS Coventry sunk by Argentine aircraft, killing nineteen. Twelve killed in missile attack on the British Merchant Navy vessel Atlantic Conveyor.

May 28-29, 1982: Battle of Goose Green. Seventeen soldiers from 2 Para killed in two days of fierce fighting, that ended in Argentine surrender with dozens killed and more than a thousand soldiers taken as prisoners of war.

June 8, 1982: More than fifty British soldiers were killed in attacks on landing craft RFA Sir Galahad and RFA Sir Tristram off Fitzroy.

June 11-12, 1982: British destroyer HMS Glamorgan badly damaged in missile attack. British forces take Mount Longdon, Two Sisters and Mount Harriet. Three Falkland civilians killed in a British naval bombardment.

June 13-14, 1982: British forces took Argentine positions on mountains overlooking Port Stanley.

June 14, 1982: General Mario Menendez surrendered to Major General Jeremy Moore as British forces marched into Port Stanley.

June 17, 1982: Argentine President Leopoldo Galtieri resigned as leader of the country's military Junta.

CHAPTER THIRTY FOUR
SO MUCH BLOOD
ARGENTINA V HUNGARY: 1982 (WORLD CUP OPENING ROUND)

The fall-out from the Belgium defeat was poisonous for coach Cesar Menotti and his players and the second outing against Hungary became a game the World Champions simply couldn't afford to lose. After an astonishing, opening, 10-1 win against El Salvador, the Magyars were full of confidence and with memories still vivid of what happened to them four years earlier against Argentina, the talk was of revenge. For the holders, the pressure was well and truly on. The media back home had gone into overdrive labelling the defeat to Belgium a national disgrace. The coach and players were being called out for being ill disciplined, no motivation, not caring about the flag. Feelings were running out of control in Argentina over the loss of the *Malvinas.* Passions raised, a hysteria had taken hold, people were looking for scapegoats. It wasn't a good time to start losing football matches after four years. Cesar Menotti was berated for an abundance of things, mostly staying loyal to many players from the previous *Mundial.* Also, photographs appeared in the Argentine newspapers of him emerging from his apartment with arms around a stunning German model. It was well known amongst journalistic circles how much Cesar had an eye for the ladies and a good night out, but timing was everything, *El Flaco* was being pilloried.

Diego Maradona was also not spared the wrath of his fellow countryman and their Spanish equivalents, who went after him with equal wrath as they did Menotti. Diego had brought across from Argentina to Spain, his family for close support, as an emotional barrier against the madness that surrounded his every move. Diego Senior, Tota, brothers, sisters, cousins and close friends would form a circle around him, as the slings and arrows were hurled in his direction. They began to be mockingly referred to by the Spanish media with real disdain as a clan. The *Maradona clan.* The inference being they were freeloaders, happy to sponge off Diego as they partied away, when the reality wasn't true at all. Those around him differed during the World Cup from what was soon to follow in Catalonia. A furious Maradona found himself receiving an opening dose of just what lay in store when he arrived full time in Barcelona and already it was driving him fucking insane.

Before the all or nothing match against the Hungarians, on Friday 19th June 1982, at the *Jose Rico Perez* stadium in Alicante, Cesar Menotti's told his team that they had no choice but, 'To die with their boots on.' An emotional, extraordinary, chest-thumping statement by him, considering just the day before the British had formally declared the war at an end and back home General Galtieri had been forced under almighty, pressure to resign his Presidency. After receiving such ferocious criticism from all angles following the opening day defeat, the World Champions came roaring back against Hungary to win 4-1. Menotti's men began in blistering fashion. A goal each for Daniel Bertoni, Osvaldo Ardiles and two for a magnificent Diego Maradona surging back into electrifying form, ripping apart the Magyars almost single-handed with a virtuoso showing. There appeared no sign of the injury that despite Dr Oliva's hands on, clearly affected him as the Belgium game had worn on, after initially appearing to clear up. Argentina appeared far more cohesive, their passing and movement that of worthy holders. A small side-note to this game, Hungary kicked off both halves, unnoticed by the Algerian referee Baldian Lacarne, not that it helped them much!

The goal spree began on twenty-seven minutes when after relentless Argentinian pressure, Bertoni scored from six yards out from a mad scramble. Maradona swiftly grabbed a second with a close range header, as the Hungarians struggled to control him. It only got worse for there was nothing more deadly on a football pitch than Diego with a point to prove. He appeared angry. Maybe the loss of the *Malvinas* gave Maradona and his *compadres* extra fuel to succeed that night, whatever caused the change, be it the war, hurt pride, or simply for their much loved under-fire coach, truly a performance delivered as a message that the holders were back in the tournament. None more so than Diego who tortured Hungary with his devastating runs tearing past red shirts, skipping tackles-a sleight of foot, change of direction and he would be gone, leaving Magyars appearing like a band of blind men searching for their canes. The third and best goal came just before the hour, no surprise it was Maradona on another, lung-bursting charge into the Hungarian penalty, hammering home past the keeper Ferenc Mezaros at his near post, who simply never had a chance, such was the power. Four minutes later Ardiles swooped on a mistake by Mezaros making it 4-0. There was a late consolation for Hungary, but it mattered little. This was Argentina's evening, the plaudits showered on Diego Maradona afterwards fully deserved.

Meanwhile, far away in the South Atlantic.
By this time Argentine conscripts and *compadres* Privates Edgardo Esteban, and Rodolfo Carrizo were off the islands and amongst the many hundreds of prisoners aboard the British frigate *Canberra*. Come full time of the Argentina/Hungary match, the result was read out over a loudspeaker for the soldiers, whom all went absolutely crazy on hearing the news. For a moment the British guards thought they were rioting and an uprising was taking place! Happily, it was swiftly realised the excitement was nothing more than sheer emotion at hearing their beloved team had won. Smiles appeared on the faces of the British watching their so-called enemy celebrate. Some even started to applaud. After all that had occurred between the two nations, football was a passion

both truly shared. Tragically, it was a shame the conflict couldn't have been settled with a ball,
 instead of so much blood.

CHAPTER THIRTY FIVE
'ABANDONED ALONGSIDE THE ROADSIDE'
ARGENTINA V EL SALVADOR (WORLD CUP FIRST ROUND)

On Tuesday 23rd June 1982, at the *Rico Perez* stadium in Alicante, Argentina secured a place in the second round of the tournament, with a 2-0 victory over the minnows of El Salvador. A penalty by Daniel Passarella put the World Champions in front on twenty-three minutes, after a shocking dive by Independiente midfielder Gabriel Calderon, that incensed the Salvadoran players. The Bolivian referee Luis Barrancos was in no doubt, but swiftly found himself under assault as the El Salvador team swarmed around like an angry mob, before defender Francisco Osorto lost his cool and kicked Barrancos in the leg! The result being Osorto received only a yellow card, as the Bolivian probably never fancied being lynched by the wild-eyed Salvadorans! This typical of a brutal encounter with no surprise, Diego Maradona, the main victim of the central American's vicious tackling, 'I had the shit kicked out of me!' Diego said post-match. It was alleged, but never proved that before the game Maradona said he was going to score ten goals against them on his own, thus enraging the already pent up Salvadorans! It wasn't until Daniel Bertoni scored a fantastic, second goal on fifty-four minutes, when he smashed home from twenty yards, after beating three defenders could Argentina relax a little. Beforehand, it had been a war!

El Salvador had been absolutely broken by their opening, monstrous, 10-1 savaging by Hungary, the following two games against Belgium that they lost narrowly 1-0 and Argentina, were all about saving some face before going home to explain just what the hell happened against the Hungarians?

It was a record defeat very unlikely to be beaten and the 15th June 1982, would go down forever as a stain on El Salvador's proud history. There were actually mitigating circumstances and the fact they made it to *Espana 82* at all, was a minor miracle-a civil war was ripping their nation apart. As for training in the midst of such, it proved almost impossible. One of the players recalled, 'If some of us arrived late, it was because we had to assist wounded people abandoned alongside the road.' In the dressing room the footballers had differing opinions on what side they supported, whether it was the left-wing guerrillas. *The National Liberation front,* or the United States, CIA-backed, military Junta government. An unspoken rule existed amongst the players not to discuss politics, for nothing was ever allowed to come before the team. Midfielder Mauricio Alfarfo who came on as substitute against Argentina, remembered how they helped to try and bring the people together, 'All I know is that when we played the qualifiers, the killings from both sides ceased. The people united at least for a day.
That was our greatest gift.'
Slowly, fighting for their lives on a football pitch, as their nation drowned in its own blood, the Salvadorian underdogs crawled to qualification. By some statistical freak, they scored just two goals in five games against the might of Mexico to claim a place making it to Spain. El Salvador were the last of the twenty four finalist to arrive

after an exhausting non-stop three day journey. From Guatemala, Costa Rica, the Dominican Republic, finally Madrid, where they grabbed a flight to Alicante. It left the players exhausted, their body clock's nine hours ahead of European central time, meaning none could catch up with sleep and with just seventy-two hours to prepare for their opening match against Hungary, they had good reason to fear the worse.

Whilst their opponents in *Espana* 82, Group Three, all resided in high quality training, residential quarters, El Salvador found themselves in a downbeat, sparse, shooting lodge outside Alicante. Two officials from the Salvadoran FA whom had blindly rented the lodge to save money took one look and simply vanished on a holiday, not seen again throughout the tournament. Feelings were running high as the players and coaching staff were made to feel like third class citizens. It was shameful. The kit they found waiting for them was laughably shabby-the bags they came in had the 1974 World Cup logo on. However, all faded into comparison when it was discovered there were no footballs to train with? When the Salvadorans complained, a FIFA official tried to claim they had been stolen! It was only solved through the goodwill of the Hungarians who gave them two balls of their own, after an El Salvador player called at their training camp, pleading for some.

This, the day before they actually played each other.

Come the actual match, on hearing their national anthem, the Salvadorans became so wound up with passion, they went onto the field in a state of mind to just attack Hungary and not with their normally, effective, defensive, safety-first approach. A huge mistake, as come half-time they were 3-0 down. Shortly after the interval, the Magyars got a fourth and suddenly panic set in for the Salvadorans were simply not used to conceding so many goals. Fearing the worst, manager Mauricio Rodriguez told his substitute goalkeeper Eduardo Hernandez to get ready, but Eduardo never fancied it, refusing point blank to go on under the circumstances! Soon it was five, then, the player nicknamed, 'Pele' back home, Luis Ramirez Zapata snatched a goal back. Zapata's celebration was way over the top and team mates rushed telling him to calm down, because they didn't want to wind up the Hungarians! Sadly for El Salvador, it did, the Magyars cut loose even more hitting another five in the last half hour! Three came from the substitute Lazlo Kiss, who broke two records that day. The only substitute to score a hat trick in the World Cup, also the fastest hat trick!

Come the end, by the time Tibor Nyilasi scored the tenth goal, those in charge of the score board were scratching their heads trying to figure out how to add another zero! In a silent, despondent, El Salvador dressing room, the shame wasn't just visible, it could be felt. Finally, after a long period of grim reflection, the Captain Norberto Huezo stood up and declared, 'From now on, we will play our normal game. We will defend with all our hearts and recover our pride!'

The following game against Belgium saw a narrow 1-0 defeat, in which the Salvadorans fought till the end and come Argentina, they vowed to leave nothing on the pitch in search of a huge upset. Then, just when they thought the footballing Gods had done with them, an earthquake hit El Salvador, causing the players to worry about their families. Two wanted to go home, but were persuaded to stay until after the game.

The Salvadorans, last stand was a bitterly, miserable, affair with some savage tackling and players of both sides arguing on the pitch. Midfielder Diaz Arevalo claimed he was called, 'A dirty guerrilla man,' by Amerigo Gallego. Arevalo hit back mocking Gallego by reminding him of the English bombing their little ships in the Atlantic. 'We got carried away, but at least we stood up to them,' said Arevalo. Post-match, more madness ensued when the two Salvadorans chosen for dope testing were offered water, soft drinks or beer to help them with being dehydrated. They went for the beer, two hours later as the players staggered out of the stadium, they discovered the team bus had gone, so the two, both drunk were forced to find a taxi!

Once back home, the reality of the 10-1 debacle became clear as the fall-out hit the Salvadorans like a cruel slap in the face. Their coach Mauricio Rodriguez never managed again and became an engineer. His assistant Jose Castro also quit, 'What happened in Spain was just too much,' he claimed. Players were mocked, ridiculed, far worse, threatened. The number ten haunting their every waking days. They were in disgrace, it would never be forgiven or forgotten. One player did always try to hold his head high when questioned about that black day, Luis Ramirez Zapata would say, 'Everyone remembers the ten, but nobody remembers my goal!' he complained. All goal scorers, even the great Pele himself, treasured every single goal that ever hit the back of the net!

As for Argentina? Only coming second in the group meant the small matter of seeing the World Champions placed in a three team group with the giants of Italy and eternal, enemy, Brazil. The world held its breath and for one twenty-two-year-old Argentinian, with the same world on his shoulders, history beckoned. All eyes would be on Diego Armando Maradona. This had been the stage he had been waiting for all his life. The opportunity to prove once and for all, that he, Maradona was the greatest player on the planet. Little could Diego realise what lay in wait for him and matters were hardly helped when the real Pele publicly made known doubts, as to what he felt was the Argentinian's true character. Writing in a column for *Clarin*, 'My main doubt is whether he has the sufficient greatness as a person to justify being honoured by a worldwide audience.' This truly hurt Maradona by someone he admired and viewed as a friend. Decades passed before Diego forgave the Brazilian for these remarks, back then, what better way to repay Pele by knocking out his nation in the forthcoming Group of Death?

CHAPTER THIRTY SIX
THE WOLF AND THE GOLDEN BOY
ARGENTINA V ITALY (WORLD CUP SECOND ROUND)

The truth was out. The glorious victory promised by the Junta regime, spoken of endlessly on a loop by every Argentine media outlet proved abject nonsense. Every picture told a story of death, desolation and humiliation. It had all been a lie, the battle for the *Malvinas* was nothing short of a slaughter, for the first time the Argentine footballers in Spain were watching on Spanish free television, with their own eyes, finally away from the clutches of State controlled television and government propaganda. The grand illusion that these young men had grown up with for most of their lives since kids had tricked them once more. Together as a squad in their Alicante hotel they witnessed it in total silence, many crying, the scenes of conscript kids many the same age as them, even some younger, humiliated, appearing frozen half to death.

The British Paras guarding them, their faces impassioned, they too had been through hell-above the Union Jack regarded by Argentinians as the Pirate banner from back in 1833, the ghost of Captain James Onslow, the gringo sonofabitch had returned. As for Galtieri and the rest of his tinpot Generals whom had sacrificed so many innocent lives on the flip of a fucking coin, praying this beyond reckless crusade would save their skin had failed desperately. For the World Cup holders, if the pressure was on previously to give their people something to hold onto before the surrender, Cesar Menotti's team now found themselves as a nation's last hope for redemption.

All the talk at the time was of their poor form in the opening three games being solely down to what had occurred in the *Malvinas* and the lies told to the players, but not all agreed. One who was present did later refute such claims. Jorge Valdano came clean admitting that was, 'Bollocks! The real problem was that the squad never gelled, and fractured into two camps. The 1978 veterans and the youngsters.' Against such a backdrop of discontent, loss and national despair, Argentina looked towards one more than any other to shine a glimpse of light onto the darkness.

The churches filled across Buenos Aires and beyond to pray for the souls of their poor boys lost in the South Atlantic, but also a final prayer that Diego would be fully fit and firing for the forthcoming match against the Italians…

Lord hear us.

ITALY: the trials and tribulations…
Paolo Rossi. The Prodigal Son. In 1980, when confronted with the dreadful accusation, twenty-four-year-old

Tuscany-born, Paolo Rossi steadfastly, refuted them. He claimed innocence, this was all some horrendous mistake. It mattered little for the evidence was overwhelming. Whilst playing on loan from Juventus for Perugia against Avellino, Rossi was found guilty of the heinous crime of match-fixing. It was alleged he only insisted in going along with the scam after being allowed to score twice in a 2-2 fixed scoreline demanded by a Rome bookies, betting syndicate. A horrified Rossi completely denied involvement claiming his comments to an opposing player during the game of, '2-2, if you want?' was said only in jest. This as a defence hardly surprisingly cut no ice with the Italian authorities, Paolo Rossi for his part in what became known as the infamous widely spread *Totonero* affair, was banned for three years. 'It was easier to find someone who hadn't been bribed,' were the words of British journalist Brian Glanville. A flowering career for the explosive centre-forward that had promised so much ground to a shameful halt. The ban on appeal was later reduced to two years, ending as the 1982 World Cup finals were only two months away, on 29th April. With their great silver-haired warrior Roberto Bettega injured and unavailable for selection, the *azzurri* manager Enzo Bearzot decided to risk all on the extremely, rusty, Paolo Rossi. With only three end of season games under his belt for Juventus, it was a major call for Bearzot to make, one he realised could well return to haunt, even finish him. Before the scandal broke, Rossi was the golden boy of Italian football, but had become badly tainted. In short he was damaged goods. Yet, despite all the flak aimed towards him, Bearzot was not for turning. Rossi was chosen for Spain, this decision meant Roma's Roberto Pruzzo, who had been Serie A's top-scorer the previous campaign missed out, only magnifying the coach's decision. Bearzot clearly no fan of Pruzzo with the comments, 'I can honestly say that if I'd had another alternative I wouldn't have called Paolo up. It was a huge risk gambling on him being able to get into the rhythm of such a demanding tournament and on his desire to make up for past mistakes. But, we desperately needed someone to poach goals in the box in a way that suited the style of play I wanted. If I didn't take him, I wouldn't have anyone capable of causing trouble in the area.'

Paolo Rossi would be handed the opportunity to wipe his slate clean. The two would share a close relationship with Rossi in time regarding Bearzot as a Father figure, the way he kept faith and talked to him when the pressure was at its most intense during the dark days of the first round, when a despondent Paolo appeared to have lost his way on the pitch, looking a broken man.

'Enzo Bearzot was an honest man with important values. He treated us like his children with no preferences and no distinctions. He was someone that praised you and other times scolded you. That is why everyone loved him. You could talk to him about everything. I recall him coming into our rooms at night to speak with us. He discussed paintings with me, for example, because he knew that I loved art.' The *azzurri* had closed ranks to all after receiving horrific abuse from their own media even before a ball had been kicked in *Espana 82*.

A friendly on the eve of the tournament in Vigo, on 8th June, against Portuguese club side FC Braga, was won 1-0, but Italy hadn't played well and their own media went after them with incredible venom, leading with tales of the players demanding massive bonuses to play were deemed a *disonore*, (a disgrace). All was a mess and the atmosphere around Bearzot's squad poisonous. In such circumstances previously, the man who acted as public relations officer for the *azzurri*, the wonderfully smooth, a true gentleman Luigi (Gigi) Peronace, would've calmed the raging waters acting as a wall between the two, warring parties. The charming and affable Gigi was also a football agent with a wonderful reputation as a fair man, one who got the job done. A very close friend of Bearzot, he tragically died in his arms of a heart attack shortly before the Uruguayan *Mundialito* back in 1980. With the awful loss of Gigi at just fifty-five-years-old, went the buffer against a carnivorous, Italian press pack.

When the games eventually kicked off, matters turned infinitely worse as Italy performed in the opening match 0-0 match against Poland, with no spark or confidence. The scandalous newspaper coverage carried on with their incessant hysteria. All bets were off when *Il Giornale* reported the two Juventus players, 'Paolo Rossi and Antonio Cabrini slept together like husband and wife.' Chinese whispers/pure gossip based on a possible homosexual affair between the two footballers printed as fact, all because the two were photographed bare-chested on their hotel room balcony. After this hit print and went worldwide, it turned out to be the last straw that broke the *azzurri* back and after Enzo Bearzot gave his blessing they went ahead with the boycott. a total ban was announced by the players of talking to the media. So, began a *Silenzio Stampa,* (a media blackout). They elected instead a spokesman, the legendary forty-year-old goalkeeper Dino Zoff to speak on their behalf. His would be a lone voice. 'Every news conference after a match became a court process,' he recalled, 'Where instead of talking about football, it became a session for defending ourselves. In the end it seemed whatever I said, they just insulted us more.'

All hell exploded again, after only drawing once more in their second match against Peru. A fantastic early strike from Roma winger Bruno Conti was cancelled out in the second half by Peruvian defender Ruben Diaz. As for the Prodigal son? Paolo Rossi was shockingly off the pace, so morose, ineffective, Bearzot hooked him off at half-time. 'I was too sick to carry on,' said Rossi later. 'In my legs, my eyes, there was no rhythm.' If possible, the *azzurri's* performance proved even more dire and lacklustre than the Polish match. No surprise as they slumped off the pitch at the end, the press were already busy slaughtering each and every one of them. Fierce criticism flew even from one of their own, when following the full-time whistle, a disgusted President of the Italian League, Antonio Matarrese, erupted in a television interview claiming, 'This team is a disgrace. I wanted to go down to the dressing room and kick them in the backside!' More wild accusation were made of footballers being drunk in bars, wild parties, even shooting up drugs. All without the merest semblance of truth. As the fires raged around the *azzurri's* circle of wagons, inside, Enzo Bearzot kept a typically, calm head as he attempted to fix the many problems on the pitch. One game remained against the Cameroon where a draw would prove sufficient to see the Italians qualify. Bearzot needed goals badly, his decision recalling Paolo Rossi had so far backfired, horribly, but he was not yet prepared to give up on the young lad whose quest for redemption was proving well beyond him.

On the 23rd June 1982, at the *Estadio Balaidos* in Vigo, Italy once more stunk out *Espana* 82, with another dismal showing, this time against the Cameroon. A 1- 1 draw was enough to provide qualification, but offered little if no hope whatsoever for their chances in the next round against the South American giants of Brazil, whom had so far illuminated the tournament with their beautifully, destructive football and World Champions Argentina. Everything surrounding the game against the Africans felt stale, even shabby. Bearzot's men qualified above the Cameroon, courtesy of Fiorentina's thirty-year-old winger Francesco Graziani's looping header past a fumbling goalkeeper Thomas N'kono on the hour. Almost immediately, Cameroon went straight down the field and hit back when the midfielder Gregoire M'Bida fired past Zoff from six yards. From that moment, even though it meant the Africans would be eliminated, both side appeared happy to settle for a draw. Dark rumours emerged after the match regarding the Cameroon's strange reluctance to go for a second goal in the final half hour and remain in the tournament, instead of being eliminated, albeit unbeaten. Why did the manager's wife return home with a large plastic bag crammed with various foreign currencies? Others whispered of the Mafia offering huge amounts of money to the Africans for throwing the match. All unproven, but something never felt truly real after M'Bida's equaliser.

As for Enzo Bearzot? Despite the criticism still being hurled in his direction, he still refused to lose faith in the underachieving team. The latest bombshell revealed by the press was that each player had received an appearance bonus of 70 million lire after qualifying for the second round. As expected this caused further outrage given the abysmal performances in the three opening matches. More than ever, the *azzurri* remained public enemy number one in their media's eyes. 'I believe in the spirit I've infused in my group,' Bearzot told a trusted journalist friend following the Cameroon match, not for public consumption. In a way, the pressure valve had loosened because nobody expected the *azzurri* to find a way past Brazil or Argentina. Bearzot was already planning ahead for the World Champions in six days' time. He felt there was nothing between the teams, except for one golden boy and a plan was forming in *Il Vecio's,* (The old Man's), mind how to deal with Argentina's most potent weapon. In a distinguished, playing career Bearzot played for Inter Milan and Torino as a *Mediano*, a holding midfielder. His one international appearance came in Budapest 1955, against Ferenc Puskas and his wonderful Magyars. Bearzot was handed the thankless task of man-marking the chubby little genius Puskas and despite Italy going down 3-2, he earned huge plaudits for his handling of Hungary's legendary number ten. For Bearzot, it came down to total concentration, make such a tussle your own personal duel. So, it was Enzo Bearzot went to speak to his defender Claudio Gentile about how he felt about being handed the monumental task of hauling in the reins on Diego Armando Maradona?

Born, 27th September 1953, in Tripoli, Libya, the twenty-nine-year-old Claudio Gentile was at the very heights of his defensive prowess. His nickname in the international squad hardly surprising was 'Gadaffi'. Gentile was Italy's and Juventus's established right-back, a true master of the dark arts. There was something of the Sergio Leone, Spaghetti western violence about the way he played the game. Gentile's appearance with the dark, swarthy, Middle-Eastern looks, murderous, staring eyes and arch villain's moustache, all suited him perfectly! Some of the tales abounding around about Gentile were the stuff of legend. On Wednesday 16th November 1977, England played host to Italy in a World Cup qualifier. That night the Manchester duo of United and City wingers Steve Coppell and Peter Barnes, were handed their debut by manager Ron Greenwood. The English won 2-0, but ultimately it was the *azzurri* whom qualified out of the group and England were forced to watch *Mundial 78* on television. Throughout the match both the impressive Coppell and Barnes came across Claudio Gentile, as he tried to stem their threat. Coppell recalled still with a shudder, 'I put a cross in and we both slid and he sort of put his hand on my testicles. I would say it was a playful squeeze, but it was a little tighter than that and it made me yelp for a little bit!' Barnes also suffered not such a painful experience, but still felt Gentile's wrath, 'He was marking me that night and spat in my face, calling me an English pig. Gentile actually was booked in the first half for pulling my shirt back and literally throwing me to the ground, as the ball rolled about five yards away, he smashed it against the back of my head, as I was lying on the floor!' Little did Steve Coppell and Peter Barnes realise, they had both got away light.

This apart,

here was a brilliant footballer. The archetypal, Italian defender. Switched on like a light when playing, intelligent, a fine technique, able to link clever, fast, more than worthy of his permanent place in the Juve and *azzurri* line-ups. Back in 1978, when Italy came up against the host nation Argentina in the First Round, Bearzot had pondered long on who to man-mark Mario Kempes. He believed there were many worthy candidates in his squad capable of such a task. Gaetano Scirea, Antonio Cabrini and Marco Tardelli to name but three, but Bearzot really wanted to find out who was really up for the challenge to go head to head with the explosive Argentinian hit-man. Two days before the match, he walked into a packed, Italian changing room after training, called for silence, and whilst smiling asked, 'Who here feels like stopping Mario Kempes?' Almost immediately, Claudio Gentile stood up looking his coach in the eyes and declared menacingly, 'Me.' Enzo had his man! The game itself saw a snarling, biting, electrifying Gentile shackling Kempes' every move. He was a dark shadow over the Argentinian number ten, who simply couldn't shake him off. With their most deadly opponent muzzled under lock and key, Italy performed wonderfully beating Argentina 1-0 against all the odds to top their group.

Spring back to 1982, with this in mind, two days before they faced Argentina once more, Bearzot approached Claudio Gentile about how he felt taking on the role of Diego Maradona's jailer? At the time Gentile was relaxing alone, watching television in their team hotel lounge, when Bearzot casually came calling to ask him, 'How would you feel about marking Maradona?'

'No problem,' replied Gentile, a response echoing his reply four years earlier. A smiling Bearzot patted him gently on the shoulder, stood up and left. He had heard enough. Immediately, Gentile sorted out some video cassettes of Diego and began to study him. Like a wolf in the woods stalking a deer from afar, his every movement, how Maradona received the ball, which way he favoured to turn, the acceleration, the dribbling, shooting-soon Gentile turned off the tapes realising there was no way he could cage such genius, instead it would be more a case of breaking him on the day. Making the golden child lose heart by breathing down his neck from minute one, sharing the shirt, foul after foul, push the law, the referee and Diego Maradona to their upper most limits. For Claudio Gentile, there would be no rules and no mercy for the boy from Villa Fiorito. Once upon a time in Barcelona was dawning for Italy and Argentina, a brutal, epic of a contest that even Sergio Leone himself would've been proud of.

CHAPTER THIRTY SEVEN
ONCE UPON A TIME IN BARCELONA

On Tuesday 29th June 1982, at the *Estadio Sarria,* home of Espanyol in Barcelona, a crowd of 39,000 waited with baited-breath for Cesar Menotti's World Champions Argentina and Enzo Bearzot's Italy to take the field. The teams had been announced, once again Bearzot had kept faith with his misfiring, centre-forward Paolo Rossi, much to the chagrin of an Italian press pack still seething with being blanked by the players, whom had taken another vote amongst the squad, that came out 18-4 to continue the boycott.

The teams.

Italy: Zoff, (Captain), Gentile, Cabrini, Tardelli, Collovati, Scirea, Oriali, Conti, Rossi, Antognoni and Graziani.
Argentina: Fillol, Olguin, Tarantini, Gallego, Galvan, Passarella, (Captain), Bertoni, Ardiles, Diaz, Maradona and Kempes.

The scene set, a vibrant, intense, occasion, the atmosphere stifling, hard to breathe. The green, white and red tricolours of Italy, the sunshine blue and white of Argentina's flags flying high-the supporters of these football, mad nations deafening as they sang their songs, banged their drums and prayed and prayed so desperately for an opening victory in this ultimate group of death. With an imperious Brazil appearing unstoppable, roaring out of the first round scoring ten goals, both sides knew a loss would almost certainly send them home. The player's faces during the national anthems etched with concentration, sweat and strain as the temperature in the *Sarria* soared to over a hundred degrees in the late, Barcelona, afternoon sun.

 It was a shootout…Nothing less.

 Straight from the kick off, Claudio Gentile headed for Diego Maradona, the duel began. A single camera was placed on the two that for ninety minutes recorded nothing but x rated-brutality! From the opening moments his would be a display of controlled violence, that didn't so much stretch the rules, but operate outside of them. A first half unfolded with nerves frayed on both sides, as flying tackles, blatant assaults and over the top lunges counted as challenges. Players throwing themselves to the floor at every opportunity. The Romanian Referee Nicolae Rainea required a third eye in an opening period where he booked five and missed twice as much again. All was wonderfully described by an English journalist John Roberts, writing in the Daily Mail at the time, 'This match contained all the exaggerated violence of a Spaghetti western, although the acting was much better.' Claudio Gentile had set about his task with a worrying relish for Diego Maradona, who ten minutes before the break approached Rainea to complain about yet another Gentile lunge, but found himself booked for protesting! An incredible eleven times in the first half Gentile was pulled up for fouls on Maradona alone. It was nothing short of a backstreet mugging. The hacking and the slashing to bring him to earth, one time, Diego careered forward with Gentile facing and as the

Argentinian went to go past, he brought him down from the knee. So blatant to the human eye, even Rainea agreed showing a yellow card to Gentile, who had the nerve to remonstrate with the Romanian claiming innocence! It was outrageous, cynical and at times defied belief-so close to Diego was Gentile around his neck, they could hear each other breathe. The Italian's wicked, vast, repertoire of dirty tricks from a simple tap of the ankles to a forearm across the young maestro's throat, all on show, put to use. Even when he appeared to show some modicum of sportsmanship by helping Maradona up off the turf, after yet another crude challenge, it was only to dig his fingernails into the back of Diego's stretched out hand. Not just Maradona suffered, Osvaldo Ardiles ended the first half with his shirt ripped to bits, due to the treatment handed out by a ferocious *azzurri* rearguard, utterly determined nothing or no one was going past them. As Rainea called the interval with his whistle, it would have felt more fitting for him to do so with a bell. Make no mistake it wasn't all one way, Argentina's own hitmen, Passarella, Tarantini and Gallego, no shrinking violets were also getting away with murder! As for the actual football? There had been only one effort on goal of note-a Ramon Diaz snapshot easily tipped over his crossbar by Dino Zoff. The rest of the half was taken up with shocking passing from both sides, sheer fear of opening up, petty squabbles, arguing with the referee and utter, bloody mayhem! As for the coach's? Cesar Menotti and Enzo Bearzot left their seats heading to the respected dressing room clearly deep in thought, thinking all still to play for. That being only if Argentina and Italy didn't end up killing each other before the end.

The Gospel according to John. It was the marriage at Cana in Galilee, where the first miracle attributed to Jesus Christ occurred. Himself, his Mother and the disciples had been invited, only for the hosts to be horrified when the wine ran out. Never fear, for their special guest Jesus saved the day by turning the water present on the table into wine.

Some transformation by any standards, but as the *azzurri* kicked off the second half, throwing off their defensive shackles, going on the attack, even that holy fable faded in comparison. Only a few days previous, Cesar Menotti when asked about Italy's qualities replied, 'One of the world's great teams until they cross the halfway line.' Cesar was about to regret such comments.

After softening the holders up before the break, Bearzot's men now went for their opponent's throat's in a footballing sense. They opened up, in midfield the Fiorentina playmaker Giancarlo Antognoni came alive. At the start of the 1981/82 season, Antognoni had been in a coma for two days after a clash with a goalkeeper. He couldn't train well, but was such an outstanding talent, a decent human being that similar to Paolo Rossi, Bearzot felt it worthwhile taking a punt on him and now Antognoni had begun to find his delightful, incisive, passing range. Another roaring back to form was the superbly, skilled, left-footed, little Roma winger Bruno Conti, who on his day could tear any defence to pieces. With the fullbacks Marco Tardelli and Antonio Cabrini also starting to charge down the flanks, Italy were a team reborn.

Something was dreadfully wrong with Argentina, there was no shortage of effort, but with Diego Maradona being hit from all angles whenever in possession, their spark had gone out. They were playing like a team of eleven individuals. Marco Tardelli let fly a thirty yard piledriver on fifty minutes that Ubaldo Fillol was forced to tip gloriously around his post-shots continually rained in on the Argentina keeper, an ever increasing fury. There felt in the stadium an inevitability about an opening Italian goal and on fifty-seven minutes it duly occurred. The fleet-footed Antognoni raced from midfield feeding the quick-thinking Conti, who in turn slipped a pass for an in-rushing Marco Tardelli, racing into the Argentine penalty to control instantly, before taking aim and firing a piercing, low-drive past Fillol into his bottom corner.

1-0 to the *azzurri!* The deadlock broken! Suddenly, their team had handed the massed Italian support a moment to be proud of, thousands of red, white and green tricolours flew with a revitalised love and enthusiasm for the cause. It swiftly became apparent that mixed amongst them on the packed, heaving sweating terrace of the *Sarria*, was more than a few hundred, yellow and blue Brazilian flags and shirts amongst them!

A sense of fear and sheer desperation cut through the Argentinian players. After all their nation had just suffered, now they looked set to fail also. Such thoughts saw them bite back and when Gentile with yet another brutal lunge scythed Diego Maradona to the floor thirty yards out to earn a free kick, Diego, full of unbridled fucking anger, let fly to smash against the Italian crossbar. The World Champions poured forward, from a floated Galvan cross, Passarella rose high with a crashing header that also struck Fillol's crossbar! Argentina had awoken from a comatose state to at least resemble some form of their old selves. Watching from a high in the stands, the supporters reacted, a familiar, incessant, chant began to resonate loud over the *Sarria,* 'ARGENTINA!'

ARGENTIN…'Thirty seconds later their voices were silenced, for Italy had broken with Graziani, who split the Argentinian defence to free Paolo Rossi. Off soared Rossi who sprinted clear with just Ubaldo Fillol to beat. Was this the moment to end the curse as he fired low, only for the keeper to block. The ball fell loose landing at Bruno Conti's feet-his touch back to Antonio Cabrini was perfection and the defender flashed a shot past Fillol high into the net from just inside the area. 2-0! Surely, game over?

In a final, desperate, rally led by Maradona, Argentina swarmed around the Italian penalty area, but the *azzurri* in *Catenaccio* mode, unbreakable on the edge of the penalty area. On a rare occasion Diego flew clear of Gentile, another blue shirt, mostly the sweeper Gaetano Scirea covered to crowd him out. The holders were on the edge, one time Maradona found himself on the floor with three Italians, still trying to keep the ball, whilst being pushed and trampled, yet still he wouldn't give it up. This had been his since he was three-years-old, but who else, none other than Gentile finally managed to poke the ball clear. As frustrations mounted, Gallego was sent off for a crazy lunge at Tardelli, Rainea at last showing a red! A dollar for Diego's thoughts as he watched his *compadre* sadly slump off after all Gentile had inflicted on him. Six minutes remained when Daniel Passarella took a chance and crashed a free kick into the net, as Dino Zoff was still preparing his defensive wall, remarkably Rainea allowed the goal to stand. Chaos broke out, the irate Italians surrounded the referee pleading with him, but he simply shook his head. 2-1.The game restarted-try as they might the Argentinians with their swift one two's that so dazzled in 78, the dazzling interplay had vanished, they were time and again picked off by Gaetano Scirea and his magnificent, unyielding, defence assembled in front of Zoff. All drained, exhausted, but determined to fight to the end. As Ardiles tried one last time to pick a hole through, Rainea put the whistle to his lips blowing for full time. An immensely brutal, at times, truly, savage, contest had ended, this wasn't about the beautiful game, Italy just had to win by all means necessary. It had been *Catenaccio* bolted with rusted nails. A smiling Enzo Bearzot in his sunglasses, dressed immaculately bore the appearance of some dapper don. In the desperate café of adversity, Bearzot had forged a feeling of togetherness amongst the squad that had shown itself against the World Champions. A philosophy of '*La forza del gruppo*', (group strength), had been entrenched in the players, how they rewarded him. After all that occurred in the early rounds, Bearzot and his players would now be heroes back home. However, there would be no easing off of relations with their press, when some ecstatic hacks tried approaching the players afterward, they went for them with a vengeance. Too much dirty water under the bridge. The time for rest and recuperation, to let injuries heal, to plan was at hand, for an even greatest test lay in wait against the Brazilians. For the moment the *azzurri* could afford to just sit back and watch as the greatest footballing derby of them all was next up. Brazil v Argentina.

Cesar Menotti's seemingly, broken team trooped off the pitch heads down, knowing that in just three days' time, at the same stadium, of all teams, it would be their most hated, rivals lying in wait to twist the knife even deeper by sending them home. Post-match, they complained loud about the tactic adopted by the Italians. 'It made us lose our concentration from what we were supposed to be doing out on a football pitch. That was playing football,' argued Mario Kempes. Osvaldo Ardiles spoke of ending the game with a shirt ripped to pieces. 'I spent all my time complaining to the referee trying to get him to put an end to it,' he raged. On being told of the South American's comments, Claudio Gentile, the wolf, simply smiled and shook his head, 'Football isn't for Ballerinas. The Argentinians don't have anything to complain about,' he retorted. 'It's obvious that when you're losing you look for excuses.'

As for Diego Maradona?

The experience at the hands of Claudio Gentile left him traumatised, such was Gentile's total dedication to his craft, he had all but suffocated during the game. For weeks later Diego claimed that on waking up in the morning, he would go in the bathroom, look in the mirror and see the Italian behind him! It was to prove in the history of the World Cup, the most blatant attempt to play a footballer out of the game, by methods bordering on thuggery. Yet, Diego never held a grudge against Gentile, 'It wasn't his fault, that was his job to stop me. It was the fault of the ref.' Later, the Italian would say of the events in the *Sarria*, 'My character was not to intimidate, it was to show I was the boss on the field. You have to be gritty and determined. At certain times you have to know how to foul.' Claudio Gentile's task had been to take out the Argentine heartbeat in Diego Maradona and once upon a time in Barcelona, with a wolf's teeth and cruel intent, he duly succeeded.

CHAPTER THIRTY EIGHT
TO THE BEAT OF A DIFFERENT DRUM

The talk in the bars and cafes of Barcelona was that they had bought the wrong player. Poland's explosive forward, the twenty-two year old Zbigniew Boniek had recently scored a sensational hat trick against Belgium and been snapped up by Juventus from Widzew Lodz, for £1.3 million. Barca supporters had watched their new boy from day one against the Belgians in the *Camp Nou* and were far from impressed. A tournament where Diego Maradona was supposed to cement his title as the greatest player in the world lingered on a disaster. There had been rare moments when Diego was irrepressible, a Rembrandt painting in motion that had jumped off the canvas causing hearts to burst with exquisite skill, but not enough to convince. The jury was far from out by a worldwide audience, perhaps more importantly, those who would be paying his extortionate wages for the next six years remained unsure.

Now, as if matters couldn't get any worse, an old adversary who absolutely hated their guts awaited in the next match to deliver the ultimate *Coup de Grace*-the ending of Argentina's reign as World Champions and in doing so silence the hype of the so-called Argentinian wonder kid, Maradona. Their own Zico, the pride of Fluminense, had won the title of the best South American player for 1981 and 1982, few would argue against the fact that it was he, not Diego who was the finest player on the planet. Not some street kid *porteno* with a few fancy tricks from a Buenos Aires shit hole called Villa Fiorito. This was the World Cup, no higher plain, here was where such arguments were once and for all debated and decided.

Diego Maradona was pilloried from all sides, more so his own. It was to be the time when Diego's paranoia with the media took a permanent grip. As Argentina mourned events in the South Atlantic, the loss of life and face, Maradona and his *compadres* in Spain were providing perfect copy for the Argentine press desperate to vent their anger and spleen and who better than *El Pelusa,* now he had flown the nest to Barcelona?

It was a reborn *Selecao* under Tele Santana, whom had found their natural rhythm on the ball once more and for the first time since 1970, gone back to traditional Brazilian values. A 7-0 slaughter of the Republic of Ireland in the build-up gave notice they were coming. From the opening moments of the tournament where Brazil were based in Sevilla, the huge, wonderful, support drenched in yellow, blue and gold had provided a mesmeric background with their mass, rhythmic, dancing and singing on the terraces. As the Samba drum beat resonated loud, the team appeared to pass the ball and move around the pitch as if in tune with it. Neutrals adored them, Their players already had become household names. The world had fallen in love with this team of hearts. Falcao, Junior, Cerezo, Eder, Zico and the tall, bearded, incomparable Socrates. After scoring ten goals in their opening, three, group games, almost everyone a footballing work of art, Brazil appeared unplayable-oh, they gave you a chance, there remained weaknesses at the back, notably the Sao Paulo goalkeeper Waldir Peres, but such was the wealth of talent in front of him, actually managing to beat them was another problem. There had been some tensions in the team causing a few niggles before the tournament began, that seriously needed to be ironed out and fixed. As the Captain, Socrates made it his mission to create harmony amongst the Brazilians, a perfect starting point for success. It all came down to a question of egos, Zico's in particularly. Although the Captain, he realised the 'White Pele' was by far their best player, so he simply let Zico play king, whilst he took the role of a prince by his side. 'Zico was the king,' recalled Socrates. 'He was much better than everyone else. When there is a king, the rest fight to be close to the king. So, it was he who should lead. It was Machiavellian, but I was the prince, and Zico,

He was the king!'

Sevilla. Brazil v USSR. Monday 14th June 1982. *Estadio Sanchez Pizjuan.* Whenever a World Cup comes around there are few more exciting feelings than the expectations before a Brazilian team play. 1982 was no exception and as the *Estadio Sanchez* quite literally melted in the late, Sevilla sun and her terraces throbbed and ebbed in a fiesta of Brazilian colour, a perfect backdrop for the latest boys from the Copacabana, attempting to emerge from the daunting shadows of Pele and his legendary, glorious World Cup winning,1970 team. Come kick off, as the two sides lined up, the red shirted Russian footballers and their vastly outnumbered supporters in the stadium must have felt like a band of nuns accidentally entering an orgiastic party involving 50,000 lunatics!

Santana's Brazil lined up, Peres, Leandro, Junior, Falcao, Oscar, Luizinho, Dirceu, Cerezo, Socrates, Serginho and Eder. It was one rich beyond words in attacking flair, but their opponents managed by the wily, sixty-year-old Russian coach Konstantin Beskov, came with a plan to tame the South Americans. Led on the pitch by the superb defender, Captain, the Georgian from Dinamo Tiblisi, Alexander Chivadze and their experienced, legendary Dynamo Kiev striker Oleg Blokhin, leading the line, the Soviets would prove a hard nut to crack. The Spanish referee Lamo Castillo blew his whistle and to no one's surprise the Brazilians enjoyed early possession. Zico had a chance going through, but his right-footed shot was well saved by the keeper Renat Dasayev parrying it away for a corner. They came again, the raiding full-back Junior stormed forward to combine with the on-fire Zico setting up the centre-forward Serginho, but he snatched at the ball and it flew haplessly over the crossbar. Much to Zico's, clear disgust. Due to pre-tournament injuries to their best two centre-forwards Reinaldo and Careca, the incredibly cumbersome, twenty-nine-year-old from Sao Paolo, was considered by Santana just about suitable to hold the line, as his array of wizards and conjurors plotted around him. A cruel description maybe, but compared to the rest of his team mates, Serginho's lack of first touch and awareness around him made the poor man appear like a drunk in a performance of Swan Lake.

When allowed the ball, the dangerous Russians shown no fear of driving forward and a wonderfully, open, game ensued with many opportunities at both ends. The Soviet were not shy, showing little respect to their much, vaunted opponents. At times the impression given by the Brazilians as the ball was moved from yellow shirt to yellow shirt around the pitch, with a sublime delight, appeared them to be saying we can score anytime, just sit back and enjoy the ride-then, on thirty-four minutes, Kiev's little midfielder Andriy Bal let fly a low-drive from well outside the penalty area that Peres somehow let squirm past him into the net. A dreadful error, despite owning the ball Brazil were one down.

Come the second half, the pressure on a Russian defence marshalled supremely by Chivadze slowly increased-yet they still held enough purpose and power to break out causing heart attacks on the terraces and the vast millions of Brazilians back home on, and past the Copacabana watching between their fingers. The clock ticked down, only fifteen minutes remained when Socrates took centre stage. Taking the ball from twenty-five yards out, *O Canhão* (The Cannon), cut inside to fly past two red shirts leaving them spinning, before in one movement flashing a magnificent shot high past Dasayev into the top corner! The doctor had solved a near crisis in the most astonishing manner! The *Selecao* were alive, well and looking for a winner. As a draw appeared likely, the Russians in the closing moments were hardly able to clear their lines due to exhaustion. It had been a long, sweltering evening in a marvellous game of football under ever, darkening, Sevilla skies. The Samba drums on the terraces still resonated loud with hope, the massed, Brazilian support as one danced and swayed, clapped, sang, the rhythm and tempo of the songs and the drums in totally harmony with the team remaining as one. Two minutes remained to play when the substitute Paulo Isidoro, (Maradona's amigo from the *Mundialito*), rolled a pass to Falco on the edge of the Russian penalty area. The Roma man without a care in the world let it through his legs to be picked up by the incoming left winger Eder, who flicked up the ball with his left foot and hit a devastating, dipping, swerving, shot that Dasayev could only dream of stopping! Yellow and green mayhem ensued! A rousing, passionate, encounter in the land of the gypsies, Southern Spain, had received a fitting finale-the Russians on their knees, the *Estadio Sanchez* exploding in joy. 2-1, it finished for Brazil, a close call, but a magnificent victory, nonetheless. Santana's men had shown you could still win at this level without changing your spots and staying in your own skin.

They were back.

Next,

was Scotland, whom after a few nervous moments finally beat the underdogs of New Zealand 5-2. They met a euphoric Brazilian side on the crest of a wave at the home of Real Betis, *Estadio Benito Villamarin* in Sevilla, on Friday 18ᵗʰ June 1982. In a brave move manager Jock Stein dropped Kenny Dalglish and went with a five-man midfield to try and match up against Brazil's creativity. Stein's team lined up, Rough, Narey, Gray, Wark, Miller, Hansen, Strachan, Souness, Archibald, Hartford and Robertson. A brave, tactical-move by the legendary Stein, one fascinating beforehand to discuss, but in reality they were mercilessly outclassed. Inside the *Estadio Benito*, the 47,000 crowd was truly a sight to behold, as the South American trumpets played, Brazilian, Scottish, Spaniards and neutrals mingled, danced, hugged and kissed on the terraces. All day around the city as Sevilla police watched warily on, there had been wonderful, coming togethers' of both sets of supporters, happily this continued up to kick-off and beyond. Their colour and noise creating a wonderful spectacle off the field. The saltire, tartan, blue and white flags, immersed in alongside the sea of Brazil's yellow and green. This wild and raucous Scottish travelling army fuelled on cheap Spanish plonk, heartfelt goodwill and a drunken dream that they were going to beat Brazil was a sight to behold. No more so than on eighteen minutes, when the Dundee United defender David Narey raced through onto a John Wark header from a Graeme Souness long pass, to smash a right-footed slicer past Waldir Peres into the net! The twenty-six-year-old Dundee born Narey had been brought in specifically by Stein to try and handle Eder, this wasn't in the script. Working for BBC Television, that hot, sultry evening in Sevilla was Jimmy Hill, his opinion that Narey's goal was simply a 'Toe poke' caused outrage amongst Scots and the controversial, provocative Hill swiftly became a marked man north of Hadrian's wall. As the Scottish supporters roared out in disbelief around the *Estadio Benito,* at what they had just witnessed, Socrates was having serious words. It wasn't right that you had to concede before starting to perform in the World Cup, for it would eventually do for you. Brazil had dominated possession, but time had come to step up and go to work.

Slowly, the movement of the Brazilian midfield interchanging-constantly like yellow ghosts across the pitch, Falcao, Zico and Eder proved impossible to mark. The Captain Socrates at their very heart, albeit one with skates on, it proved bewildering to deal with for the chasing, increasingly, bedraggled, Scots. On thirty-three minutes Alan Rough could only stand and watch Zico's beautifully, placed free-kick from the edge of the penalty area soar majestically past him! Scotland survived till half time, but as once more that Samba beat took a hold, like witchcraft, the Brazilian players seemingly in sync with the rhythm, as they treated the ball like some holy relic that must never, ever be given away on fear of death. Three minutes into the second half, Junior's in-swinging corner was headed down powerfully past Rough by the towering Oscar, outjumping Souness and the deluge broke. It became just a question of how many. The tempo was stepped up a breathless pace to leave the brave, but horribly, outclassed Scots chasing shadows. A footballing carousel that took you round and round as the Brazilians turned up the heat looking for more goals. The explosive box of tricks, Zico, sublime skills, impossible vision, that rarity, a two footed genius was proving impossible to control and could easily have earned himself a hat trick, before the third goal arrived for Brazil with trumpets blazing on sixty-five minutes.

To a bouncing, exhilarating, soundtrack of a hypnotic, Brazilian mass, orchestra on the terraces, Peres rolled the ball to Falcao, he in turn found Socrates, who fed Serginho-a clever turn from the under-firing striker, again enduring a frustrating night, but this time around, Serginho left the much-lauded centre-pairing of Liverpool's Alan Hansen and Aberdeen's Willie Miller standing, rolling a pass to Eder, arriving wide-left of the penalty area. Noticing Alan Rough well off his line, the twenty-two-year-old little winger from Brazilian club Atletico Miniero, executed the most sumptuous chip over the Partick Thistle man's head to drop like a golf shot high into his goal. 3-1, Eder celebrated with the crowd, Socrates jumped on top of him, the *Estadio Benito* ignited in a plethora of noise and excitement that echoed twelve years all the way back to the *Azteca,* in the blistering, melting heat of the Mexican sunshine.

Tele Santana's team were performing to the beat of a different drum, no one but they could hear and had not yet finished with the traumatised Scots. Stein attempted to stem the tide by bringing on Kenny Dalglish, but even a talent such as he was helpless when you couldn't get the ball. A deserved fourth goal arrived for the Brazilians three minute from time and it was arguably the best of the

evening. Again, Socrates involved setting up Roberto Falcao, (The Roma fans christened Falcao the (*'Eighth king of Rome'*), to thrash a ferocious, low drive from thirty yards sizzling past a besieged, Alan Rough.
Brazil 4 Scotland 1.

The noise cascaded down from around the *Estadio Benito*. A truly, memorable, evening finished with Brazilian and Scottish supporters partying the night away together in Sevilla, each sporting the shirts and flags of the other. Post-match, though hurting in both the size and manner of defeat after being utterly outclassed, Jock Stein still couldn't hide his admiration of the Brazilians.

'It will be good for soccer if Brazil win it. It is never easy to accept defeat but this one is different. The Brazilians are so good.' Stein went on to say, 'They are willing to let you take control of the ball and then set out to kid you into passing where they want it to go.'

Hardly surprising that none other than the great Scottish journalist Hugh McIlvanney described in poise, mere, mortal writers could only ever dream of adhering to match. 'The hurt Scotland feel over the four goals dazzlingly inflicted on them by Brazil should be no more tinged with shame than the sense of inadequacy experienced by every golfer who has been buried under a flood of birdies from Jack Nicklaus, every fighter overwhelmed by Sugar Ray Robinson, or all the Grand Prix drivers who have ever had Juan Fangio's exhaust fumes blowing in their faces. When you lose to the best, self-recrimination is a graceless irrelevance.'

Best just to leave it there…

CHAPTER THIRTY NINE
'GOOD LITTLE BOYS'
ARGENTINA V BRAZIL (WORLD CUP SECOND ROUND)

On Wednesday 23rd June 1982, Brazil's final, first round group game saw them despatch New Zealand 4-0, with one eye closed to qualify unbeaten. Two goals for Zico, one for Falcao and at long last the lambasted Serginho found himself on the scoreline, before being substituted in the second half. A former Brazilian coach Joao Saldanha was clearly no fan and working as a journalist in Spain, was cruelly spiteful in his criticism of Serginho, 'He is not the kind of player who should be leading the Brazil attack. It was beautiful when he went off against New Zealand. Suddenly, the ball was round again.' So, it was to no one's great surprise, that even though the Brazilian's second round opponents were two classic, huge footballing nations in Argentina and Italy, Tele Santana's team were being made clear favourite to clinch a historic, fourth World Cup victory.

Whilst their great rivals bathed in the spotlight of world-wide adoration, Argentina licked their wounds and prepared for a last stand to defend their title. They had only three days to prepare for the do or die clash against Brazil, which would again take place in the *Sarria*. The World Champions had to win, otherwise they were going home to a whole cesspit of abuse. As for Diego Maradona, still bruised, dazed and battered from his mauling at the hands of Claudio Gentile, he was under no illusion that what lay in wait against Brazil, was going to be equally brutal. The hatred between the two countries on a football pitch impossible to measure on any reasonable scale, it was simply off it and with events only four years previously still rancidly, vivid in Brazilian minds, when they were eliminated on Argentine soil, convinced because of a soiled fix. For them this early chance for revenge was heaven sent.

On the eve of the game, Socrates spoke to journalists of the bad feeling that existed between the two nations. 'It's pure rivalry,' he began.' They're right by us, but we're two very different cultures, we're different people. Argentina's origins are European, but Brazilians are very much a mix with the Africans. I think this rivalry is going to be eternal. There's a brutal difference in sporting behaviour between the two countries. Argentinians are very much more aggressive, when they take to the pitch, you just know he doesn't think about consequences, just victory. Brazilians are much like good little boys, you know, they're not really violent against anyone. It's the difference in culture between the countries. We play football for fun, for entertainment sake, for the spectacle, for the beauty, whereas,…Argentinians play to win.'

'Good little boys?' Diego Armando Maradona was soon set to strongly disagree with the doctor's, wildly, idealistic version of Brazilian football.

Barcelona. *Estadio Sarria.* On Friday 2nd July 1982, Argentina and Brazil stepped out into a smouldering, blazing, atmosphere bathed in the colours of both nations. A carnival of sorts, uproarious and warlike-the Brazilian samba drums and trumpets, the songs and the chants all tinged with not so much exuberance, but more expectations. Don't lose, don't you dare fucking lose to these! Meanwhile, their Argentinian counterparts roared out equally loud with sheer, blinding, defiance. A cannon could have fired over the *Sarria* and wouldn't have been heard. Brazil picked up where they had left off in Sevilla, as Menotti's team were straight away pushed back. Again, Socrates dictating the pace and style, In preparation for the 1982 tournament, he totally changed his lifestyle. The Captain even gave up the favoured two packs a day of cigarettes and love of the booze in order to be at his physical peak when *Espana 82* began. It took the Brazilians just twelve minutes to open their account when the destructive Eder smashed a ridiculously, swerving, free-kick that crashed off the underside of the crossbar and Zico from close range, jumped over Ubaldo Fillol, to get in front of Serginho and from a yard out scrambled the ball over the line! To the delight of their supporters and the millions of neutrals whom had adopted them, Brazil had not just come to party,

They had come to play.

Astonishingly, they appeared to go up yet another level second half, as the ball was passed around the disgruntled holders with a snake-like precision and pace, designed to both cause deadly harm and break the hearts of opponents. Menotti's team were hurting, running on empty-they bore the look of men that knew the game was up. Although continuing to fight staunchly, they were simply being outclassed. Their one shining light, Maradona, in whom all Argentina's hopes had been invested was enduring another frustrating, afternoon, being kicked, pushed and brutalised by yellow shirts, whom similar to Belgium in the opening match were passing him around to rough up. Nothing was coming off for Diego, the anger as the treatment grew increasingly worse, clearly began to show. Something was going to blow. With their best player outgunned, isolated,

Menotti acted and dragged off a wholly, ineffective Mario Kempes to replace him with Ramon Diaz, yet still Argentina struggled to mount any serious threat. On sixty-eight minutes, matters turned infinitely, desperate for the fading World Champions. Zico and Falcao combining to perfection-the White Pele creating a beautiful pass for the eighth king of Rome to produce a cross of such perfection, even a lurking Serginho couldn't miss, heading in past a beaten Fillol at the far post. 2-0, the clock was ticking down on Argentina's reign. They were close to breaking, six minutes later it was 3-0, when Zico with another glorious pass took out four Argentinian defenders to find the on-rushing Junior, who had sprung from defence to finish with marvellous ease past a deflated Fillol. It was fiesta time for the Brazilians! Scenes of joyful ecstasy on the jumping, dancing, terraces at putting paid to their greatest rivals broke out. Let the trumpets and Samba drum herald the downfall of the fucking Argentinians-a ghastly stark contrast to the sights of the mass, crying, outraged, fallen holders. Their blue and white face paint masked by tears. The team taken apart, dissected, embarrassed and humiliated by the old enemy now dancing on the grave of their world crown. A day to forget, one that simply couldn't get any worst for Argentina. Not, quite…With just three minutes left to play Diego Armando Maradona finally exploded and all hell let loose in the *Sarria*.

As if dethroning the Argentinians was not of sufficient pain to extract, the Brazilians succeeding in destroying the one player they truly feared. A
 concerted series of fouling from the opening moment to the near last, saw for an exasperated Diego, who snapped and launched a wretched, crazy, waist-high, lunge on the poor substitute Batista, who had only been on the pitch for

two minutes. He was in place of Zico, just recently wiped out by a horrendous Daniel Passarella tackle that should have seen the hurting and angry Captain frog-marched off to the nearest Spanish jail! Nineteen years later in an interview Passarella claimed, 'I should not have played at the 1982 World Cup. A lot of kids died in the *Malvinas* and I, as the Captain, should have done something to stop us going on the pitch.' *El Gran* had clearly lost his head on realising not just the battle against Brazil, but indeed the wars both on and off the pitch had proved disastrous. Passarella dealt with it in typical fashion, boots flying! Maradona would later say he was looking for Falcao, Batista was simply a case of mistaken identity! Socrates' 'Good little boys' had got their man and the Mexican referee Mario Vasquez flashed a red card to send Diego Maradona off. Two penalty calls could be said to have gone against him, one most definitely when he was cleaned out in the box by Junior, an incredulous Maradona ended up doing a backward flip in disgust when Vasquez waved it away, just giving a corner. As Diego trooped off the field in abject disgrace, head down, close to tears, Alberto Tarantini walked towards him and planted a gentle kiss onto his head. Tarantino whispering the kind words, 'You'll be back Diego.' Yet, there could be no guarantees. Maradona's spirit was broken, a wipe of the shirt on his face and out of sight-four years was plenty of time to mend a broken heart, but at that moment, Mexico 86 was far away as the stars. Who knew what the future now held for *El Pelusa*? Maradona crossed over the touchline, making the sign of the cross, then he kissed the tiny silver crucifix around his neck before looking up to the heavens. With so many expectations upon still fledgling shoulders, Diego's world had crumbled and come tumbling down. He exited in disgrace his first World Cup.

Around Barcelona, alarm bells were starting to ring loud, as to just what was coming their way the following season? Years later, a smiling Socrates in an interview was asked the eternal question, Pele or Maradona? 'That's what people always want to know,' he replied. 'Well, I can tell you, the only time I played against the artist Maradona in the World Cup, I won.'

Italy were set to knock the smile right off the doctor's face...

CHAPTER FORTY
THE GAME
ITALY V BRAZIL (WORLD CUP SECOND ROUND)

As Argentina returned home with their reign as World Cup holders over, already neutrals were preparing a coronation to place their crown onto Brazilian heads. Tele Santana's beautifully, composed, riotously, dangerous team of hearts required just a draw to qualify for the semi-finals against Enzo Bearzot's Italy. Such was the quality and confidence flowing through Brazil, it was felt only a madman would hand the *azzurri* any chance to silence the samba drums. Maybe so but sometimes there's a very thin line between madness and genius and amongst Bearzot's supremely, organised, courageous, highly technical side, a quiet confidence was growing.

Only a madman?

Italy had found themselves chastised by the world media for their brutal tactics against Argentina and the showdown in the *Sarria* was being hailed in many circles as some almighty good versus evil battle for the soul of football. Brawn against beauty, maybe somebody should have asked Diego Maradona just who was who? Scottish journalist Patrick Barclay wrote, 'Brazil have shown signs of approaching the 1970 standard in this tournament. Set this against the moral bankruptcy of the Italians against Argentina, and you have the reason why the international footballing community will be behind Brazil.'

Hours before the game even began the *Sarria* teemed with supporters of both nations. The Samba beat rolled melodically on in the afternoon sun, as a mass blanket of yellow shirts danced like maniacs swamping the terraces. The Italians were also present in large numbers, the green, red and white tricolours flying, clearly evident around the ever-filling stadium. Thirty minutes before kick-off, the *azzurri* players emerged from the tunnel to check the pitch and soak up the incredible, atmosphere and on seeing their heroes the *tifosi* hordes exploded! Horns blew, flags waved and firecracker sizzled and deafened in the torrid, hot, Barcelona sun. The footballers watched in astonishment at this wonderful, heart-stopping, act of defiance and loyalty. Anymore inspiration if it was even required to win the day was surely increased ten-fold at witnessing such scenes.

The Italians were up for a fight in Barcelona.

Amidst blinding, smoke bombs and a cacophony of noise. Rockets, horns, bells, trumpets and drums, anything that resonated loud accompanied the teams appearing into sight. 44,000 people held their breath as that fine, Israeli referee Abraham Klein signalled to each of his linemen to begin what was to be the finest game of football ever witnessed in the history of the World Cup.

Italy started where they had left off against Argentina. Bruno Conti probed intelligently coming inside, looking for a way through. With just under five minutes on the clock, the classy Roman wide-man swept a ball over to the other side of the pitch to attacking full-back Antonio Cabrini. The Juve defender put in a dipping cross to the back of the penalty area, where arriving like a thief in the night was Paolo Rossi, stooping low to aim a precise header past Waldir Peres into the net! Finally, the Italian centre forward had begun to repay Beazot's, unstinting loyalty. The *tifosi* bombs burst loud, their voices soared loud on the terraces. From Naples to Rome to Milan, Italians were going crazy with Paolo's goal! The Brazilian defenders appeared aghast, none saw him coming and that was a worry.

 Brazil restarted, eager for swift retribution. Socrates glided like a gazelle with the ball over the half-way line, his, long, spindling legs eating up the turf, yet he still possessed the ability to appear the epitome of serenity-Socrates' pass found Serginho, who was struggling to hold off the clawing mantles of Claudio Gentile on his back. The big centre-forward fumbled losing possession, only for Zico to take over, and flick a lovely ball through for Serginho to run onto with just Dino Zoff to beat. As the tens of thousands-legions of Brazilian Supporters held their collective breath, the hapless, striker risked eternal infamy by miskicking, blasting, horribly wide. It was the miss of a drunkard, whose eyes and legs were twelve sheets to the wind. Zico gave Serginho a searing look of disgust, whilst barrels and buckets of abuse and disdain was hurled upon his head from the supporters.

 Once more the ball was square.

 On twelve minutes, to the utter delight of all those who adored the beautiful game, the Brazilians pieced together an equaliser of the highest, possible order. Again, who else but Socrates who forced the Italians to back-pedal. Playing a pass inside to Zico, who produced a moment of sheer effrontery, a devilish back heel that had everyone off their seats in the *Sarria*. As if spinning on ice, Zico tore past his man-marker Gentile, (This time around Bearzot told him ten minutes before kick-off, the task was to be his!), and played in Socrates, who had kept on running. The Brazilian Captain had his Father to thank for his unusual name. He was from a very poor family in the Amazon who taught himself to read. A man with no education, but he built a huge library and was interested in ancient Greek philosophy. So, be the name, Socrates! On he went into the penalty area, before unleashing a low drive that flew past Dino Zoff, beaten by simple power at his near post. Audacious, a footballing work of art. Zico's balletic twist and turn to leave the limpet-like Gentile on his back, as if he was a blind man walking into a wall was beautifully outrageous. Commentating for BBC television, John Motson called it, 'A goal that sums up the philosophy of Brazilian football.' A breath-taking equaliser that once more ignited Brazil's supporters and settled their nerves in the *Sarria*. Paolo Rossi's early strike had surely been a mere blip, because, after all,

it was only Paolo Rossi.

Incidents followed thick and fast, with the game swiftly unravelling into a compelling contest, both highly emotional and dripping with drama. As the Brazilians poured forward, Italy were unyielding. Led by Gaetano Scirea, the *azzurri* rearguard were in that mood-The referee Klein shown Gentile a yellow card for a gruesome foul on Zico making it clear to the Italian he wasn't going to put up with a repeat of what occurred in the game against Argentina. Oh, how Diego could only have prayed for such a guardian angel. On twenty-four minutes this match from the footballing Gods took on another twist that left all watching open-mouthed. A careless Cerezo inexplicably gave away possession to Paolo Rossi, twenty-five yards out, who unable to believe his luck, ran on and fired powerfully past Waldir Peres into the Brazilian goal. Such was Cerezo's outpouring of grief at his shocking error, the tears fell and a furious Júnior threatened to hit him in the face if he didn't stop crying! Such a joker's goal from Brazil's point of view to lose, suddenly, despite the magic and wonder that existed elsewhere in the team, it became apparent that against the right opponents, they were truly fallible. Waldir Peres in goal, his mistake against the USSR. The aberration by Cerezo, the abomination masquerading up front as a centre-forward in Serginho. Brazil only had to breathe out of place and the Italians were exploiting it.

 This extraordinary game once more had swung back in Italy's favour. Paolo Rossi was mobbed by his teammates like the prodigal son he now certainly was. Bearzot had leapt of his seat when Paolo shot them in front. His boy was back in business. True faith. Brazil began again, now having to score once more, or unthinkably they were going home against a team whom defended a lead, with all the ferocity of a lion protecting its cubs. Cerezo immediately tried to make amends crossing for Socrates, who powered a header straight at Dino Zoff. Ten minutes before half-time, the Italians were forced into making a substitution, when the stalwart Collovati was injured and on to take his place came Inter Milan's defensive prodigy, eighteen-year-old Giuseppe Bergomi, with his coach's full trust to handle Serginho. Bergomi took up position alongside Gaetano Scirea. Shortly after coming on, the youngster complained to his Captain Dino Zoff that he was having difficulty breathing, due to the almighty pressure valve squeezing tight all in the stadium. Zoff calmed him down and Giuseppe Bergomi went on to play the finest game of his young life swiftly laying down a marker on the Brazilian centre-forward's shins. As half-time drew close, a let off for Italy occurred when Gentile ripped Zico's shirt off his back, a clear penalty, but Klein had already blown up for offside.

Finally, the interval arrived giving both teams and supporters time to breathe and recover from what had been an enthralling first half of football. The 2-1 lead for the *azzurri,* albeit partly self-inflicted had clearly scarred Brazil's confidence. A scoreline not in anyone's script, except maybe Enzo Bearzot's. The second period opened with the Brazilians going through the gears forcing Zoff into three saves of rapid succession. The finest by far when he came hurling off his line to thwart Cerezo. Now playing like a man possessed because of the horrific error for Rossi's second goal. Zico and Gentile were involved in a persona duel, a monumental struggle, although the Italian was being forced to curtail the outright violence used against Maradona. For Klein wouldn't stand for it. Instead, Gentile imposed himself on the Brazilian number ten, stretching still the laws of the game just long enough so they didn't snap altogether! Zico escaped from his manacles for a fleeting moment, though enough to play in his worst nightmare Serginho, who again failed to control the ball, fumbling, only managing to fire off a weak effort straight at a relieved Zoff. The Brazilian supporters howled in derision as yet another God-given opportunity went begging. They poured scorn down on the head of the clearly, distressed Serginho, so far out of his depths it was sad to watch. The pressure increasing-the clock forever onwards. Now involved on a one man mission to save the day for his nation, Cerezo again went close as Brazil hammered away against a magnificent, Italian defence. Bearzot's men however were also now full of confidence, no longer afraid of launching forward on swift breakouts. One such saw Graziani race clear on the left, before crossing for an unmarked Paolo Rossi-with time to spare and surely win the game, Rossi inexplicably shot wide. A horrible miss, the boy from Prato buried his head, Brazil were still alive. As their supporters bayed, prayed and pleaded for an equaliser, the flames and fire atmosphere inside the *Sarria* threatened to overwhelm all present. The flair and sorcery of the Brazilians trying all in their might to unlock an *azzurri* team, increasingly looking to finish them off on the counter-attack. Twenty-two minutes remained, when a Brazilian plying his royal trade in the eternal city, escaped from Italian shackles to send his countryfolk dancing once more into carnival mood. Dribbling in from the left-hand touchline, Junior swept a pass across field to the advancing Roberto Falcao-Italy dropped off. Falcao cut in as Cerezo again involved, ran outside of him into the box taking out Cabrini, Tardelli and Scirea, leaving space for his team mate to thrash an outstanding left-footed drive from the edge of the penalty area! 2-2! Off he soared, eyes bulging, arms raised, before vanishing under a sea of yellow.

The supporters erupted, the entire Brazilian bench ran onto the field to join in the celebrations. Once again it was advantage Brazil as this marvellous, emotional, contest moved into its final quarter.

To make matters even better for the dancing sea of Brazilians, amongst whom there were many crying tears of sheer emotion, Serginho was substituted by Santana and on came the winger Paolo Isidoro, who took up a midfield position, releasing Socrates to move forward. Brazil showing absolutely no inclination to shut up shop, for it was simply not in this team's nature, or indeed did they possess the ability to do so. The Italians were left with no option but to open up. Bearzot regrouped his troops-Giancarlo Antognoni began to make positive skirmishes into Brazil's half. In the ongoing tussle between Gentile and Zico, the Brazilian had begun to tire badly due to the constant close attention of the Italian's Octopus-like grip. Still, the chances fell for the *Selecao,* Isidoro foiled by a remarkably, brave stop by the forty-year-old Zoff. His had been a true *Capitano's* role. Italy surged forward and a corner was earned. Fourteen minutes remained when Conti's cross flew high into the Brazil box and landed at the feet of Marco Tardelli. The defender knocked the ball back into the six yard area, where it was pounced upon by Rossi swooping to fire past Peres! 3-2! The Brazilians fell to the ground in disbelief. Paolo Rossi had snatched the most sensational hat trick. Those many Italian journalists whom handed out incessant abuse to the player and coach, that had stuck by him throughout his goal drought, would now queue to kiss both their hands. Rossi, the one-time outcast had repaid Bearzot in a manner he could hardly ever have expected. The *tifosi* could hardly bear to watch the historic events unfurling before their very eyes. This was by no means the team they had become accustomed to. Bearzot's newly, discovered attacking philosophy might have been good for the soul, but it was wreaking terrible, havoc with their hearts.

Tele Santana stood on the touchline urging his side on for one last great effort. The yellow masses had temporarily fell silent, but soon the samba drums resonated once again to beat out their rhythm, never had those yellow shirts on the pitch needed them more, for there was still time. Anything could yet happen.

Gaetano Scirea had marshalled the Italian defence with all the strategic brilliance of a five-star General. Now, as the Brazilians launched their final bout of assaults, the magnificent Scirea prepared those alongside him for one last great effort. Brazil came forward with a fury, now bordering on panic, as the clock ticked continuously towards their footballing Armageddon. Socrates had an effort disallowed for offside. Throwing caution to the wind, the South American were being effortlessly picked off by the *azzurri*, as they broke out with deadly intent. From one such counter-attack, the sublime Antognoni shot home past Peres from nine yards, only to also see it called offside by Klein. The twenty-two-year-old Florence golden boy now seemingly fully recovered from his medical scare, had been that day the equal of any Brazilian on the pitch. Two minutes remained-Brazil laid siege to Italy's goal. Their supporters screaming themselves hoarse in a vain attempt to force yet another equaliser and ultimate salvation, but the Italians were simply unbreachable. The noise level increased to even further levels of delirium when an Eder free kick jetted into the penalty area and Cerezo rose high to smash a header goalwards, only to see Dino Zoff break his heart to save. Toninho Cerezo could not have done anything more. Another corner, Eder sprinted across to take it. Many could hardly bear to watch as he put in a wickedly, curling, cross that Zoff launched himself heroically into a mass of jumping, writhing, bodies to punch clear. The *azzurri* players pleaded with the referee to end their torment, but still it continued. This was no longer *Catenaccio,* more sheer, desperation. Finally, Abraham Klein called time on what had been a truly, epic occasion.

The game...

The Italians rushed as one to embrace the hero of the hour Paolo Rossi, who found himself swamped by jubilant teammates and officials alike. Tears flowed rivers from both sides. Even amongst neutrals, the passion and drama of the day had seeped under the skin. Commentating for BBC television, Bobby Charlton finished the game in tears and colleague John Motson was forced to carry on alone, as Charlton struggled to control his emotions.

The Brazilians were inconsolable. Eder slumped in a heap, Cerezo sat crying, whilst a clearly, shell-shocked Socrates could only watch on at the joyful Italians. Zico lay on the ground utterly distraught, his ferocious struggle with Gentile ending in abysmal defeat. As fine a team of hearts they may have been, beautiful on the eye also, but in the late sunlight of this Barcelona afternoon, Brazil were out. A side brimming with world class individuals had been struck down by its inability to stop careless-defensive errors. Over-confidence, bordering on arrogance had in the end proved their downfall. Adios, to their footballing philosophy and imagination. Adios, to their adoration of the beautiful game. Adios, to their broken-hearted yellow and green drenched army of supporters. Adios, to the pulsating rhythm of the samba soundtrack, finally falling silent. As for the contribution of the wretched Serginho? Least said the better. Zico was disgusted by what happened, calling it out as, 'The day football died. We played artistic football with beauty, all about goals and attacking, Italy were the opposite, completely preoccupied with stopping us playing.'

It would be another fourteen years before the *Selecao* got their hands again on the World Cup. This Brazil of Socrates, Zico, Falcao and Eder was destined to stand alongside the past greats of Hungary and Holland, as amongst the finest never to win the biggest prize of all.

Once back in the dressing room, Telê Santana told his broken team, 'The whole world has been enchanted by you. Be aware of that.' Later, entering the post-match press conference, the entire room, over three hundred people stood to give Santana a standing ovation. A wonderful sentiment, but again all counting for nothing when the traumatised Brazilian players boarded the plane back home. Johan Cruyff once said, 'There is no better medal than being acclaimed for your style.'

They never played together as a team again.

As for Enzo Bearzot and his never-say-die Italy? He wasn't convinced by the argument being presented that their victory had been nothing more than a triumph of pure pragmatism. 'There was some mean-spirited talk. Our third goal was scored after a corner with all the Brazilians in the area. I repeat, all the Brazilians in the area! Yet, we were still accused of playing counter-attacking football?' Back home Bearzot and Paolo Rossi were praised to the heavens. The sins of the past forgiven, if never totally forgotten in Paolo's case. From being labelled a fraud in the opening rounds, Enzo Bearzot was now hailed a tactical genius. Former accusers lining up to praise his achievements in guiding Italy past Brazil into the semi-finals. The brave decision to stick with Rossi as he struggled to find a modicum of form now being viewed as a classic piece of man-management. However, Bearzot had been badly burned by the criticism, he knew well defeat by their next opponents Poland would see the same journalists turn with a venom once more. Happily, for Enzo and the *azzurri* this was not to be, for the Italians swept the Poles aside with some ease. Two goals from the rejuvenated Rossi sufficient to see them into the World Cup final against West Germany.

On a glorious night in Madrid, at the *Estadio Bernabeu*, goals from Rossi again, Marco Tardelli, and Allesandro Altobelli saw the trophy return to Italian soil, for a historic third time matching Brazil. As for the prodigal son? His spell in the wilderness ended in the summer of 82. Paolo Rossi was going home, redemption had been gained.

To finish…

'Our loss to Italy was not simple. Some say that we were the greatest side never to win the World Cup. They tell us that to this day. People remember our team because we lost, not won. But nobody tried to copy Italy, the pragmatic team which lifted the World Cup. The beautiful team, with the art and creativity, lost. Besides, the match finishes, but life goes on.' Doctor Socrates.

CHAPTER FORTY ONE
LIGHTNING IN A BOTTLE

The Battle of the *Bernabeu*. Madrid, Saturday 5th May 1984. It was never a vendetta started by Diego Maradona, but as he floored the insulting Basque player Sola with a left hook, it appeared one the Argentinian was determined to end. As fists flew and Barca players came hurtling to his aid with a barrage of punches and kicks, the melee turned into a full-scale riot. Players fell, no neutrals. Back came the *Butcher of Bilbao,* with a second attempt to cripple Diego Maradona. Down he went-only for the butcher to be dropped himself, from an unexpected, Kung-Fu assault from Diego's, Barca amigo Migueli. Utter mayhem continued unabated as the two sides tore into each other settling scores. Maradona was in the heart of the fighting with his fist and feet. The slum kid had returned to basics-this was Bruce Lee and Rocky in a Barca shirt and he was being deemed an absolute, fucking, disgrace! Pure hatred. Bilbao and Barcelona. For two years Diego Maradona led a blazing, trail of drama, mayhem, heartache and intrigue on Catalan soil. Wherever he turned the smell of cordite followed. Back in the *Estadio Bernabeu*, as Madrid's baton-wielding riot police hid behind their shields and showers of objects from the terraces, bottles, coins, even shoes rained down upon the fighting players, Spanish football experienced the final engrossing episode of Maradona's trials and tribulations in Barcelona. To understand such a dramatic ending, you really have to go right back to the day Diego appeared at the *Camp Nou,* to begin a new life in the old world, leaving all he ever loved or understood behind in the new.

Before the adventure in Barcelona began, there was a brief respite with family and close friends on the beautiful, never-ending, white sandy beaches of Atlántida in Uruguay, where the Maradona's owned a villa. There he relaxed with Mum, Dad, Claudia, brothers and sisters. Diego would take long walks amongst the countless pine trees lined all along the *Playa La Brava,* with Chitoro, pouring out his heart on what lay ahead. He would listen carefully, offering a few words here and there, but every single one would be taken on board by his son. Chitoro was Maradona's shield of wisdom against all the bullshit and crap constantly being whispered into his ear by those who cared about little else, but making dollars out of him. He offered Diego advice based on love, one steeped in reality, for this was his boy. As for Barcelona? The old man told him, 'Do what you do, that is better than anyone else in the world. Be, Diego Armando Maradona.'

'Barcelona is the team for me. It is the biggest club in the world, better than Juventus.'
Diego Maradona

Early doors. On Wednesday 28th July 1982, FC Barcelona's, traditional pre-season unveiling took place on the *Camp Nou* pitch. The main attraction so far as the vast, media presence were concerned was undoubtedly the Argentinian Diego Maradona, whom Barca had paid out a world record fee of $7.6 Million and for thus were expecting miracles from. 'The transfer of the century' it was being hailed as. The Spanish weekly sports magazine *Don Balon* declared on their front cover, 'Boom Maradona, six million dollars talking, running and scoring goals!' The press and media were present in the hundreds, fighting amongst themselves for a mere soundbite from their incoming superstar. Diego's arrival this time around in Catalonia from Argentina, was a far, more, peaceful affair. In fact, film footage of him at Buenos Aires on the way out, he appeared like any other tourist off to visit the sights of the old world, alongside his girlfriend Claudia. No hysterical, biblical scenes of fans screaming out the war cry, 'MARADONNA!' Whilst similar, on arrival in Barcelona, there was hardly any fuss, as the young couple made their way through customs. Oh, the camera crews and Journalist lay in wait, but more out of duty. An air of uncertainty now lay over Diego, who was in many way after Argentina's miserable *Espana 82,* yesterday's news. His crown, like Argentina's had slipped with the shameful, dismissal against Brazil. The jury remained out on the true greatness of Diego Armando Maradona, for his performances in Spain left people with far more questions than answers.

The Camp Nou. As the player's names were being announced over the stadium tannoy, a 60,000 crowd greeted Maradona's with polite applause, but hardly anything like overwhelming support for the new boy. Instead, it was their blond-haired, German midfielder Bernd Schuster, who remained firm favourite amongst the *cules.* Schuster was back to play following a career, threatening injury. After a brilliant start to his Barca career, Schuster's world fell apart in an away match against Athletic Bilbao. He suffered a broken left-knee in the *San Mames,* after a horrendous challenge by defender Andoni Goikoetxea. Later to earn everlasting, infamy in attempting to mutilate Diego Maradona from his ankle. Schuster would later recall how Goikoetxea had been whispering to him throughout the match, 'I'm going to fucking do you.' True to his word, the Basque centre-half carried through the sinister threat. He was already the holder of a notorious reputation, even in such a ruthless league that took no prisoners, Goikoetxea stood apart. The leader on the pitch of this Basque fortress in the northern mountains. A notorious Barca graveyard. Now, fully recovered a beaming Schuster waved to the adoring masses as they cheered wildly his name. It was clear

Maradona had some way to go before being held in the same regard as the German.

One definitely not happy with the Argentinian's signing was Barca's third allowed overseas' player, the Danish superstar striker Allan Simonsen. With only two foreigners permitted to start, Simonsen was convinced his time left at the *Camp Nou*, barring injuries to Maradona or Schuster would be spent on the bench. As a former European player of the year and still only twenty-nine, the electric-heeled Simonsen was already looking at getting away. Talks with President Nunez had begun about having his contract annulled as a gesture of good faith for three relatively, successful goal-scoring seasons. He had taken it as a personal insult when Diego Maradona was signed, for a fabulous footballer who lit up the *Camp Nou* whenever called upon, Simonsen had no wish to remain and be sacrificed at the altar of FC Barcelona. Bitterness, hurt pride and no little anger at this obvious push towards the door meant his career in the *Blaugrana* was all but finished.

Smiling and joking with his new team mates Diego Maradona appeared relaxed, ready to make a mark. To prove his worth and fee, to silence the many critics. Already he had become close to several of the players. Marcos Alonso amongst them, 'The first day he arrived in the dressing room, he picked up some rolled-up socks and started to do, oh, I don't know, a thousand keepie-uppies or more, we thought, if he can do that with some socks?' One who Diego become extremely friendly with was twenty-three-year-old winger Francisco Carrasco. The two shared a room at the Barca training camp in Andorra. The Alicante born Carrasco was impressed by the affable Maradona. His sense of humour and humility, a seemingly, utter lack of arrogance. A proper team player. The two soon became inseparable, full of pranks, their friendship one of the few aspects of his time at Barca remembered fondly by Diego. 'My accomplice,' he later said with a smile, when asked about him. Carrasco couldn't help but fret about his new Argentinian *compadre,* for the merciless pressure that came from adorning the *Blaugrana* shirt, had at times threatened to overwhelm and drown him. Carrasco knew compared to what would be expected of Diego, his experiences would be lightweight. He could sense trouble coming down the line, for the demanding Catalans would insist that in the *Camp Nou,* Maradona performed a miracle or two in every match. Anything less, they would howl and abuse. Also, he worried that Diego's wild off-field antics with the clan, whom had now joined him was a slow, burning fuse, that in time would explode. A young boy already rich beyond his wildest dreams, out and about in a city, where rich desires and dark temptations lurk with the power to bring to heel, kings and princes. Never mind a kid from the slums who could kick a ball around. Carrasco spoke to Maradona about how he had to take care when in the clubs and nightspots of Barcelona. For if you were struggling on the pitch, that would be the bullet used to try and kill you.

…One has only to recall the sad ballad of Hugo Sotil…

In 1973, Barca signed from South America an unpredictable, young Peruvian footballer Hugo Sotil, who when on fire could rip apart any defence in the world with his dancing feet and dribbling ability. Sotil was that rare breed, he played with a smile and true sense of drama and was adored by the *cules* for doing so. For him the game like life itself was fun. No one, not he or his team mates, the crowd, or most importantly the opposition knew what was coming next. Alongside the majestic Dutch master Johan Cruyff and Catalan hero Carlos Rexach, the charismatic Sotil helped destroyed Real Madrid 5-0 in a historic massacre, that is still spoken of today in hushed awe around the city.

Sotil also loved to party, he even more loved to drink. The dance floor to him just a natural extension of a pitch. A love of the ladies, matched only by a ball. A taste for alcohol that sadly became all-consuming. In time the magic waned a little, as the consumption took hold. The cheers turned to jeers, the ballad of Hugo Sotil turned sad, as he was cast out and replaced by another great Dutch superstar, Johan Neeskens. Discarded like a lame dog that no longer made his owner smile sent packing. Sotil left broken, a tragic tale of a footballer blinded by the dangerously, tempting, bright lights of Barcelona.

Carrasco feared greatly for his new friend...

Diego Maradona's initial attempts to settle into his new environment was hardly helped by constant disagreements, running battles with the Barca coach, forty-seven-year-old strict, German disciplinarian Udo Lattek. Following a year in charge, Lattek retained the temporary trust of his President. Arriving in Barca after success at Bayern Munich and Borussia Monchengladbach, the intelligent, utterly, single-minded Lattek was under no illusions of the task ahead. Daunting enough that he followed in the exalted footsteps of the Barca, legendary, figure Helenio Herrera, Lattek would also be at the mercy of a trigger-happy Nunez, desperate for immediate success. He had made it known to the German that there could be no excuses for failure in the coming season, it was the title or

the sack. Doing it his way, Lattek would either prosper at the *Camp Nou,* or suffer the inevitable. With this mindset he set about dealing with the magical, but for him, extremely, irritating new Argentinian. Theirs' was a tale of two continents, two worlds' apart. A clash of cultures, personalities. Though widely regarded as a forward-thinking revolutionary, Lattek was no Cesar Menotti, he ruled with an iron fist. For him the so-called beautiful game was a myth, wishful, foolish talk by old footballing romantics who refused to let go of the past. In the early eighties, counter-attacking football won leagues and trophies. It was all about speed and power, serious raw strength. Just ask the Brazilians? Already, this theory was being proved correct by the Basque triumphs in overhauling the old order of Madrid and Barcelona. For Lattek, the time of the artist, of flair and guile was drawing to a close. Attitudes such as these were hardly likely to endear him to a free spirit like Maradona, whose reluctance to conform to Lattek's coaching methods infuriated him. An insistence on hours upon hours just spent on the running track in training left Diego despairing. He would also be made to run from goal to goal with a medicine ball under each arm weighing eight kilos each. As the season began, the bigger the game, the more weight in the medicine balls was increased. Come the Real Madrid clashes, they were doubled! Maradona simply craved for a ball, that was his lifeblood, the touch and the feel of it, all being denied him by his new *Mister.* Silently, he fumed, when would they realize that Diego Maradona was a footballer,
not a fucking weight lifter.
 In training Diego found himself knocked about in training by his new team mates like a spinning top. So ferocious

and physically demanding was Udo Lattek's pre-season preparation, the Argentinian felt like he was being readied to go to war, not to play football. 'In the training sessions you could easily end up getting kicked in the mouth!' recalled Diego. This wasn't football. Everything was alien to what Maradona had ever experienced-he was used to a pre-match ritual that involved plenty of rest and concentration on ball work. With Lattek, Diego was lucky if he ever saw one. In an effort to stamp total authority over the training ground, Udo Lattek also made a point of confronting Jorge Cyterszpiler on his daily trips in with Maradona. Lattek told the agent he was no longer welcome. With the coach receiving Nunez's full backing, not wanting to appear big time in front of his new *compadres*, Maradona had little choice but to take this one punch on the chin. A small victory, one of the few moments when Lattek's bark was heeded by Diego. For him, no big deal, for further down the line there would be much bigger battles to be fought.

Whilst huge scepticism over Diego Maradona's huge transfer fee remained rife in Catalonia and most notably Madrid. If these same cynics had been lucky enough to witness him up close during training sessions, their opinion might have been somewhat different. For they would argue Barca had indeed got themselves a bargain. Many a time his fellow players were left open-mouthed, applauding as in an attempt to impress, the new boy turned on the style. One instance captured by television cameras brought even a half smile to the otherwise, permanently, growling expression of Udo Lattek.

Stood behind a small five-a-side goal, Diego Maradona helped himself from a bag of footballs, before chipping one over to land on the other side. As a watching crowd looked on in astonishment, a laughing Maradona put out his arms, as if pleading with it to return. Then, as if attached by string, the ball suddenly spun and rolled back into the goal! Stood next to Maradona that day was Barca left-back Julio Alberto. Talking later about Diego's conjuring tricks Alberto remained in awe, 'Diego was a magician. Some of his tricks left us scratching our heads. His left foot was the equal to any wand.'

On Monday 8th August 1983, Diego Maradona's opening appearance for FC Barcelona came away against lowly German side SV Meppen. A 5-0 rout ensued in the *Hindenburg* stadium, with Maradona scoring a penalty before being replaced at half-time. However, the real action began six weeks later on Saturday 4th September 1982, when Barcelona travelled down south to Valencia, as the league re-commenced.

The line-up. Artola, Gerardo, Migueli, Alexanco, Manolo, Victor, Urbano Schuster, Quini, Maradona and Marcos.

Playing in the opposing white strip was Maradona's Argentinian team mate, goalscoring legend, Mario Kempes. He had returned to Valencia after being sold to River Plate two years earlier, the fans welcoming him back with open arms. The two shared an embrace on the pitch beforehand. Kempes wishing his *compadre* the best of luck, but only after they had left Valencia! In a pulsating contest at the intimidating *Mestella*, Barca finally went down 2-1, this after Diego had put them in front after twenty minutes. A scramble in the box saw the ball finally falling loose to Maradona's left foot and from fifteen yards out he drilled a low-shot past the keeper Sempere into the corner of the net. Maradona was off and running. Bernd Schuster should have doubled the visitor's lead shortly after, but uncharacteristically, the German mishit from just six yards-a let off for Valencia. Moments after the interval, the game was level when the home defender Miguel Tendillo charged upfield and raced unmarked through the middle of a sleeping, Barca rearguard to equalize. The game continued with opportunities at both ends, Maradona flirted in and out, well-marked-brutally when required, a quiet debut apart from the goal, then, disaster for the visitors ten minutes from time, when Valencia's Santiago Idigoras headed home the winner from a free kick. 2-1 and the *Mestella* erupted!

Catalan disappointment at this opening defeat was huge, their mood miserable. Off the pitch that week, a lousy atmosphere enveloped all at the *Camp Nou*. A midweek fixture away in Florence against Fiorentina hardly helped, a 0-0 draw, one of many friendlies President Nunez had lined up to recoup the Maradona transfer fee. It was Boca Juniors revisited-contracted to a series of what appeared a never-ending stream of matches, with Diego the number one attraction worldwide, Barca would be constantly flying everywhere to some far destination earning huge bucks. To pay for Maradona, Nunez would use Maradona, simple as. Pure economics.

An ill wind blew over the *Camp Nou* on the morning of Barca's opening home fixture again Rayo Valladolid, when Diego Maradona refused point blank to partake in a team walk! Choosing instead to remain in the hotel room and reserve his energy for the game. Lattek's appearance at his door demanding Maradona joined in, cut no ice with him, 'I don't walk,' claimed Diego, who received surprised and much appreciated backing from his team mate Bernd Schuster, claiming it was a 'Stupid idea.' An angry Lattek raged, 'There will be sanctions,' only for the Catalan born, club Captain, Jose Sanchez, who had been stood watching outside the room, with fellow defender Migueli, replying to Lattek, 'Oh, no *Mister*, there will be no sanctions.' Not willing to risk the wrath of open revolution, a fall out at such an early stage of the campaign with the Captain and his two leading players, Lattek backed down. A huge loss of face. Even though the season was just one game gone, a chasm of mistrust had already come to exist between Maradona and his coach, that would only widen as time went on. Troubling early times.

Later that day at a nervous, heavily, expectant *Camp Nou,* Barca took out any feelings of frustration against an unfortunate Rayo Valladolid to hammer them 3-0 and welcome into their midst a new hero. Beforehand, the tension of the occasion laid etched on Diego Maradona's face, as he waited nervously for the game to begin. On this day, so far away from home. Compared to Barcelona, Villa Fiorito might as well have existed on another planet. Here, for Diego, it truly began. He had a point to prove and was desperate to show these doubting Catalans just what their dollars had bought. They didn't have to wait long for within a minute Maradona had left two Rayo defenders for dead, before crossing low for Barca's number eleven Marcos to slam home at the near post. Hitting the *Camp Nou* ground running, Diego Maradona proceeded to rip apart the visitors. The white shirts of Rayo treated like training cones, as he tore time and again down the left-hand side, providing ample opportunities for his wasteful *compadres.* Right on half-time, Maradona converted a penalty to double the score, a ridiculously confident effort, as he slid a left-foot shot low into the net. The torture for Rayo Valladolid continued long after the break, as every time the Barca new boy received the ball, gasps of expectations swept across the vast terraces of the *Camp Nou*. He was simply unplayable, dribbling down the right wing, before whispering 'Adios' into the ear of full-back Pepin and off he flew! Racing at blistering speed into the area, Maradona noticed Pichi Alonso unmarked and his inch-perfect cross was finished with aplomb.

3-0, as an opening performance in the *Blaugrana,* on this arguably the greatest club stage in world football. This Catalan cathedral of dreams where they gathered to worship, but also to destroy, if the mood arose, Diego Armando Maradona had brought the house down.

The new kid was off and running.

Four days later, they hit another eight against Apollon Limassol, from Cyprus, in the European Cup Winners Cup. Three for Maradona, a brace for Schuster, as they tortured the Cypriots throughout. The two players performing, as if telepathic, whilst plying their magic on that rarefied plane high above mere mortals on a pitch. A quickness of body and mind, the sleight of foot, the hidden pass that makes idiots of good defenders, buffoons of ordinary ones. Now, as Maradona cut loose with Schuster alongside him, the *cules* truly began to realise what all the fuss was about. So began an unbeaten run that saw Barca fighting it out at *La Liga's* summit with Real Madrid and the new order of Basques, Real Sociedad and Athletic Bilbao. Sadly, for Maradona, a muscle problem saw him sidelined for three matches, but he returned on the bench for the derby match against Espanol at the *Camp Nou*.

An hour of frustration followed, as their city neighbour dug deep and defended for their lives in an effort to defy their more illustrious, ultra-powerful, big brother. As the game wore on and frustrations rose to furious decibels,

Diego Maradona urged his coach to throw him on, but even though personally he had little time for Diego, Udo Lattek wasn't prepared to risk his main asset in a game he still felt confident of stealing. However, as the clock ticked ever further down and with no sign of Barca making a breakthrough, Carrasco was withdrawn and to deafening applause, on came Maradona.

The effect on both the home side and crowd was immediately inspiring. As if ignited by an electrical current, he sparked and flitted around the penalty area, unable to dispossess and suddenly the movement that came from his positioning caused gaping holes. The by-now, close to exhausted, Espanol defenders, for so long content to just sit deep fending off incessant, but predictable Barca pressure, suddenly discovered they had a dervish on their hands. Only nine minutes remained for the *Periquitos* to take a priceless point from Barca, when, almost inevitably, the fans rose from their seats as Maradona fed in Marcos and the day was won.

With Diego Maradona fit again, Barca were on fire! No more so than when they crushed a fine Red Star Belgrade 4-2 away in the European Cup Winners Cup. A performance that shone like a beacon. Two goals apiece from Diego Maradona and Bernd Schuster giving hints that Udo Lattek's side was coming together much faster than many expected. Maradona in particular was imposing his technique and ability to set the tempo of a match onto a Barca crammed with those willing to die for the cause, but maybe lacking that creative spark. Such as Viktor, Alonso and Carrasco, all high-quality footballers, full of furious running, fine technique, and determination. Archetypal Lattek-style players, but with Maradona, and Schuster adding the fantasy, the Catalans suddenly began to resemble a fearful proposition. A 2-1 second leg victory at the *Camp Nou,* saw Barca comfortably through, but it was what occurred in Belgrade that will live long in the memory.

A Maradona goal of such sublime quality and vivid imagination that even the fanatical Red Star supporters, despite spitting blood rage found themselves applauding for a full two minutes. An astonishing moment that stunned all present in the Yugoslav *Marakana*. It came after forty-seven minutes to put Barca 2-0 up. After running through from the half-way line, Diego noticed the Red Star goalkeeper Stojanovic slightly off his line and executed a chip-shot of unerring precision over the dumbstruck Yugoslav's head. Stojanovic could do nothing, but watch and shrug his shoulders. The travelling Barca *cules* basked in the happy glow of such a thrilling performance by their team. They argued that not only did they possess the world's greatest player in Diego Maradona, but also had the second with Bernd Schuster. For generations past the *Camp Nou* was home to true legends of the game. Samiter, Kubala, Czibor, Cruyff and Neeskens. This glittering Belgrade display offered proof that the two present incumbents for potential hall of fame, albeit precariously early in Maradona's case, were already proving worthy successes to the heroes of year's past.

As ever, despite having the ability to turn water into wine on a football pitch, off it, trouble followed Maradona like an unwanted shadow. His battle with Udo Lattek on-going, Lattek referred to his star player as 'Este chico Diego' ('This kid, Diego), with the resigned air of a coach knowing he was wasting his time.

With a genius came a certain arrogance when dealing with men such as Udo Lattek, whose attempts to make them change was always doomed to failure. Imagine lecturing Mozart or Morricone to tone it down a little, telling Caruso or Pavarotti you need to cut out the fucking passion...Birds were meant to fly, Maradona was never going to change.

Lattek won the odd skirmish, one time he simply had enough and fuck the consequences with the President, Cyterszpiler, or who else from this cesspit of Catalan and Argentinian ego's, that would come screaming in his face. Driven to distraction by Maradona's couldn't give a flyin' attitude to timekeeping, the German ordered the team bus to drive off for an away fixture without their star player. 'Once, he didn't turn up on time when the team were due to leave. I had two options, wait for him and lose my authority, or go without,' recalled Lattek, years later. 'A small victory for me, but he won in the end.'

Feeling tired and in need of rest, Diego asked his coach if he could have some time off to recharge batteries? After being told of Maradona's request, President Nunez flatly refused. Happy to inform Diego of this reply, Lattek did nothing more than laugh in the player's face when doing so. Civil war loomed in Barca's ranks and all would erupt on an infamous Paris evening. The beginning of the end for Udo Lattek and a reminder for Nunez that not only did they have a genius on their books with Maradona, they had also acquired for a world record fee, a ticking time bomb.

On Sunday 13th November 1983, FC Barcelona were due in Paris for another friendly match against Paris St Germain. However, the same morning doubts arose as to whether Diego Maradona would travel for the player had gone on strike! There was just one demand, that every Barca player going to France, including substitutes, be paid the same win bonus as he. If not, then Maradona wasn't going. Non-negotiable. Pay up. Knowing the French would complain bitterly if they turned up minus their star attraction-the one who the Parisians were all coming out to watch. That the good name of FC Barca would be tarnished, as would more importantly their bank balance, Maradona got his wish. Left with no option, irate club officials agreed to Diego's blatant blackmail and he happily boarded the plane to a standing ovation from his team mates!

That evening at the *Parc Des Prince*, a full house was treated to a sumptuous display from a Barca team proving more than worthy of their additional win bonuses. A 4-1 victory not doing them justice, as they slaughtered the home side. At its beating heart, Maradona was magnificent. He appeared reinvigorated basking in the warm glow of his *compadre's* good feelings towards him and the small matter of knowing that somewhere, back in Barcelona, Nunez would be besides himself with anger. Yet, still he had not finished with the President, for the night wasn't over. The bright lights of the Parisian night was calling, Diego Maradona was in the mood for a party!

Totally ignoring orders from both the fuming coach, Lattek and Barca directors, he gathered around him travelling clan members and team mates to descend like Vikings upon the Parisian nightspots. Anarchy had come to FC Barcelona. The festivities lasted till dawn and come the following morning, all had been captured by the *paparazzi*. Also, French and Catalan journalists whom tracked them throughout. Every club, disco and strip joint. They clicked, snapped and watched on in disbelief. He didn't, he couldn't, he wouldn't dare? He did!

Diego Armando Maradona. No rules.

As the wine flowed, pills popped and tongues loosened, stories so wild it would not have surprised the Catalan news editors to wake next morning and discover they were at war with France. On being awoken and told of the breaking news as it occurred, President Nunez felt he was in the midst of a Diego Maradona nightmare. Raging, he issued a statement personally blaming Maradona. Measured, but in itself so damming, Nunez may as well have placed an apple on the player's head for journalists to shoot at.

'I will have a word with Diego Maradona, because our fans want to see impeccable behaviour off the pitch.'

Like a red flag to a bull with a toothache, Maradona immediately hit back,

'I will do anything, or go out anywhere I want. So long as it does not damage my capacity as an athlete on the pitch, it is no one else's concern.'

In an attempt to act as peacemaker, Jorge Cyterszpiler phoned President Nunez and asked him why on earth he had come out blaming just Diego, when so many more were involved? 'Because I am the boss,' came Nunez's terse retort. To which Cyterszpiler replied, 'You are also a son of a bitch!' before slamming down the phone.

Blessed are the peacemakers.

An intolerable situation simmered on affecting all in the *Camp Nou*. Barca's next game, a hugely, frustrating 2-2 draw at home to Celta Vigo was greeted with derision and cat calls from a Catalan crowd clearly unimpressed with the antics of their team and still unsure where their true feeling lay in regards to alleged ring-leader Diego Maradona. A late, face-saving penalty equaliser by Diego, not sufficient to prevent his car being attacked by angry *cules* on leaving the stadium. A worrying incident that left

deep, mental scars on him. For it was suggested by Cyterszpiler, maybe this had been more than just some hot heads angry at Maradona, for besmirching the good name of FC Barcelona. That instead it was a political act meant to teach him a lesson? If so, it worked to only stiffen Maradona's stance that he wouldn't be controlled. For as free spirits go, attempting to silence Diego was akin to capturing lightning in a bottle. Luckily, fast coming into sight an occasion to focus all hearts and minds. One that bonded those with Barca in their hearts like nothing else. An old friend awaited their arrival in Madrid.
El Clasico had shown its wary face.

CHAPTER FORTY TWO
THROWING ROCKS AT GHOSTS

It was said to be payback time. A revenge for being the last major city to fall against overwhelming, Nationalist forces. He took their flags and freedom. Barcelona became infested by spies and informers. People scared witless to even think, let alone speak out against the despised Generalissimo Franco. However, there was one place. A sporting arena where Catalans would gather in tens of thousands, in safety of numbers to vent their anger against what had become of their city and Region. *Les Corts,* the, then home of Barca became a Catalan haven to resist. If only through songs and derisory chants aimed towards Franco, it helped to ease the pain for a loss of identity.
So, began the war on the pitch.

It was a welcome that came laced with falsehoods, respected Presidents shaking hands when they would rather wring each other's necks. 'Wipe your feet on the way in. Respect the history, don't touch the silverware, shut the fucking door on your way out.' Politicians, judges, kings even, coaches players and supporters, all stressed days and weeks before with the morbid thought of defeat. Invading every waking moment, the last before sleep. A game so very much more than life itself. Pompous sounding maybe, clichéd without doubt, but true. Where all that matters is to win. Honour and fair play can take a long walk and keep on fucking going. The biggest game in the world.

El Clasico.

…For weeks leading up to the match, Diego Maradona's team mates, the President, every single Catalan he encountered lectured Diego endlessly on the importance of an occasion, that was quite literally death or glory for FC Barcelona. They told him of a city bombed mercilessly during the civil war, over 4700 killed. They told him of a Barca President Josep Sunyol executed at sunrise by a Fascist firing squad. They told him of a people robbed of dignity and identity, as they were forbidden to speak their own language. They told him of the Generalissimo and his favourite football team...

They told him of Real Madrid.

The previous March witnessed the Madrileno's greatest ever player, the legendary Alfredo Di Stefano take the helm at Real Madrid, after a short stint at River Plate. Di Stefano did not have long to wait in welcoming his fellow Argentinian exile to the *Bernabeu*. One already being hailed as heir apparent to the *Blond Arrow,* as their nation's finest ever player. A mantle Di Stefano remained fiercely proud of and was very reluctant to give up. His was a personal, ancient rivalry with the Catalans stemming back four decades...

Once upon a time,

the legendary Real Madrid President Don Santiago Bernabeu, was a man driven by a vision. He envisaged a footballing Camelot carved out of white marble reaching high into the Madrid heavens. Blessed with the vision and wealth to create such beauty, Bernabeu searched for men of sufficient quality to defend its walls. The call went out for the best. Soon, the white knights had gathered under the Madrileno's banner. Yet, despite such riches of talent Bernabeu sought that little extra. The spark to flame the fire. Rumour reached him of a young footballer plying a remarkable talent in the relative backwaters of the Colombian league.

An Argentinian called Alfredo Di Stefano.

In 1953, Don Santiago sent his fixer/maker of dreams Raimondo Saporta to convince Di Stefano his future lay in Madrid. Armed with a suitcase of money and the promise of footballing immortality in the Madrileno white shirt, Saporta arrived in Bogota and swiftly sought him out. Unknown to Saporta, there was another equally desperate to attain Di Stefano's unique services. One who despised Real Madrid, Santiago Bernabeu and everything they stood for. Representatives of FC Barcelona had arrived in Colombia determined to land their target and put one over General Franco's favourite plaything.

With Catalonia suffering the wrath of Franco's, jackboot-nationalism, to rip Di Stefano from Real's grasp at the last would be a small, if sweet victory. A tug of war occurred. Both sides offered treasures, but neither were able to land the esteemed one's signature. Each found legal loopholes to prevent the other succeeding, before finally the Spanish FA stepped in offering Solomon like advice to solve an intolerable stand-off. Alfredo Di Stefano would play two seasons apiece in both Barcelona and Madrid. Left with scant option but agree, the warring parties reluctantly went along and Di Stefano headed for the mountains of Catalonia to begin his Spanish adventure. He began in wretched form for Barcelona and almost immediately whispers were that the Catalans had been sold a fraud. Looking uninterested, sluggish, an impostor, it was quickly agreed this player didn't possess the sufficient quality to play for FC Barca. Contact was made with Madrid, whom were told Di Stefano was available. With unholy haste, a new deal was drawn up and overnight Alfredo Di Stefano became a Real Madrid player. The following week he made his debut for the Madrilenos, against of all teams Barcelona, scoring twice in a 5-0 rout! Di Stefano was magnificent as he covered every blade of grass, constantly marauding, wreaking havoc, then defending when needed. Appearing a class apart, even in such sumptuous company. The Catalans had been fooled. Di Stefano had already been sold the dream by Raimondo Saporta. What occurred in Catalonia simply a ruse to free him from Barca right of contract. So, began a glorious period for Real Madrid, whom orchestrated by Di Stefano, won five Europeans cup in a row.

A team claimed by many as the greatest of them all and still.

A host of wonderful players, beguiling artists. Raymonde Kopa, Francisco Gento and the irascible genius of Ferenc Puskas. Knights in white satin, though none more special than the one who became known as the *Blond Arrow*. That was Di Stefano on the pitch with a ball at his feet. Now, he was forced to depend on eleven others whom could never hope or aspire to play at the same level of himself, Puskas or Gento. Though possessing fine players, international stars such as the German sweeper Uli Stieleke and the

Spanish international forwards, Santillana and Juanito, they were sadly, unlike the great Alfredo's past colleagues, merely human. Whereas, lining up for Barca would be a footballer destined to sit alongside these football kings.

On Sunday 27th November 1982, a magnificent Diego Maradona inspired Barca to a famous 2-0 win against Real Madrid at the *Estadio Bernabeu*, fuelling hopes for the Catalans that this would be the year their championship drought ended. If there had been doubts amongst the *cules* regarding Maradona, they faded a little that night as the kid from Villa Fiorito lit up this grand old stadium of their hated rivals in a manner not witnessed since the likes of Puskas and Alfredo di Stefano. Two classic breakaway goals in each half from Carrasco and their centre-forward Quini won the day. Both were fashioned with wonderful passes by Diego Maradona, as he electrified and ran riot against a Madrid team that simply couldn't handle him. Barca's first began by Bernd Schuster, his blond hair flowing, the German won back possession on the penalty area edge, before feeding a racing Maradona wide on the left wing. Immediately, Diego spotted an unmarked, team mate Esteban Vigo's surging run through the middle and Vigo's inch-perfect pass put the Barca midfielder Carrasco clear to round Real keeper Agustin, before unleashing a flashing drive high into Madrid's net.1-0. Moments later, Maradona went clear once more leaving white shirts trailing, before setting up Carrasco to hammer a shot straight at the keeper. Then, a stupendous free kick as his effort flew agonisingly close causing gasps from the Madrid crowd. They were petrified, Diego was on fire, slippery than an eel, impossible to mark.
It was like throwing rocks at a ghost.

Barca's much deserved second came on eighty-six minutes. Maradona dribbling clear of four chasing Real players on the half-way line before releasing Quini to run through and finish gloriously with a flighted chip over a stranded Agustin. Barca ruled in Madrid. 2-0, their number nine Quini celebrated by raising both arms to the heavens. For this night they had smiled upon the Catalans. Much as Real Madrid were abject, a pale imitation of the white ghost's past. Destroyed on home turf, their worst nightmares realised. FC Barcelona had been sensational. The game ended for a sorry Madrid with just nine men, as frustration overflowed at being totally outclassed. First to be dismissed was defender Francisco Bonet, for an outrageous tackle on the brilliant Carrasco. Another that night who had terrorised Madrid with his rampaging runs. Then, with seconds remaining, the Dutch midfielder Johnny Metgod was shown a red as he launched a two-footed tackle at Viktor. So incensed was the *Bernabeu* crowd with their team's miserable showing, that come the final whistle, thousands of white cushions were thrown onto the pitch in disgust. It had proved impossible to stomach and any other but Alfredo Di Stefano would have seen their head roll that night in Madrid. Oh, for a *Blond Arrow*?

Above all, ignoring the Madrileno woes and tales of yesteryear, it was a master class from Maradona in the biggest derby of them all, that would long be remembered. Also, whatever personal feelings Di Stefano felt regarding his fellow Argentinian, on a truly shocking night for Real, he never shown it. Despite endless attempts by the Catalan press to trap Diego into saying something derogatory about Di Stefano, not once did he bite. For this was a man he really did hold, like Pele, in the greatest of respect. Diego was cute, savvy, wise enough to know one doesn't bad mouth Argentinian royalty like Don Alfredo and spoke only in whispered tones of reverence regarding the great man. Despite the bitterness of defeat, a dejected Madrid coach made a point of later seeking out Maradona and congratulating him on his outstanding performance. 'Well played Diego,' he said to him. 'Although it was a shame you had to play like that whilst wearing a Barca shirt!'

Seven days later,

the proud Basque champions Real Sociedad were beaten at the *Camp Nou*, courtesy of a fifth minute, Maradona wonder goal. A sublime left-footed finish over Sociedad's international keeper Luis Arconada, into the far corner, before he raced away to accept the acclaim of the roaring Catalan crowd. I love you, I love you not? A passionate affair still in its infancy, too early to call, whether happy ever after, or see you in hell. Destined to tug heart strings, memorable, and painful, for with Maradona there was never no half measures. With the ball priceless, six goals for Diego Maradona in fifteen games may have appeared a fair return on such an enormous investment, nothing more. However, Maradona's positive influence on the pitch, his work ethic and stunning, individual performances astonished even the hardened Catalan critic.

More so impressive, considering the absurdity of all that surrounded him away from the ball…The intensity of a media, whom had become obsessed with his every word and move. The fall outs with Nunez and Lattek. The alleged, widely reported, drug-fuelled-nights down on the *Ramblas*. Partying amongst the beautiful people, Barcelona's jet set, whom watched in disdain as the Argentinians gatecrashed their once, exclusive nightclub VIP areas. Most notably the *Up & Down club*, a playground, unlike any other. Where footballers partied away the midnight hour with drunken politicians, socialites, aspiring actresses and any number of chancers desperate to make a killing. It was here gossip erupted into near meltdown over a reported glazed-eyed Diego Maradona. Tales of coke, white powder...Away from the ball?

Barca spies whom were instructed by their President to follow his every move dreaded reporting back that the man who their club had spent a king's ransom on appeared already out of control. Allegations that when confronted by a furious Nunez, Maradona predictably screamed outrage. Cyterszpiller instructed immediately to threaten libel against any whom dared publish. Away from the ball, nothing but a plague bubbling under.

CHAPTER FORTY THREE
DODGE CITY (THE BANDIDOS!)
'There was no clan, they were just my friends.'
Diego Maradona

FC Barcelona rented for Diego a huge residence in the rich, Catalan neighborhood of Pedralbes. Whilst hardly a village church hall, where the Maradona clan would gather to sing psalms and quote from Bible passages, was, if some of the more outrageous, scandalous, gossip to be believed, an incestuous pit inhabited by Argentinian demons and whores, constantly wasted on drugs and drink! A description wildly, colourful and maybe just a little somewhat off the mark, but there was no doubt some of the Maradona clan's antics that allegedly occurred in Pedralbes, caused even the most open-minded Catalans to shake their heads in disgust. Dark whispers, tall-tales of prostitutes queuing outside to enter, copious amounts of wine and white powder flowing freely. Crazed carrying on's. Orgiastic frenzies the likes hardly associated with the ultra-socialites and serious, minded residents of conservative Pedralbes. Porn movies shown on loop courtesy of a huge cinema screen. Screeching cars way past midnight blasting out music, Jose Iglesias (Maradona's favourite), as they raced through Pedralbes like it was a Grand Prix circuit. The curtain-twitching Catalans seethed. Beavering journalists digging for controversy never had to look hard. The six and a half thousand miles from Buenos Aires to Barcelona, was quite literally half a world away for Diego Armando Maradona, but on *Sant Francesc de Pedralbes street*, there was a little piece of the Catalan capital, that was for a short while, most definitely, his Argentina.

Maradona hated the word clan, but that's exactly what it was, a circle of amigos, an unhealthy concoction overall of the heartfelt good, the very bad and the downright, fucking ugly. From family blood and lifelong *compadres* who would die for Diego, to those along for what they could get, to outright shysters. The mansion was home to three floors, ten bedrooms, a tennis court and a giant size swimming pool, that had been repainted at Maradona's request, in FC Barca colours. Here the pampas cowboys partied, cavorted and for a while turned an elegant, sleepy, tranquil, small area of Barcelona into an Argentinian Dodge city.

The music was turned up twenty-four hours a day.

A madhouse!

At any time there could be thirty or forty people around the place. These made up mostly of girlfriend, Claudia, parents, Tota and Chitoro, (occasionally). Diego's brother's Lalo and Hugo, sister, Maria with her husband Gabriel Esposito. The masseur/ pill man, Miguel Di Lorenzo who was known as Galindez, after the famous Argentinian light heavyweight World Champion boxer of the seventies, adored by Diego Maradona. Di Lorenzo had known Maradona since he was a young colt at Argentinos Juniors, the two were close. Miguel was also the double of Galindez, hence the nickname! Like Diego, the boxer Galíndez hailed from the Buenos Aires ghettos. He was forced to retire at just thirty-one, after a great career, because of two operations to repair his detached retinas. Galindez then tried to pursue his other dream of becoming a stock-car race pilot. On 25 October 1980, he participated in what would be his first and last *Turismo Carretera race.* (A popular, touring car racing series in Argentina). After going to the pit for repairs, Galíndez was struck by a car that lost control, he was killed instantly, a death riddled in controversy. Galindez became a folk hero in Argentina and for Maradona, a true hero.

Also living in the mansion, Jorge Cyterszpiler, with a Spanish girlfriend, his brother Silvio, plus a cameraman working for Cyterszpiler, who was following Diego around for a film being made by *Maradona Productions.* An old amigo from the Cebollitas days, Osvaldo Dalla Buona and many others of various acquaintances, friends of friends, not forgetting a huge staff of caretakers, cooks, gardeners and two maids!

This was no happy household where everybody lived and loved together in peace and harmony, like a Carpenters song. It was vile and nasty, bitter rivalries, paranoia and petty jealousies existed. There were two sides constantly fighting for the boss's attention. Those of Claudia's, much more prudent trying to rein in the excesses taking place in

Diego's name. The amount of paper iou's left across Barcelona in his name were simply outrageous. Claudia was driven to ensure that no bastard took her boyfriend and future husband for a fucking ride. Then, there was the nemesis, Jorge Cyterszpiler. Both slaves to love for Maradona's charms, with different ways to his heart. She wanted rid of Jorge, a mistrust based on what she saw occurring around her. The beautiful mansion in Pedralbes hardly fit to call a home, despite its splendour. She knew those with their hands in the till and though Claudia could never claim that of Cyterszpiler, she thought him not worthy of looking after Diego's money. Especially, when in time it would become hers to worry about. As for Jorge, he longed understood of her feelings towards him and had been paying Maradona's brother-in-law, Gabriel, to spy on Claudia, whilst he was out and about in Barcelona and beyond on business. It was through this Cyterszpiler discover that Claudia wanted to fire him and put Maradona's Father in his position. As families go, it was enough to make the Borgias appear functional, as for Diego?

The change in him had become apparent since landing in Catalonia, for there was already a touch of the Caesar about *El Pelusa*-which when you consider people had been falling at his feet since he was ten-years-old could well be understandable. In Argentina, it started to show as the world media closed in to become all-consuming. At home he would be the same charming, generous, child-like even Diego, doting on Tota and Chitoro and immediate family, but once back in the public eye dealing with the other reality, the fame, then the shutters came down. The Maradona who was a force of nature, the Diego of still, Villa Fiorito. Two different people in one body. Now, in

Barcelona it had become hard to see where one started and the other began. Each day surrounded by knaves paying homage, on waking up in the morning and standing in front of the mirror, just who did he see? The young, happy-go-lucky Diego from times past, or the one who had to be obeyed at all cost? His every wish, whim catered for. If he wanted the moon Jorge Cyterszpiler would've bought him the fucking moon. 'You are the greatest Diego.'

'They don't deserve you Diego,'

'You can have anything, or anyone you want Diego, anyone?'

The story went Maradona desired Princess Caroline of Monaco. She was said to be at the time, 'His great passion'. Diego had an idea. He ordered Cyterszpiler to convince President Nunez to organise a friendly in Monaco and then he could make his move! Nothing ever came of Maradona's romantic notions, but it did show the mindset that he now possessed.

Then there was the other girls…They always came from Madrid, hostesses brought to Barcelona through a travel agency employed by the club at that time. An unnamed source who lived at the house claimed, 'They said that they brought them to Diego, who was the one who was responsible for the expenses, but in reality they were for us.'

Dodge City indeed…

Just when all appeared to be coming together for Diego Maradona on the pitch, disaster struck when he was diagnosed with Hepatitis, in early December. It was a Barca doctor Carles Bestit, Diego Maradona had been seeing over a sprained ankle who suddenly noticed something not right with the player's eyes and had him sent for immediate blood tests. Doctor Bestit visited Diego at home with the results that he had Hepatitis and that a lengthy period of recuperation would be required, just as he was finding his feet. Maradona was horrified with the news. He was starting to feel good vibes on the pitch, an understanding with team mates, a togetherness that came only in the midst of battle. Diego's diagnosis went down with President Nunez like the demise of a close relative. Appearing weary, unshaved, unkempt even and flanked by a seething Nunez and a solemn Jorge Cyterszpiler, Maradona announced his illness at a live television press conference. He viewed the vast majority of Catalan media outlets as Nunez puppets. Mouthpieces for the constant lies and slander about him that filled their daily headlines. Not all was true. As to how the Hepatitis came about? For the entire twelve weeks he was ill, they surrounded his Mansion. Watching, waiting and praying for the hint of a scandal to print. If none occurred, the problem was solved easily by making it up. Diego Maradona bit back only once, despite the insane number of untruths wrote. It occurred when alleged by one gossip rag that it wasn't Hepatitis, but indeed Gonorrhea he was suffering from? Then, Cyterszpiler acted for this had to be shot down fast and very swiftly the article was removed. In later years Maradona admitted his drug taking began seriously in Barcelona, the stories once thought incredulous, now appear to have had real credence.

Diego's three months, enforced absence seriously affected matters on the field for Barca and by the time he returned in mid-March, there was a new face at the helm of FC Barcelona. The authoritarian Udo Lattek had lasted just over twelve months, before bad results tested President Nunez's patience and once more he snapped. Lattek was not helped by fellow countryman Bernd Schuster, referring to him in a newspaper interview as a drunk. A proud man, Lattek hurt badly on being axed by Nunez, always claiming like the rest, he wasn't given enough time. However, behind the scenes his unpopularity knew no bounds, few were sorry to see him depart. The endgame arrived following a despairing 2-0 defeat at the *Camp Nou,* to lowly Racing Santander. The final match in a disastrous run which also included humiliation in the UEFA Super cup, against unlikely European champions Aston Villa. A trophy specifically targeted by Nunez, who in his mind, if won handed much needed prestige to FC Barcelona on foreign shores. After a narrow 1-0 win in the *Camp Nou,* courtesy of an Alonso strike, the Catalans travelled to *Villa Park* and in a bad tempered contest with three players sent off, (Allan Evans for Villa, Julio Alberto and Marco Alonso for Barca), they held out until the eightieth minute, when Villa's blond striker Gary Shaw levelled the tie with a precise, low-drive past Javier Urruti. As the Catalans tired badly in extra time, they came under tremendous pressure from the English champions, whom deservedly scored twice more through a Gordon Cowan's penalty that was originally saved by Urruti, but Cowans followed in to score. They were finally finished off by a diving header from Scottish centre-half Ken McNaught. It had been an embarrassing night for FC Barcelona. The heavy defeat and the shabby, petulant behaviour of their players, left the huge Barca travelling contingents angered and ashamed. None more than their President who that night began the search for Lattek's successor. The German was a dead man walking.

El Flaco received the call.

President Nunez proved a man of his word, for in came the by-now, former Argentinian World Cup, winning manager Cesar Menotti, who having grown sick of the criticism, in the bitter fall-out of their disastrous campaign resigned. A promise made by Nunez to Menotti that his efforts in persuading Diego Maradona to sign for Barca was honoured. This, a man so monumentally different to Lattek, both in personality and footballing beliefs. Menotti's magnificent achievement in leading Argentina to a first World Cup meant he would be forever remembered as a legend on home soil, but memories fade, the vicious treatment he received in post-Argentina, *Espana 82*, shown how fickle the game, life could be. The Catalans came calling and Cesar joined Maradona in Barcelona.

Menotti set his teams out to play a high-pressing system with defenders pushing forward to constantly keep opponents pinned back. A swashbuckling, tactical approach, that fit like a glove the attacking talent at his disposal in Barcelona. This Nunez was looking for after the rigid, tactical set ups of Lattek. He so needed to appease the *cules*. Also, Menotti's appearance at the *Camp Nou* meant a smile was never far away from Maradona's face, for despite the age gap, these two men were kindred spirits and had grown close over the years. Diego was a follower of *Menottism*, Cesar called the game, 'A joyous fiesta in which human beings must participate, because it expresses their feelings and delivers the happiness of being alive. I want to win because my team played better, not because I stopped the other team from playing.' They also shared a love of the the Catalan forbidden fruits. After dark, away from *paparazzi* camera clicks and prying eyes. A secret world leaving nothing to the imagination, that *El Flaco* adored. It was alleged that the reason he changed

Barca's training hours was to fit in his more extracurricular activities. Menotti moved training sessions to the afternoons and early evenings, citing 'Biorhythms.' When in reality it was more so he and Maradona could sleep off their previous night's antics.

…Cocaine? 'The first time I took it was in a Barcelona night club, I felt like Superman.' In later years, Diego admitted Barcelona was where it all began. 'It was the biggest mistake I've ever done in my life.' His amigo and Barca team mate Carrasco claimed it was only on the last night before leaving for Naples that Diego partook, but too many had already hinted the white powder was being lined up for Maradona well before the Neapolitans came calling from the Italian south. 'I did it because I thought it was smart. Lots of players were doing it.' So successfully was Diego in covering up his cocaine habit, that the city's lord mayor paid him to co-operate in an anti-drugs campaign. Diego Maradona was twenty-two-years old and felt invincible, what was a little coke well away from the pitch, when everywhere he and his Argentine posse frequented was drowning in it? Cocaine was the beloved, preferred drug of the Catalan upper classes-the chosen music of the Barca night throbbed, bounced and danced to it. The temptation for Diego to partake as he entered the bars and clubs flanked with his amigos from the new world, irresistible. This prince of the slums amongst the Catalan partying elite with a gift from God to almost make him their equal. Almost. For to them he was still a *Sudaca*, as was those surrounding him, new world, new money, Maradona remained a fucking peasant in their eyes. Cocaine...

In January 1983, as Maradona was struggling to recover from the Hepatitis, he received a much-welcomed visit from the new national coach of Argentina, forty-five-year-old Carlos Bilardo. A man whose footballing beliefs were in stark contrast to his predecessor Cesar Menotti, who had been at the helm for the previous eight years. *El Flaco's La Nuestra* was set to be replaced with *Bilardism*, a back to the future style of play, given an eighties makeover, a 3-5-2, tactical set-up. A devoted pupil of the dark arts and former huge player of the infamous, successful, Estudiantes team of the late sixties that brought new meaning to the words, win-at-all-cost. Adored by their supporters, reviled elsewhere. Carlos Bilardo had travelled to Barcelona with a double purpose in mind, one to break bread with Diego Maradona and two, tell him he wanted Diego to be his Captain for the new era. The ruthless Bilardo's plan was to build a team around its talisman, Diego-fresh blood. Legendary names, World Cup winners, champions-all set to be jettisoned. This decision to cut loose players such as Daniel Passarella and Alberto Tarantini, saw Bilardo fall out spectacularly with Cesar Menotti. Two men whose initial attempts to produce a united front, such was their totally differing, footballing ideologies, was never going to last. It didn't and the two would be constantly at each other's throats in the years to follow. Fully appreciative of Carlos Bilardo's support at a time when he was at a new low, Diego Maradona agreed wholeheartedly to take on the Captaincy. For him there could be no higher accolade. The kid from Villa Fiorito set to lead his nation in their qualification group for Mexico 86. Undoubtedly, Diego's star had slipped and once more he had mountains to move in his quest proving to the many doubters that Maradona remained the greatest player in the world, despite the painful experience of *Espana 82.*

On Thursday 3rd March 1983, Diego returned to action after the Hepatitis bout, against Real Betis in the *Camp Nou.* Looking far short of fitness, his touch heavy, passing constantly going astray. It was apparent this dreadful, draining disease had taken a heavy toll of Diego and there were none more frustrated, and angry than he at not being able to do what normally came naturally. His mood made worse with Barca's inability to beat Betis, who escaped with a 1- 1 draw. All adding to what was a miserable Catalan evening. Post-match, a desperately worried Maradona was told by Menotti to 'Calm down.' That despite what was written in newspapers, or spoken about on the television, he was only human. Wise word for his young countryman, 'Stay cool Diego, because the magic will return.'

The first real test for Cesar Menotti's reign as coach arrived on Saturday 26th March 1983, when Real Madrid travelled to the *Camp Nou,* determined to extract revenge for the 2-0 loss on home soil. Goodwill in Madrid towards their coach Alfredo Di Stefano still shone bright, but even someone of his standing, and magnitude would fall under increasing pressure if they lost again. Far as the *cules* of Barca were concerned, another victory against the Madrilenos, then Cesar Menotti, could lie in bed all day and party till the sun shone over the Catalan mountains. There was no greater, or sweeter bloodied head on a platter than Real Madrid. To deliver a double would see massive amounts of good grace handed to Menotti. This was a rivalry that went so much deeper, a war on a pitch, they were soldiers in football boots and not with guns anymore.

Franco may have died eight years earlier back in 1975, but his dark, foreboding, Fascist shadow forever drew a veil over *El Clasico*. So much death, so many bad memories.

In 1943, Barcelona and Real Madrid met in the semi-finals of the Spanish cup, shamelessly renamed in Franco's honour as the *Generalissimo's Cup*. The first leg at *Les Corts,* saw Barca gloriously hammer the Madrilenos 3-0, to the delight of an adoring Catalan crowd. Mocked mercilessly throughout, hammered out of sight, Real Madrid returned to the capital in disgrace. Two weeks later Barca travelled to the *Estadio Chamartin* and shortly before kick- off, their team received a special visitor in the dressing room. The murderous, chief of security state police, Jose Finat y Escriva de Romani. A man with more blood on his hands than a war surgeon told the terrified footballers that they were only allowed to play because of General Franco's generosity. He had forgiven temporarily their lack of patriotism on display in the first game. In other words, they tried too hard to win? Now, in front of the General they had been given a second chance. He pointed out three of the Catalans in the Barca side whom had left Spain during the civil war. Domenec Balmanya, Josep Raich and Josep Escola. They sat in horror as the chief told them the files regarding their suspicious disappearances may be reopened. The message clear, blatant and obvious. Lose. In such threatening circumstances, Barca were crushed 11-1.

The game began badly in the *Camp Nou* for FC Barcelona, when Real forward Juanito, struck with just twenty minutes gone to silence the home crowd. Hated by the *cules* for his constant barbs towards the Catalans, few enjoyed scoring against the *Blaugrana* more than Juan

Gomez Gonzalez. Juanito. 100,000 watched in mortal horror as the white ghouls celebrated on their sacred turf. Like uninvited guests at a Catalan wedding they had insulted the parents, groped the bridesmaids, drank the best wine and were threatening to stay the night. Redemption arrived moments before half time, when Diego Maradona pounced from close range to flash a diving header past Garcia Remon into the goal.1-1! In that one instance Diego proving that courage as he launched himself, amidst flying Madrileno boots and fearful lunges, was but another string to his golden bow. As the second half wore wearingly on, a raw fear of making a mistake cut deep on both sides. A stalemate occurred with each trying desperately just not to lose. Then, with thirteen minutes remaining, the ball fell to Bernd Schuster, whose raking pass put Maradona away into the penalty area. Running at full speed Diego made it to the goal-line and hooked the ball back into the middle for the Barca forward Periko Alonso. Showing calm and great skill, Alonso controlled and delicately slid past the keeper Garcia Remon, before hammering into the net and igniting the stadium! Mobbed by ecstatic teammates and over enthusiastic ball boys, whom all wrestled him to the floor, Alonso appeared close to tears, when once more visible. The final whistle hailed wild scenes of delight in the *Camp Nou*. Real Madrid were beaten again, Cesar Menotti was set for the evening of his life in the Catalan capital, as *El Flaco* and all of Barcelona were set to party all night long.

CHAPTER FORTY FOUR
FIRE AND WATER

After only finishing fourth in the league, with yet again no sign of truly competing for the title, this for a club

Barca's grandeur was embarrassing once more. So, it was the opportunity to win silverware in the King's Cup against Real Madrid, became all-consuming to save a disastrous season. However, four days before, team preparations for the match were thrown into chaos when Diego Maradona found himself immersed once more in controversy. After being refused permission by President Nunez to play in the great German defender Paul Breitner's testimonial, Diego saw red. Again, the ball was put away and he went back to war with his President. Nunez claimed that Real Madrid had banned their star players from playing in Germany, so, therefore Barca were entitled to do similar and say no to Maradona. Throwing verbal rocks, hurling abuse and name calling ensued between the two, for being told no was something he never took lightly to. Since being ten-years-old, it was a word rarely spoken to him. Nunez could fight dirty and he did so by inviting the Catalan President Heribert Costa to the training ground, where he would speak to Diego, before a mass barrage of Catalan, television, radio and newspaper media. Costa gave Diego an unwanted history lesson on why Real Madrid had to be beaten. How FC Barcelona's pride was at stake, how he must think of nothing, but the King's Cup! Then, the killer line, 'We need you Diego. We need you.'

What could he do after this?

Maradona was livid. He shared many of Breitner's left-wing views, his deep, heartfelt concerns for the less poverished-Diego deemed it such an honour to be asked, along with Bernd Schuster. Whatever, fucking Nunez, his new public enemy number one said, or any other Catalans, Maradona was determined he was going. Only to receive the news off Jorge Cyterszpiler that he had originally handed Maradona's passport over to the club for safe-keeping and now Nunez was refusing to return it. Diego blew a gasket. The feeling being, if the President wanted a war, he was getting one. Set on a confrontation, Maradona with Bernd Schuster alongside him drove to the *Camp Nou,* but on arrival, when he asked if Nunez was around, Diego was originally told the President wasn't there, only to then notice Nunez's car and chauffeur. Maradona insisted, but was then informed that the President had no wish to speak to him. By this time, he was irate and with Schuster alongside headed off to Barcelona's spectacular trophy room. There the two found their path blocked by none other than Diego's old *compadre* Nicolau Casaus. On originally arriving in Barcelona, Maradona stayed with Casaus at his home. He later described him as his 'Second sporting Father'. However, that was then. The two embraced before Diego asked this old man of who he was so fond for his passport back? 'No Diego, I can't, the President doesn't want you to have it.' With blood boiling, Maradona told Casaus they had five minutes to return his passport, otherwise, he would start smashing all the trophies. One, by one. The time passed and with still no sign of it, Diego picked up the Teresa Herrera trophy, an enormous vase won in some long-gone, pre-season tournament and to Casaus' horror, dropped it, smashing the crystal trophy into a thousand pieces. After threatening to break another, two minutes later, a Presidential aide of Nunez shown up with his passport. Mission complete, the two left the *Camp Nou,* watched from afar by a furious President Nunez surely thinking, 'What the fuck have I bought?' Ultimately, Maradona and Schuster never travelled to West Germany to play in Breitner's testimonial, due to the Spanish football Federation intervening and inventing a clause. For Diego though, a round well one on points against Nunez, but it was clearly going to be a long and bloody fight.

Already resigned to an inevitable early parting of the waves, a sad Nicolau Casaus knew a day of reckoning wasn't far away after this incident. Maradona and Barcelona were simply fire and water. The highly loved Catalan heaved a heavy sigh. Unlike his fellow board members, he couldn't help but like this kid who walked with giants, shot and spoke from the hip and came blessed with a talent only God handed out to so precious few. Casaus knew this tempest that raged in their midst, a blessed curse was destined to be gone soon. It made him sad, for in the end his beloved Barca would end up losers. No one had attempted more than he to mend bridges between Maradona and the President. Casaus had visited the player at Pedralbes and even he had struggled to get an audience with a man treated like a demi-god by those surrounding him.

Since arriving in Barcelona, everything in Maradona's life was being controlled by Jorge Cyterszpiler, the 'them and us' standoff's suiting perfectly his own personal agenda. Those attempting to see the player would claim it was easier to get an audience with King Juan Carlos of Spain, than Barca's number ten. Like so many others in his inner sanctum, Cyterszpiler knew without Maradona, the life he currently enjoyed ended. Jorge simply couldn't afford to lose control. He needed their friendship to remain strong and didn't need Diego being told by such a wise old owl like Nicolau Casaus, that maybe you should look closer at those around you before lashing out elsewhere? He had enough problems already dealing with Claudia, keeping her at bay, for business wasn't so good as it should have been. *Maradona Productions* was having serious money troubles and that meant problems ahead. Cyterszpiler was a worried man, but he daren't tell Maradona what was occurring. Jorge just daren't. Let the rollercoaster continue, he would fix things. The dollars would soon be pouring in again, for those who claimed there was no such thing as a sure thing were wrong, or had never heard of Diego Maradona. A license to print money, Jorge Cyterszpiler just needed to up his game and find that magic tough once more.

Or else?

Nicolau Casaus could sense this feeling of selfish bullshit around many of those surrounding Maradona. 'Diego was a simple boy, the best player in the world, who was surrounded by parasites that in time would drive him crazy.' For Casaus, the little Argentinian maestro was basically a good kid with a big heart, who just lived to play football, but it was a total refusal to bow down to any type of authority, that meant any hope of him in some sort of servient relationship with Nunez was simply unimaginable.

Maybe this came into play after what occurred with the Falklands/Malvina war? The fact he and the other players had been lied to so much and all those years before of being under the total mindset/control of a Fascist Military Junta. He'd had time to think now and was finished with all that. Never again. Fuck Videla and fuck the rest of his scumbag Generals. The torturers, the death squads, the green fords, the death flights, fuck them all. Here was now a young man free to make his own mind up, rich and talented beyond the heavens and with the power to say fuck you to any who dared ever try keeping him down again.

There was though something else that worried Nicolau Casaus deeply. A new arrogance now existed within Diego, something that hadn't been there when they first met in Argentina. This seemingly, absurd belief that because he had been born with such special gifts from God, it allowed him special dispensation to dally also in the devil's delights. Casaus knew well of the rumours regarding the drug taking. Cocaine. For when one is so blessed as Maradona, it appeared even the almighty tended to deliver with one hand a wish and the other a curse, just to ensure they remained human. He prayed the Diego that he knew and loved could wise up before the ultimate fall through the trapdoor into hell.

On Saturday 4th June 1983, at the Kings Cup final in the *La Romerada* stadium, Zaragoza, a Real Madrid side obviously sick to death at the sight of Diego Maradona ripping them apart decided *no mas* and proceeded to try and cut him in two. The treatment meted out to Barca's magical number ten verged on psychotic at times, as their defenders took turns to scythe him down. None more than the renowned *Madrileno* hatchet man Hector Camacho, whose eagerness to seemingly cripple Diego, deservedly drew comparisons with Claudio Gentile at *Espana 82*. Some of the tackles bordered on assault, even causing gasps amongst the Madrid supporters. Yet, despite the outrageous attempts to curtail him, Diego kept going. Time and again, the more he was hit, the more Maradona pleaded for the ball to run those desperate to stop him into the ground. Turning, twisting, one touch, then away. A sleight of touch and two white shirts left confused in his blistering wake. Barca deservedly won 2-1, for it was they whom at least attempted to play football, whilst Madrid appeared more intent on separating Maradona's head from his body. A first-half goal by Viktor, finished impeccably from twelve yards and set up by Maradona was cruelly cancelled out in the second half, when a horrendous mix up in the Catalan defence, resulted in the deadly Carlos Santillana shooting low past Javier Urruti. 1-1, suddenly Barca were rocking. A game they dominated had now slipped precariously from their grasp. Yet, there was still to be a twist. A riveting contest between two sides split by a chasm of history that sucked normal human beings into acting like lunatics, was settled for FC Barcelona with a dramatic and truly glorious goal. Ten seconds remained when Maradona found full-back Julio Alberto, who raced down the left-wing, before crossing superbly for Marco Alonso to slam a stunning header back past the coming keeper Miguel Angel into the net. A goal that brought every Madrid player to their knees, the ultimate insulting gesture to the Madrid bench from a pumped-up Bernd Shuster and Catalonia partying once more till dawn. Any victory over the old enemy was cause of great celebration, but to leave them crying, despairing in defeat? When even their ace card, the man in the middle didn't have time to pull an invisible penalty out of his top pocket. Franco may have been dead eight years, but conspiracy paranoia regarding referees wearing white shirts beneath their black, remained alive and well and residing in Catalonia. Despite the magnificent finale, that night will be forever remembered as when Maradona refused to bow down to hatchet men. Instead, he left them flailing and ultimately beaten. High in the VIP box an emotional President Nunez with television cameras upon him stood with tears rolling down his face, as Barca's Captain Jose Sanchez lifted high the King's Cup. This what it meant to beat Real Madrid.

Nunez accepted with a smile the token, congratulatory handshakes of opposing Real officials, knowing that inside their stomachs were churning with the rotten stench of defeat.

Two weeks later, these eternal adversaries met again twice in quick succession for the two-legged final of the Copa Del Liga. A battling 2-2 draw was earned first by the Catalans in Madrid and it would be in the *Bernabeu* that Maradona left an indelible, lasting epitaph in a Barca shirt. With the Catalans already 1-0 up though a Carrasco header, Maradona ran clear from the half-way line, chased by a desperate posse of white shirted defenders.

On past the keeper Diego raced, until only an empty net stood before him. Instead of scoring he stood waiting for the on-rushing defender Juan Jose to rush in, then incredibly dribbled around the stunned Madrileno, also before tapping the ball home. With this one act of genius in taunting the great white Satan, Diego Maradona entered the annals of Catalan folklore. Astonishing scenes followed as many, even in this place so hostile to FC Barca, applauded Diego's most wonderful goal.

Maradona's wonder strike to give Barca a 2-0 lead looked to have already killed the tie, but a late rally from Real Madrid forced a draw and still all to play for when the two once more went for each other's throat in the *Camp Nou*.

So, began the final game of the season with an opportunity to finish it in the finest manner possible. With the stadium ablaze in Barca colours, screaming for Madrid blood, Menotti's team set about their last task in blistering fashion and on nineteen minutes, the early pressure was rewarded. Julio Alberto's long cross into the box was latched upon by Bernd Schuster, who when set to shoot found himself bundled to the floor by a desperate white shirted scrum. Up stepped an ice-cool Diego Maradona, to convert the penalty with a typical, swish of the left foot past a diving Agustin, into the bottom left-hand corner.

Barca were rampant as the Madrilenos found themselves pinned back. A second for the Catalans came just before the half hour. Again, it was Alberto, his darting run and final pass met by centre-half Alexanco's head from six yards out powered into the net. 2-0 and the Madrileno's roof was caving in. A third looked a certainty and if not for a magnificent, almost disbelieving save from Agustin, a rout may have ensued. With his back to goal surrounded by Madrid players, Maradona dribbled the ball up and somehow to the amazement of all in the *Camp Nou*, managed to flick it over his head and find Viktor at the far post. The Barca winger's thundering header from point-blank range was blocked and turned over the bar by a superlative Agustin. Determined to end their campaign on a special note, Barca continued to go for goals in the second half. Schuster, Viktor, Carrasco and inevitably a scintillating Maradona wreaking havoc. All running from midfield, creating opportunities a plenty that were either squandered, or foiled by a heroic Agustin. Nine minutes from time, Barca paid a heavy price for their inability to kill Madrid off, when Santillana pounced onto a knock down from nine yards out to smash low past Urruti, handing his team an unexpected lifeline. A last moment of great tension for the *Camp Nou* crowd followed, when again it was Santillana who let fly from twenty-five yards, only for Urruti to save and with that went Madrid's last chance. The final whistle sounded to signal a double haul of trophies at the Madrileno's expense. Once more, the Barca Captain Sanchez, strode forward, this time raising aloft the Copa Del Liga. Against a heart-stopping backdrop

of 100,000 cheering *cules* waving Catalan flags and
banners, Sanchez took the acclaim before handing the
trophy to a beaming President Nunez.

'Now for the title,' he exclaimed excitedly to the television
cameras. With Maradona exploding back into top form and
Menotti looking to have the Midas touch, FC Argentina
ruled at FC Barcelona.

CHAPTER FORTY FIVE
THE BUTCHER
'FORBIDDEN TO BE AN ARTIST'
Marca headline…

1983-84. A new season dawned,
and the Barca *cules* pondered once more the coming nine
months. Each year that passed without that elusive title, the
pressure increased on players, management and most
tellingly the club President. An emotional, quick-tempered
man at the best of times, Nunez reacted to disappointments
and failures like a child having his favourite toy taken
away from him. A desire for scapegoats to take away the
spotlight off himself shown itself in the constant sacking of
coaches. Now, suddenly there was genuine optimism at the
Camp Nou, for with Cesar Menotti at the helm, whose
easy-going presence created harmony amongst the ranks
and Diego Maradona looking for all his worth the best
player on the planet, hopes were high that the hellish nine-
year famine was set to end. Yet, this was FC Barcelona,
cules had learned in the short time Maradona had been
amongst them to expect the unexpected. He had their
adoration, but not trust. Fingers crossed, prayers said,
lucky charms worn. Most importantly, all eyes would be
on Diego, for he held the key to their dreams.

On Sunday September 4th 1983, history repeated itself for Barca as once more their campaign began with a defeat. A hammering in the deep south by a scintillating, Manuel Romero's, Sevilla. A 3-1 final score not doing justice to a home side, whose second half performance left the bedraggled Catalans looking unable to tie their own bootlaces, never mind compete for the title. Leading 1-0 at half time through a rare goal from their tough Basque centre-half Jose Ramon Alexanco, Barca's collapse in the last half hour left the coach Menotti, the travelling hordes and an ashen-faced President Nunez, who was having to endure swapping pleasantries through gritted teeth with grinning Sevilla dignitaries, totally lost for words.

It was to be a week before the memory of the Sevilla savaging could be eased, when the *Camp Nou* welcomed Osasuna, in what the goal-hungry *cules* were hoping would be akin to shooting ducks. That Barca won only by a single goal was itself a miracle, for they should have scored ten. Terrible finishing by the Catalans and chance luck proving Osasuna's best friends. Instrumental in creating opportunities, only for his Barca team mates to invent seemingly new ways to miss them was Diego Maradona. Unusually ineffective in Sevilla, but back close to his teasing best on home soil, Maradona picked locks and terrorised throughout. The lone goal for Barca coming on thirty-four minutes from Jose Carrasco, after Osasuna's overworked Brazilian keeper Vicente Biarrun, had spilt a Bernd Schuster twenty yard thunderbolt. A 1-0 massacre, if such a thing existed. Their next two matches saw Barca truly catch fire, as they clicked into top gear with nine goals in two away fixtures. Four by Diego Maradona, as he struck a hat trick in a 5-1 dismantling of German side

Magdeburg in the Cup Winners Cup. Then, as the Catalans returned to La Liga, Maradona created all three and scored one as they stormed to a 4-1 win on the beautiful, Balearic island of Mallorca. In the dressing room before the game, however, Maradona was less than happy. He had brought no less than six pairs of boots, yet somehow none felt comfortable. With time running out and a pent up Diego steadfast refusing to get ready for kick off, *El Flaco* had to use all of his considerable wit to charm Maradona out onto the field! Happily, it all worked out. A nice touch before the game began when he appeared smiling to sign autographs and have his picture taken with the disabled fans. With half of Mallorca, fervent Barca, support for Menotti's team in the *Estadio Lluis Sitkar* was immense. The red/blue amongst the crowd draped in huge numbers. RCD Mallorca began well going one up through their Northern Ireland international Gerry Armstrong. Signed by Mallorca, after his magnificent performances in *Espana 82,* including the winning goal against host nation Spain, saw Armstrong snapped up by *Los Bermellones*. There was to be another that day who grabbed the headlines, for after the Irishman's eighteenth minute close-range strike, a Diego Maradona inspired FC Barcelona gave their Mallorca based *cules* a day to treasure. Firstly an equaliser as Maradona and Bernd Schuster combined for a masterpiece. Diego's defence splitting thirty yard pass taken on the chest by the German in the penalty area, before he finished with a touch of style. As if determined to match his team mate's exquisite effort, Maradona produced only seconds before half-time one to rival, if not outdo Schuster. A left-wing cross from Marcos taken in his stride by Diego, who dribbled sweetly around the stranded keeper Tirapu making it 2-1. Further second-half goals from Esteban and Viktor confirmed Barca's superiority and set them up for an almighty showdown at the *Camp Nou* against the men from the north.

Spain had new champions,

the uncompromising, proud Basques of Bilbao and on Saturday 24th September 1983, they travelled to the *Camp Nou* determined to prove worthy of their newly anointed title. Coached by a man who made Udo Lattek look like Mary Poppins, thirty-three-year-old Javier Clemente had installed in Athletic Bilbao, a ferocious, win-at-all cost philosophy. It was a style of football totally alien to Cesar Menotti and his criticism of Clemente was harsh, at times very personal. Not one also to hold his tongue, the Basque man was never slow in firing back. 'Menotti should keep his mouth shut and just concentrate on his pursuit of women!' Against this fervid, bad tempered, backdrop of slurs and insults, the fanatical home *cules* handed the Basques champions a welcome usually reserved for just Real Madrid.

On the pitch, Barca were electric, the football free flowing, fast and cutting through the visitors at will. Stoked by the fearful memories of times past he had faced the Basque, Bernd Schuster performed like a man possessed. Fired up beyond belief, Schuster appeared determined to beat Bilbao on his own, as he dictated the midfield, whilst still finding time for a personal vendetta whenever the tackle arose. With Maradona also in the form of his life the Catalans attacked from every angle. The home side were rampant-the football needle-sharp, cutting razor-like through determined, but outclassed opponents. Despite the missed opportunities mounting for Barca, there was no panic, for it appeared just a matter of time. Finally, on thirty-eight minutes, Maradona again carved open the Bilbao defence with a wonderfully flighted pass for Alonso to run onto and fire home from twelve yards. Then, just as Athletic thought they had made it to half time, another cross into their box and up popped the raiding left-back Julio Alberto, to double Barca's lead and cause consternation in the *Camp Nou*! Bilbao were in great danger of being massacred, humiliation appeared in the wind for the newly crowned Spanish champions. In the dressing room Clemente demanded they act like men, to go down fighting. If ever a team existed that quite literally played from the heart, willing to sweat blood for the cause it was the Basque. Still refusing to accept outsiders to represent their colours, choosing instead to pick only those born in the region, the hurting Bilbao players were not used to such a gruesome mauling. Their pride battered and bruised, someone would pay.

On fifty-seven minutes, Diego Armando Maradona was cordially introduced to Basque centre-half Andoni Goikoetxea. Racing to win possession just over the halfway line, Maradona reached the ball, only to be caught by a crazed, frightful, lunge by Bilbao's number five Goikoetxea, who came hurtling in like an express train, to not only catch Diego's ankle, but almost destroy it. A challenge that caused even the hardest-bitten present in the *Camp Nou* to wince, for it was a tackle that came laced with intent to cripple. Only moments previous, Maradona had spoken to Goikoetxea urging him to calm down, after a bust up with Schuster. Little did he know his name was top on the butcher's hit list. The searing pain on Maradona's face was visible to all to see, as he lay clutching his foot. An attempt to stand, saw him fall back onto the turf. Placed gently onto a stretcher, it was clear there was real fear this was a career-ending moment. Those on the terraces, the millions of Barca followers around the world held their breath, as a distraught, tear-stained Maradona disappeared down the tunnel, out of sight, with the dreadful possibility of never re-appearing. A horrific night for *El Pelusa* in the *Camp Nou*.

Stung by the brutal taking-out of Maradona, Barca shuddered momentarily, only then to recover their composure unleashing a furious assault upon the Basque. No more than Diego's *compadre* Jose Carrasco, whose many thundering runs at a wilting Bilbao rearguard came laced with revenge. Across the pitch, Carrasco's mood was shared equally by Bernd Schuster, who having begun the match with an attitude verging towards psychotic, now busied himself tormenting the visitors with a devastating array of passes, short and long that hurt Athletic much more than any act of violent retribution. Two minutes from time, the *Camp Nou* exploded once more when Carrasco, giving a fine Maradona impression careered past two chasing opponents and crossed for Alonso to head a deserved third. Now, the Catalans could claim they had truly tamed these northern wild men. Yet, still it wasn't over and perhaps fittingly as the referee got ready to end the match, Carrasco charged through Bilbao's shattered defence to smash in number four. Close to tears at what had befell his close amigo, Carrasco roared at the broken Basque players, 'That was for Diego!' A 4-0 victory over the reigning champions would normally have been sufficient to send them dancing into the streets of Barcelona. Statues covered in red/blue flags, fountains would be swamped, full of drenched, singing and drinking, ecstatic *cules*. Not that night…

An emotionally charged post-match conference, saw an outraged Menotti vent his anger against the Basque, whom he claimed, 'Maybe someone has to die in football for this to change?' Whilst Athletic coach Clemente declared himself to be proud of his players. The initial, medical report said on the night of the incident that Maradona suffered a 'Fracture of the peroneal malleolus of the left ankle.' The operation was carried out immediately. Astonishingly, Goikoetxea received only a yellow card for his outrageous foul, as Menotti called for him to be banned for life. Later on review, the defender received a ten-match ban by the Spanish football authorities, An infamous legacy was born for the man who was to become known as 'The Butcher of Bilbao.'

…When Andoni Goikoetxea next played at the *San Mames*, it was a European Cup match against the Poles of Lech Poznan and he was cheered to the rafters by the Athletic Bilbao faithful. The butcher repaid such faith by scoring the goal in a 1-0 win. Come the end of the match, Goikoetxea was carried off on the shoulders of his team mates! One man's villain, another man's hero…

On hearing this, Diego fumed. As for Javier Clemente? He left Barcelona bloodied, but unbowed, still letting off verbal grenades at the Catalan's and in particularly towards Maradona's direction. Determined to defend his players to the last, Clemente was not prepared in any way to condemn Goikoetxea's actions. Instead, he chose to question the true extent of Diego's injury, 'Let us see how he is after a week before we all cry.' An insult to anyone's intelligence, a suggestion that maybe Maradona was not so badly injured as claimed? This as he lay in a Barcelona hospital writhing in pain, fearing his career was over.

Clemente's harsh words when relayed to him days later,
cut deep and would never be forgiven,
or forgotten.
'FORBIDDEN TO BE AN ARTIST'
   …MARCA headline the next day…

The year of 1983, was when the Basque Separatist
movement *ETA* killed forty three people, in random
bombing attacks across Spain and for some in the Spanish
media, the shocking assault by the butcher on Maradona
was wrongly viewed as a microcosm of such murderous
events. Thus, only adding to the tension and it has to be
said, hatred between the two sides. The context so
distorted to try and prove a link between the terrorist
attacks and Goikoetxea and Maradona. Their take on it
being that Bilbao played anti-football, which was the
'Separatist' way, then compared it to how Barca and Real
Madrid approached the game. Thus confuse the issue,
create paranoia and fear, leave a little doubt and just
enough uncertainty to create hostility in a country already
scared to death. Job done, congratulations, sell a bundle
more newspapers off the back of the events of that early,
September evening in Barcelona. Those unhappy
bedfellows of sport and politics once more coming
together, causing nothing, but fucking lies, hurt and
distress.

CHAPTER FORTY SIX
THE RECOVERY
   Diego Maradona's fractured ankle was operated on that
same night, a two-hour procedure performed by Barca's
own surgeon, Adrio Rafael Gonzalez, in which three pins
were inserted. It was deemed a success, but what lay ahead

for Maradona was three months of painful rehabilitation with huge doubts muted on whether he would ever return the same player? Diego placed all trust in his old, and much trusted 'Magic man', the Argentinian Physician, Doctor Ruben Oliva. To help overcome the butcher's lunge, the medicine man's miraculous healing touch would never have been needed more. Astonishingly, after only six days, Oliva's magic appeared to be working, as he told the player to place his foot on the ground. Feeling relatively little pain, Maradona's healing had begun. Then, on 30th October 1983, just over six weeks since the injury, a miracle occurred in Barcelona. Always pleasant, but firm, Oliva suggested to Maradona that he throw away the crutches and take a stroll through the plush streets of Pedralbes. At first Maradona thought he was joking, but the stern look on the normally jovial Oliva's face, said different. Trusting his *compadre,* Maradona did as instructed managing to walk unaided. This, to the utter disbelief of the entire Maradona clan, whom watched on clapping, cheering and crying. Not all wept with joy. On being told this news the operating surgeon Doctor Gonzalez erupted with rage, 'They have decided to take a terrible risk,' said the doctor, referring to Oliva and Maradona. 'If you start to put your foot on the ground before time, the danger to the ankle is too excessive and unnecessary. This is the best player in the world, what the hell are they doing? Madness.' However, despite such scepticism, recuperation under Oliva's supervision was going well, but another problem was set to rear its ugly head.

When out injured, Maradona was prone to dark periods of depression, the black moods surfacing during the early stages of his three months recovery period, killed stone dead the twenty-four-hour party atmosphere that normally rocked the Pedralbes mansion. Everybody trod quiet and chose their words carefully so as not to annoy or upset. Maradona even banned the football on television. For once the neighbours slept well and the lights went out early in Dodge City. Jorge Cyterszpiler knew he had to get Diego away from the stifling, paranoid Barcelona air. Otherwise, knowing how low Diego fell when unable to play football and with too much time on his hands, he became a dangerous animal. More to himself than anyone else. Buenos Aires was calling. Firstly, they had to run it past their least favourite Catalan.

 As Cyterszpiler secretly suspected the President laughed off his idea as ridiculous, a non-starter. The decision to use Oliva had infuriated President Nunez from the beginning. It was explained to Cyterszpiler in no uncertain terms this 'Witch doctor' couldn't be trusted. Only the club's own medical staff would be allowed to supervise the recovery taking place in Barcelona. As for Buenos Aires? Under no circumstances would Diego be allowed to leave the country. Nunez was determined to lay down the law. His club, his rules, unfortunately, for the President, this particularly footballer couldn't care less. If there was anything guaranteed to get under Maradona's skin, it was this type of authoritative bullying. His response, not surprisingly was to send word back to Nunez that 'Maradona took orders from no one.' Plans to recuperate in Buenos Aires had already been arranged, they were going home. It was Jorge Cyterszpiler who came up with a compromise. They return to Argentina for three months during which no wages would be paid. Maradona would not receive a single dollar until he returned and proved his match fitness. Then, it would be back-dated. If not, the cheque remained blank. An offer Nunez could hardly refuse. His own experts had predicted six months before Maradona would again be fit to play. This way he saved three months wages and the last laugh over Cyterszpiler, who he had grown to truly detest, almost as much as Maradona. Why not let these dumb Argentinians and their back-street medicine man go and play with their magic potions for a while? Easy money. Little did he realise the magic that Oliva held over Maradona, or indeed what existed in his healing hands?106 days later Diego Armando Maradona returned to Barcelona fully fit and raring to play once more! Not knowing whether to laugh or cry, Nunez handed over the cash with a false smile that would have done credit to the Mona Lisa.

CHAPTER FORTY SEVEN
THEY CAME TO FIGHT

Jesus Christ may have turned water into wine, walked on the Sea of Galilee and fed five thousand people with a few loaves and fishes, but Diego Maradona's incredible recovery from a most hideous injury was insulting the intelligence. A heady concoction of a murderously driven Maradona to regain full fitness and Doctor Oliva's ability to plant positivity in every aspect of Diego's recovery, saw the miracle come about. Barca's doctors cried impossible, the joyful cules screamed out his name and the butcher growled, 'I'll see him in Bilbao.'

On returning from Argentina, a reporter at the airport commented that he had grown a bad beard whilst he'd been away. All wild and bushy. A slight hint that maybe he hadn't been living the life of a recovering sportsman? 'I'll take it off before I get back on the pitch,' smiled Maradona. 'I'm back, just you watch!'

On Sunday January 8th 1984, Diego Maradona entered once more onto the *Camp Nou* turf to take on Sevilla. Looking pensive as he appeared into sight, a thousand cameras blinding, a clean-shaven Maradona made a lone entrance down the touchline almost hopping, as if fearful of putting the damaged ankle back onto a football field. Nervously crossing himself, his face etched in tension, he then broke into a jog over the white line, sprinted five yards before almost appearing to explode in relief. Diego Maradona had returned and in a fantastic performance, he shown the many doubters his star still shone bright. There were times as the tackles flew high and dangerous, that 100,000 winced, but each time Diego bounced back up, continuing to torture opponents. An early glimpse proving the magic had not deserted him, as he dragged the ball clear with his instep from two Sevilla defenders. Then, on seventeen minutes the moment Maradona had dreamed of ever since the butcher tried to cut his ankle off. Taking the ball on the penalty area edge, Diego played a one-two with Viktor, whose return pass sliced through the Sevilla defence. On went Maradona before slamming a glorious, low-drive past the keeper Francisco Buyo, at his near post, causing the *Camp Nou* to explode with joy! Typical Diego, sharp and alive, sublime technique, almost impossible to stop by legal means. Five minutes later Marcos Alonso had doubled Barca's lead. A shot from Bernd Schuster deflected back onto the head of the twenty-five-year old winger, who from five yards couldn't miss. Payback time for the opening day defeat was being handed out to Sevilla. Shortly after Maradona so nearly added a third, his second after dribbling around the Sevilla keeper, who in a rush of blood had raced out of his goal, only to then foul Diego when clear through. To howls of derision on the *Camp*

Nou terraces, Buyo escaped a sending off to remain on the pitch. Three minutes into the second half, Sevilla were back in the match when midfielder Enrique Montero converted a penalty to half the deficit. Game on. At 2-0, with Barca coasting, Cesar Menotti was already preparing to substitute Diego Maradona on the hour to let him receive a much-deserved, rapturous acclaim of the crowd. Only for Montero's penalty causing a swift change of mind. On sixty-eight minutes, Menotti was shown to have either mystical powers, or possess the devil's luck when Maradona struck again. Taking a pass off Carrasco, he cut in across the length of Sevilla's penalty area, before unleashing a ferocious shot that deflected over Buyo's head into the net. 3-1, as grand comebacks go, Maradona was beginning to match Frank Sinatra. Finally, with Menotti feeling the game was safe off he came and all in the *Camp Nou* stood to applaud handing out a most wonderful ovation for their divine, if troublesome number ten. One that had Maradona in floods of tears. Most probably the emotion overflowing and the nerves finally calming, after the fear his ankle might not have been strong enough to take the punishment handed out by the Sevilla defenders.

At long last it appeared the Catalans had taken fully to Maradona, who had shown remarkable courage to fight back against a horrendous injury, that would have finished most players. Three weeks later, the ultimate test for both body and spirit. An early chance to bury the demons as he faced once more the butcher. On Saturday 29th January 1984, 50,000 Basques vented their feelings in the seething cauldron of Athletic Bilbao's *Sam Mames,* to hand Barcelona and Diego Maradona in particular, an extraordinary, hostile welcome. Cesar Menotti's derogatory comments had also not been forgotten, he too suffered the crowd's wrath. If the Basque thought such an atmosphere of hostility and intimidation would unsettle the Catalans and upset their free-flowing style they were wrong, for this time around Barca came to fight. None more than Maradona, as here in the storm's eye he faced down those, one in particular who came so close to ending his career. Andoni Goikoetxea, the Butcher of Bilbao. So, began a game that was to go down in Spanish history as amongst the most violent ever, with FC Barcelona interested only in matching fire with fire.

From the opening whistle Maradona went looking for revenge, oh, there were many attempts to again bring him to ground, but as if touched by angels, he skirted over trailing legs, fearful lunges and flying elbows. An inner voice letting him know when they were coming, a slight feint, shrug of the shoulders, he was gone. Goikoetxea pondered, it crossed his mind, but like an ageing carthorse chasing the finest thoroughbred, he just could never got near. Diego ran him ragged. Barca triumphed in a 2-1 win with Maradona scoring both-the first on twelve minutes. A typically, brave surging run through the heart of Bilbao's defence before forcing home after an initial save from the keeper Zubizarreta. Then, a second half winner. A Barca corner met by Viktor, whose knock on was finished by Diego with a flashing header from six-yards. In between there was carnage. So much that at one point in the opening period, the referee called the two Captains together in an attempt to calm tempers, for an all-out riot felt at times only one bad tackle away. Bilbao fought back and for a while in the second half threatened to overwhelm Barca, but the Catalans this night were unyielding, for every foul, they hit back twice as hard with interest. The

San Mames. A place swamped in a fanatical sea of red/white flags. The supporters roaring abuse at the Catalans. Swept along on a tidal wave of Basque pride. They were champions and Menotti's team had come to take the title off them. Over their dead bodies would this be allowed. A noise almost animalistic in its nature rose from the terraces, echoing high across the vast surrounding Mountains. 'No one gets out of here alive' wrote Jim Morrison. He could easily have been referring to the *San Mames*. The final moments were chaos, but Barca survived in not so much to win a football match, more a war. Two sides that by now despised the sight of each other, their paths would cross one last time before the season was over. An endgame. As for Maradona? He survived relatively unscathed and even found time to earn himself a yellow card for a shocking late tackle. A calling card from Diego to show he was back. Between the crashing tackles, spitting, madness and furore, that now existed between these two clubs, Maradona shown he was a truly special talent. Not only amongst the best ever seen, the bravest also.

How long Diego would be performing his miracle in Barca colours was debatable, for other clubs, notably in the far south of Italy had taken notice of his constant warring off the field with the club's hierarchy. They loved a rebel did this certain club,
and they adored Maradona.

Eleven games remained as La Liga approached its climax. Barca were well placed with an excellent chance of taking the title, as they found themselves in a three-way shoot out with Athletic Bilbao and Real Madrid. After the epic 2-1 victory in Bilbao, the *cules* had dared to dream that at last the waiting was over. Not before time Barcelona once more would take its rightful place as champions of Spain. First though there was the small matter of an away fixture against Real Madrid. Never a minor detail in Barcelona. For any self-respecting Catalan, deep forebodings always accompanied a match at the *Bernabeu,* yet this time around there was a frightful abundance of confidence. For they had Maradona. Barca warmed up for the showdown in Madrid with a 5-0 home mauling of Rayo Valladolid. Only one up at half-time, Barca cut loose in the second to find their shooting boots. Two for Maradona, both clinically finished with his left, Schuster and Carrasco twice more ensuring all present at the *Camp Nou* left with real hope in their hearts that come the *Bernabeu*, all would be well. In reality, maybe they should have known better, for one thing history had taught them. Never expect good tidings in Madrid.

FC Barcelona entered into enemy territory on Saturday 25th February 1984. Their welcome to be expected, brimmed over with derisory contempt and an unhealthy dosage of sheer, unadulterated hatred. A thirst for Catalan flesh that came with echoes of the Coliseum in ancient Rome. Unleash the lions upon the Christians, sit back and enjoy the blood fest. Roared on by a Madrid crowd, baying for Catalan heads, Real hero Juanito delivered them an opening first cut on just sixteen minutes. Taking aim, the Madrileno number seven drilled a powerful, low-shot past Urruti at his near post to create bedlam in the *Bernabeu*. He claimed after the game, 'Playing for Real and scoring against Barca is like touching the sky!' Juanito never took many holidays in Catalonia.

An open game ensued with Barca throwing men forward in search of an equalizer, in doing so leaving themselves wide open to lightning, fast Madrid counter attacks. Controversy raged when a blatant foul on Diego Maradona in the penalty area was ignored by the officials. Diego was chopped down when clear on goal. Franco's curse striking-giving more credence to the paranoia that still ran deep in Barcelona, regarding referees. Same old.

Welcome to the *Bernabeu*.

Real held their lead until the sixty-third minute, when finally, incessant, Barca pressure reaped a reward. A flying run by Carrasco down the left-hand side that took him inside the box, before crossing for Maradona, who in one movement controlled the ball and flashed it in an instance past the keeper Agustin. 1-1! Due parity was returned to the scoreline. Fifteen minutes remained to play in the *Bernabeu* and with each going hell for leather to win the game, disaster struck for Barca, when from twelve yards out, Real talisman Santillana hit a hopeful shot that looked to be drifting hopelessly wide, only to take a wicked defection off Alexanco, before flying over a stranded Urruti's head. Cruel for the Catalans, unreserved joy for the Madrilenos. The points and bragging rights belonged to Real Madrid. A 2-1 victory celebrated until next time the whistle blew on *El Clasico* and the war began once more.

Being of the mindset someone had to be at fault, Nunez sought out a scapegoat for the *Bernabeu* loss, it came as little surprise who his eye finally fell upon. One fitting the bill perfectly for the Barca hierarchy. The President had developed an unfortunate habit of blaming Diego Maradona for every defeat. A ranting Nunez confronted Maradona in the dressing room in Madrid, screaming that his off-pitch lifestyle was partly the reason they had been beaten. The nonplussed Diego sat momentarily before launching himself at the President, only to be dragged back by shocked onlookers. Nunez continued, claiming his behaviour was not that of those who adorn the *Blaugrana*.

He also dropped hints regarding Maradona's Hepatitis. Just how did this come about? Could it possibly have been the result of a decadent, lifestyle? The many affairs with local girls, drugs and drink fuelled sessions with prostitutes. The countless unpaid iou's with his name on left around the city, that might as well have just read, 'Fuck you Barca? Finally, in full view of all Maradona snapped and demanded to Nunez that he sell him. A seething President refused, insisting he would be forced to honour out the contract, but as Diego raged it became clear his time in Barcelona was drawing to a close. Dark clouds were gathering over the *Camp Nou*.

A storm had begun to gather in Catalonia.

CHAPTER FORTY EIGHT
LOVE ON THE ROCKS

Following the sorry defeat in the *Bernabeu*, FC Barcelona, minus Diego Maradona beat Real Betis 3-1 at home to soothe wounds, keeping them four points behind La Liga leaders Real Madrid. A war of words had broken out in the press and media, as President Nunez, and a hurting Maradona both attempted to drown the other out in dirt and slander. A situation already at boiling point, tipped in the President's favour during the opening half of Barca's UEFA cup quarter-final first-leg, at the *Camp Nou* against Manchester United. Maradona's time in Barcelona was drawing to a close, yet there still remained a few battles to be fought. Shortly before kick-off, a terribly ailing Maradona almost collapsed and was rushed to a nearby infirmary suffering chronic back pains. A fierce argument ensued between Diego's physician Ruben Oliva and Barca's medical doctors, in which Oliva felt the only cure for such an ailment was complete rest. However, with Maradona himself insisting he be allowed to play, the decision was taken for him to be given a heavy dosage of painkilling injections. All this taking place away from prying eyes, in particularly the 100,000 Barca *cules,* whom eagerly awaited his arrival onto the *Camp Nou* pitch, to rip the legendary English side to shreds.

Astonishingly, these two great European institutions had never met in competition. FC Barcelona's self-styled status as the biggest club on the planet, challenged by the Mancunians own standing world-wide. As the game wore on it became obvious that something was wrong with Maradona. To the unknowing eye, he appeared uninterested, drunk even, as every time he received the ball, it was given away. Remarkable to watch, sad and tragic.

A love on the rocks.

The boos that rained down from the *Camp Nou* upon Diego's head came charged with the acid venom normally reserved for visiting Madrilenos. The jeers and insults. This time he had gone too far. A manic lifestyle, the ballad of Hugo Sotil revisited. Maybe their President was right after all? Noting but a *Sudaca* who should be washing dishes or serving Catalans fancy lunches in a restaurant. Not shaming the good name of the *Blaugrana.* A freeloading junkie living on borrowed time who wasted gifts that could only have been enthroned by a higher force. Soon, the entire stadium roared their disapproval. High in the Presidential box Nunez smiled. Payback time. Little did his accusers know Maradona was experiencing side-effects of the jabs given only hours before. Good intentions had exploded in Diego Armando's face.

Substituted shortly before half time by Menotti, whose own fate hung precariously in the balance and desperately needed a result against United. The unfair, derisory chants and abuse that poured down from high upon him, must surely have made Maradona think what was the point? Himself and the Catalans were chalk and cheese. Black and white. How much blood for the cause did it require to be granted a break by these fucking people? A career almost wrecked with a sickening ankle injury, held together by nuts and bolts that pained him daily and would forever more. Enough pain-killer injections to knock out an elephant, yet, still they doubted?
Time to go.

With the loss of Diego Maradona, FC Barcelona found themselves in an almighty fight with a Manchester United team managed by the flamboyant Ron Atkinson, that had come to attack. Luck struck for the home side with an unfortunate thirty-sixth minute own goal, by young United defender Graeme Hogg, making his European debut. However, this failed to kick-start Barca, in fact United at times pinned the Catalans back, as they looked for a precious away goal. The Manchester United and England Captain Bryan Robson-for once an unlikely culprit, when thinking he was offside went clean through with just Urruti to beat, gently chipping his shot against the crossbar. Only to be horrified on discovering the referee had not actually blown? A dismayed Robson later apologised to the United fans for his error, but in time he would more than make up for it. A cacophony of whistles across this vast stadium deafened, as United threatened a deserved equaliser right until the last seconds. Barca looked to have settled for an unsatisfactory 1-0 victory. The nervous *cules,* edgy, fidgeting and dismayed at their team's inability to kill off the English. Only then to receive a stunning late bonus. With almost the game's last kick, twenty-four-year-old Catalan born winger Juan Carlos Rojo, let fly an unexpected, screaming volley from thirty yards into the top corner past keeper Gary Bailey. A supporter waving a huge Barca flag provided the backdrop for Rojo being submerged under his team mate's grateful embraces. As the *Camp Nou* exploded with joy at their boy's magnificent effort, equally loud sighs of relief were heard across Catalonia. None celebrated more than their President, who became swamped in bear hugs before pulling clear to punch the air in relief. A 2-0 result satisfied the *cules,* as the *Camp Nou* suddenly resonated with a new-found confidence that this tie was already over. Barca had never in their history lost a European tie after being two goals up. Job done. The journey to Northern England now merely nothing more than a sightseeing tour. The Catalans would agree Manchester United had played well, but were deemed by most not of sufficient quality to suggest Barca had reasons to worry about the return-leg. An arrogance hardly backed up by events in the *Camp Nou,* where many neutral observers thought United had been extremely unlucky and indeed deserved a draw.

El Flaco...

A familiar problem now engulfed Cesar Menotti's every waking hour, the imminent meltdown of Diego Maradona. As Catalan public opinion raged wildly against Maradona, he feared greatly whether his young Argentine *compadre* could handle the amount of venom being hurled towards him. For close to eight years this kid had been foremost in his life. Someone he loved and at time loathed in equal doses. A Father and son relationship in many ways. Here in Barcelona, allies in a strange land, but where did he draw the line between friendship and being the boss? It was Menotti who defied public opinion and risked lynching by leaving Maradona out of the 1978 World Cup squad. He was convinced the pressure placed upon this youngster's shoulder would have seen him buckle, who knows if a petulant teenage Maradona could ever have recovered? He knew 1978 was not Diego's time. Plans were already in place, Maradona's day would inevitably come in the Mexican sun. This was a remarkable man who with his nation enslaved by a Junta government engineered a World Cup win for the Argentinian people-a brief light in in a sea of darkness. A gang of psychotic Generals who could never agree on the time of day, but left Menotti alone to coach and manage his squad without largely any interference. Yet, it was never a mutual respect for they hated each other's guts. In normal circumstances of the day Menotti's open, left-wing political ideals would have seen him tortured and murdered, like so many thousands of other innocents holding similar values. The truth was the Generals needed him and he wished to help his nation in a time of wanton despair. A marriage of convenience in a place engulfed in hell. Amid extraordinary pressure, so long as Argentina kept winning Menotti was untouchable, beyond even the murderous grasp of men whom would torture, rape and execute, then sit down with a glass of wine and relax watching Argentina win football matches. Menotti's last line to his team before the World Cup final, 'Don't look at the faces of the Generals, look at the crowd for they are who we play for.'

This was *El Flaco*.

He heard other coaches talk of pressures in Spain and laughed. Pressure? Yet when it came to Maradona, despite all he had experienced, this kid tugged at his heartstrings like no other. For he had witnessed the beginning and though he couldn't foresee the next few years, Cesar Menotti was pretty certain where it was all going to end.

And that broke his heart.

Following the sorry fiasco against Manchester United, Maradona disappeared from sight in the Barca line-ups, claiming injury. A furious Diego retired to Pedralbes, as still the Catalan press screamed disgrace. Helped by an understanding Barca President who fed them whatever lines they needed. Nunez simply loving to thrust the knife deep into Maradona with a frightening zeal. Hardly surprising, dark moods now befell Diego and he engaged in a one man strike against all things Catalan. A stand-off occurred with neither Maradona nor Nunez reluctant to blink first. So sour had the relationship become between player and club, many in Barca's hierarchy had already washed their hands of the troublesome Argentinian. Threats and name calling raged from both sides, but it was the Catalan's decision to stop paying Maradona's wages that saw the player rise like Lazarus from his alleged sick bed for the penultimate league game at home to Valencia, before the trip to Manchester. A temporary, if extremely fragile truce was called as Barca concentrated fully on what was expected to be a relatively, straight forward task against United. By this time a depressed Maradona had instructed Cyterszpiler to get him out of Barcelona and fast. Contact was made with Juventus, whom were keen to broker a deal, as were AC Milan, but there was also another, just remaining quiet, waiting in the shadows and biding their time. Unbeknown to anyone they had secretly been courting Diego for months. One who appealed to Maradona's rebel heart. Like him an underdog with teeth.

The team and heartbeat of the downtrodden Italian south. A message was sent from Jorge Cyterszpiler in Catalonia, the words, 'Pay us what we want and Diego is yours.' From the shadows of Vesuvius, the Neapolitans had emerged to show their hand.

Napoli had come calling.

CHAPTER FORTY NINE
ONE NIGHT IN MANCHESTER

Manchester. None in the rainy city truly thought their team possessed much hope of pulling back the 2-0 deficit suffered in Catalonia. However, with United coming off a 4-0 victory over Arsenal the previous Saturday to put them top of the English Division One, hope sprung eternal amongst Mancunians that Ron Atkinson's side could yet pull off a small miracle. Atkinson had told his team to forget about the first-leg, just concentrate on winning the game at Old Trafford. Barca may have had Diego Maradona, albeit, a punch drunk version, but United's Captain Bryan Robson was entering his prime, if they were going to have a chance against Barca, it was he who would have to be at the heart of it. There was great excitement in Manchester of being able to watch Diego Maradona live, their own troublesome wonder kid from yesteryear, the beguiling Irishman George Best tended to enjoy a party or two whilst wreaking mayhem on the football pitch. The game against Barca would be a wonderful opportunity to draw comparisons. It was back in 1980, Maradona last set foot on English soil. Gracing Wembley with a performance that left all whom witnessed it utterly convinced they had been in the presence of a genius. Now, he was returning, the Mancunian public looked forward to seeing with their own eyes a player being labelled the best of his generation.

FC Barcelona came to England and no one, prophet, priest, journalist or fortune teller, dared even to give United a prayer to make it through. Strange, for a club, all but destroyed back in 1958, on a Munich runway. One that had rose phoenix-like from the ashes to win the European cup only ten years on, could never be written off so easily. There was something in the Manchester air.

They were daring to dream. A precedent had been set way back in 1957, when Sir Matt Busby's ill-fated *Busby Babes* lost 5-3 away to then Spanish champions Athletic Bilbao. It was claimed then that United had no chance of coming back in the second-leg, but on an unforgettable, Manchester evening, Busby's team produced a blistering performance that left the Basques lost for words at the finish, as they were blown away 3-0. Barca had been warned. Also, Ron Atkinson had arranged for the FC Barcelona party to be put up in a city centre hotel, right in the heart of Manchester, where it was never quiet! Not many Barca players slept well that night.

The Line Ups: Manchester United. Bailey, Albiston, Moran, Hogg, Duxbury, Muhren, Robson, Wilkins, Moses, Stapleton and Whiteside.

Barcelona. Urruticoechea, Concepcion, Moratalla, Alberto, Munoz, Alexanco, Pichi Alonso, Schuster, Juan Carlos Perez Rojo, Maradona and Marcos Alonso

Missing from the Barca line up due to injuries and suspensions would be Carrasco, Migueli and perhaps most importantly the Captain, Jose Sanchez. Losing two from his regular defence worried Cesar Menotti, for he didn't share the general consensus in Barcelona that this tie was already over. Fortune telling it appears being one of Menotti's many talents.

Wednesday 21st March 1984. A 58,000 capacity crowd paying record profits of £200,000, gathered by the River Irwell praying for a miracle. Old Trafford under floodlights catching in their misty glare, the ghosts of past, great, European nights. Georgie Best running amok past defenders, Denis Law's acrobatic overhead kicks, Bobby Charlton lashing in a thirty yard screamer. Here in a stadium notably not of the grandeur of the *Camp Nou,* but equally rich in passion and memories. A Mancunian field of dreams. The Stretford End behind one goal was a seething mass of red and white. Normally, that was where United's most vociferous support would roar out, but on the evening that Barca came to town, the entire stadium was ablaze with a rousing, raging, passion not witnessed for years.

'Don't you dare sell Robbo,' was the consensus amongst Manchester United supporters, as the rumour mill persisted the Italians were coming. Foremost AC Milan and Juventus, Sampdoria also. Robson's signature was hot property and before the match thousands of supporter had petitioned the club daring them to even think about selling their Captain. For the Chairman Martin Edwards to even consider such, was to them treacherous. Edwards had been warned!

Wearing change colours of yellow shirts with a Barca dash of red/blue stripe and blue shorts, the Catalans prepared to fend off the coming storm. So, unfolded one of the darkest nights in FC Barcelona's history. As expected, United flew at Barca from the off-Maradona received a full chorus of boos right from his first touch of the match that continued throughout. Their precocious, barnstorming, eighteen-year old Northern Irish international Norman Whiteside, who missed the first-leg through injury making his presence known early, sending the bruising Alexanco crashing into an advertising board. The tough centre-half not used to being put away in such a manner slowly got up and looked around to see the teenage lad from Belfast growling at him. Welcome to Manchester! Moments later, a mistake by Javier Urruti almost ended in disaster when stranded off his line, Whiteside chipped him from twenty yards, only for the ball to drop agonisingly onto the crossbar and over. It was a siege-the Catalans appeared nervous as the noise generated from the Old Trafford terraces drove on the home side. Any attempts by the Barca duo of Maradona and Schuster to keep possession and bring calm to a frenzied atmosphere was immediately seized upon by the ferocious Bryan Robson and Remi Moses, who snapped, wrestled and tore back the ball to begin yet another attack. It was pressure relentless, finally, it bore fruit on twenty-two minutes, when from a corner flick on, the dynamic Robson swept in the opening goal. As Old Trafford exploded, Diego Maradona stood alone in the centre-circle with hands on hips, a sombre figure staring back at the penalty area. His team now needed him more than ever, because suddenly a realisation had dawned on all concerned with FC Barcelona, it was going to be an awful, long, night under these northern English stars.

A first-half dominated almost totally by United saw Maradona shine only sporadically. His few touches of class rare, as mostly Diego was hounded, harassed, elbowed and mauled by the man-marking of Graeme Hogg, ably assisted by the small, but ferocious, bushy-haired Moses, never giving him room to breathe. Only once did he truly escape when a pass from Schuster freed

Maradona and his instant snapshot across the goal was hit straight at United keeper Gary Bailey. This apart, Diego was a ghost.

The Mancunian cavalry charges continued after the interval with Barca not being allowed to settle, constantly pressed across the pitch. Mirando Gerrardo was experiencing a hellish time at left-back. On fifty-minutes, he again found himself in trouble when pounced upon by red shirts. A panicking Gerrardo passed inside to Moratalla, who immediately played the ball back to an unsuspecting Schuster. The German's attempt to play his way out of trouble rebounded badly when the thundering hoofs of Whiteside caused panic in the Barca rearguard and a nervy Javier Urruti became forced to mishit a dreadful clearance. From that instance, the Catalans comedy of errors only worsened as Remi Moses raced over to the touchline and picked up the loose ball, before firing in a cross met first time by the sweet right foot of United midfielder Ray Wilkins. Disaster struck for Urruti when he failed to hold the England man's fierce, low-shot and again waiting to pounce was Bryan Robson to score, taking the roof off Old Trafford! Urruti looked aghast, for his error now levelled the tie at 2-2, leaving the Catalans in serious danger of elimination. It was turning into a one man show, not Diego Maradona, or Bernd Schuster, as might have been expected, but the United Captain. Five minutes later, Barca were on the floor. Again, United's talisman creating havoc, as he delivered a wonderful left-footed cross-field pass into the feet of defender Arthur Albiston's path. At full pace, Albiston tore down the left-wing before finding Norman Whiteside at the far post. Out-jumping three Barca defenders, Whiteside's header flew back across the face of the goal to be met by the right-foot of United's centre-forward Frank Stapleton, who smashed it into the net from four yards. 3-0! The Catalans were being taken apart by a rampant Manchester United. Not an hour played, Barca's two-goal lead had evaporated. Luckily, they still possessed thirty-five minutes to save their skins. Shortly before the third goal, Maradona for once escaped the red shackles of Hogg and Moses, only to lose the ball, instead of trying to retrieve possession, he simply stood and stared as the action moved away. Something was dreadfully wrong with Diego, his manner to all watching that of a player no longer caring for the Barca badge, but more so, having being pumped with so many pain killers before the match, he probably didn't even know what stadium they were playing in. Come the restart, with Barca now in desperate need of a goal, Maradona at last appeared to shift into some kind of gear. Yet, this was a night when even a magician like he appeared human, as a red swarm descending upon him whenever the ball went near. There were moments, precious few when Diego caused gasps on the terraces with either a drag down, or a hidden pass, but nothing came to fruition. One chance when he broke clear on the right to set up Schuster and his lifted effort missed Bailey's far post by inches. As the game entered its dying stages, the noise from the Old Trafford terraces increased to even higher level of delirium. Ron Atkinson relates, 'I can virtually remember every moment of the game. I've never ever been in any football match anywhere in the world that had the atmosphere this match had. Absolutely unbelievable.' It was a night not witnessed in Manchester for many a year and Barca were not being allowed to ruin it. One last time Maradona tried to raise his game flying into the United area, only to then dismally throw himself to the floor, as he raced between defenders Mike Duxbury and Kevin Moran. A terrible dive, one which saw Mancunian wrath rain down upon him. A sad sight for those who had come to view this much talked about footballer. Finally, the drama ended, amidst wild, emotional scenes, the home supporters flooded the pitch to lift high their Captain, who with his magnificent performance that night entered into the annals of Manchester United legend. Robson found himself carried off in triumph. An epic occasion and one that even today United supporters still recall as amongst their finest hours. Bryan Robson said afterwards, 'It was the best atmosphere I have ever witnessed at Old Trafford.' As for Barca, they skulked off, well beaten and home to a firestorm of criticism. It was one night in Manchester swiftly to forget. Norman Whiteside remembers, 'Every time the question comes up about the best game I played in, for atmosphere, it was the best game ever. I've played in World Cups, in cup finals, but that night at Old Trafford, it was electric. All those clichés such as the roof coming off, getting goose bumps on the back of your neck, like having an extra man- they were all true that night. I remember the likes of Paddy Crerand talking about the great European nights, I was wondering what to expect, I was only a kid and I hadn't experienced it yet. Afterwards, you realised what he meant, it truly was one of the great European nights at Old Trafford.'

CHAPTER FIFTY
SHOOTOUT

In Barcelona,
the now, traditional recriminations began. Barca's shameful defeat in Manchester was placed solely on the

couldn't care less, shrugging, shoulders of Diego
Maradona. Little praise was given to the Mancunians,
instead the Catalan press chose to crucify Maradona. By
this time he couldn't care less. A point Diego let known
publicly by rebuking his President, calling him a 'Son of a
bitch.' The pin was out of the grenade, it was all just a
matter of time.

 The team responded well to the Manchester United
mauling with a 1-0 victory in the Basque region, against
former champions Real Sociedad. Yet, there was no
Maradona in the line-up. Left behind in Catalonia, where it
was claimed he was injured. Instead, Bernd Schuster
stepped forward to become the Barca hero, it was the
German's penalty that won the day. A result to fire much-
needed confidence in Menotti's team and one to keep
Barca's season very much alive. A late run for glory
ensued as further victories, 4-1 in the *Camp Nou* over
Cadiz. Then, on Saturday 7th April 1984, away to
Zaragoza, Diego Maradona rose from his self-styled exile
in Dodge city, Pedralbes, to rejoin FC Barcelona's chase
for the title. There, a late strike from Carrasco putting them
just a point behind the champions Athletic Bilbao and the
scent of glory in Catalan nostrils. The following home
match against UD Salamanca was all but decided, when
the Catalans scored twice in the opening ten minutes. First
Barca's centre-half Josep Moratalla, who was only playing
because of an injury to Migueli, thumped home a header.
Then, as the *Camp Nou* held its breath, Barca were
awarded a direct free-kick twenty-five-yards out, all eyes
turned to fall upon one man. It was time for Diego
Maradona to see if the magic still shone bright. Sulking,
miserable, desperate to leave, picking fights, still, when
that first whistle blew, nothing else mattered but the ball.

For this was Maradona. The Salamanca keeper Juan Lozano nervously crossed himself when seeing who was about to line up the shot, as Diego took one glance, before lifting the ball into Lozano's top right-hand corner. A wonderful effort by Maradona, who despite all that had gone on remained the heart and soul of this Barca side. Still loved by his team mates, so noticeable as every home player drowned him in a red/blue sea of hugs. Yet, the cheers from the *cules* though expectedly loud, were not the passionate, emotional, rip-roaring response that threatened to tear the roof off the *Camp Nou*, following previous Maradona goals. Clearly, a love affair in its dying embers with neither feeling the need or desire to make up.

As for the title, FC Barcelona with two games to play were now just a point behind leaders Athletic Bilbao. All was still to play for as next in the penultimate game were local neighbours, Espanol. What pot of gold they would have given to derail Barca's La Liga dream? As FC Barcelona's anthem *El Cant del Barca* thundered out over the *Camp Nou* loudspeaker, the two clubs whose only resemblance was they shared the same city prepared to do battle. A convincing Barca 5-2 victory with Carrasco scoring four ensured the race for La Liga would go down to a dramatic last day. However, such sweet tidings were soured by an incident late in the first half that meant the following day's headlines would not be focusing on Carrasco's magnificent four goal tally. Instead, the papers were full of stories about a young man who just couldn't stay out of trouble if, he was invisible.

The sending off of Diego Maradona.

Diego had begun well by setting up Carrasco. A typical piece of juggling by flicking the ball over his head to take out three defenders, giving his *compadre* an easy finish from four yards out. Shortly after he flashed a snarling, thirty yard free-kick inches wide of the net. The hunger and desire that many *cules* claimed Maradona no longer displayed in the *Blaugrana* was being shown up, as he demanded the ball off team mates. Always available, chasing back to help out in defence. There appeared something almost manic about his demeanor. As if he was making a point by saying, 'This is what you are going to be missing.' Then, the madness. Retribution, a red daze. Reacting to one too many painful lunges from the Espanol defenders, Maradona snapped and for a second just went crazy. Attempting once more to play in Carrasco his pass went astray and to the bewilderment of all, a frustrated Diego swiped viciously away the legs of one of his tormentors Maldonado. A melee followed, before the referee Senor Perez stepped in and with great pomp handed Diego Maradona a red card. A poignant moment, a snapshot to record for the history books, this was to be Maradona's last appearance in Barca colours at the *Camp Nou*. A sad finale, as he trudged with head down, slowly off the pitch and out of sight for the last time.

Another reason for Maradona's dark moods was the flamethrower ignited in his direction by Jorge Cyterszpiler, who finally came clean to tell him they were all but broke. Cyterszpiler pleaded his innocence to Diego. How he had been plagued with bad luck since arriving. Jorge explaining the reasons for a whole host of business ventures involving the *Maradona Productions* brand flopping badly. Also, that the player himself was to blame? The Hepatitis and broken ankle limiting precious time on the pitch. Plus, Maradona's belief that money grew on trees, as he squandered fortunes funding his entourage meant a move away was now essential to fuel their millionaire lifestyle. In truth, the situation was much darker than even Jorge Cyterszpiler admitted, for they were in fact millions in debt. The books were a disaster as the numbers went red. The biggest monstrosity had been an attempt to produce a film of Maradona's life. Cyterszpiler hired at ridiculous expense, a top American production company based in New York, that specialised in state of the art movie sound and cinematography. The idea to release in different languages worldwide with the grand, well thought out title of, *The Life of Maradona*. It was to feature footage smuggled out of Argentina by Cyterszpiler and his own personal film crew that followed Maradona around Barcelona 24/7. One can only imagine the scenes that were cut. Cyterszpiler sensed a commercial blockbuster, he fantasised about breaking box office records. Hollywood! What Jorge actually came up with was a dud beyond words. Tragic sales- a warehouse filled with unsold copies. All at an estimated loss of over a million dollars. However, amid the wreckage of so many financial debacles, Cyterszpiler did manage to negotiate a lucrative contract with Coco Cola. It involved a television advert showing an exhausted, sweating Diego Maradona still in football kit walking down the tunnel. A young boy races after him clutching a bottle repeatedly asking if he would like a drink to quench his thirst? Three times Diego declines, only in the end to give in. Cue the final shot of Maradona gratefully swigging the Coca Cola with the famous adage emblazoned upon it. The sight of Diego turning down the coke became an in joke amongst his house guests at Pedralbes. Ironic, terribly sad. Coca Cola apart, Jorge Cyterszpiler's investments, mainly back in South America, specifically, Paraguay, where he spent huge sums after being informed by so-called 'trusted

advisors' that they were sure things, proved beyond calamitous. There were times even Cyterszpiler felt cursed. For he had acquired the unfortunate gift of turning money into dust. The total reverse from once upon a time ago. So, desperate had Cyterszpiler become, he even was forced to ask for a large loan off Cesar Menotti, just to stay afloat. This all kept from Maradona by Cyterszpiler, who was busy enough fighting his own wars, if the truth were made known to him, Diego may well have jumped off the *Camp Nou* roof. Everything considered,
  the Argentinians were in a mess.

  Negotiations with Napoli had suddenly become not just an option, but an absolute priority-it had to happen. The Neapolitans had promised a treasure chest in assurance for Maradona's signature, the trouble was he needed two treasure chests just to keep the tax man off his back, never mind the more dubious creditors that had to be sorted and soon. Catalan drug dealers for one. In Diego's wild and crazy world nothing was ever denied him. Now, they were paying the price for such indulgences. Maradona listened to Cyterszpiler's tales of woe and in the end did forgive his old amigo. He told him not to worry, that they would get it all back. If not in Barcelona, then, the next port of call. Yet, there was also a warning to Jorge Cyterszpiler, that there could be no next time, or he was fucking done. This wasn't the kid, Jorge had grown up,
no more chances.

  With Diego Maradona now suspended, FC Barcelona went into the final La Liga Sunday, knowing that a win away at Athletic Madrid's *Vicente Calderon* and Athletic Bilbao and Real Madrid both failed to equal their result, then they would be champions. It was a fantastic scenario, one that had all of Spain enthralled. There was also the prized incentive of winning it in the Madrileno's backyard. To have a party in the Bernabeu forecourt! Despite growing excitement in Barcelona, the bookmakers, no fools to fortune made Cesar Menotti's team rank outsiders to end the day as champions. For in a season where Athletic and Real had all but dominated, along with Barca, it appeared inconceivable that the two could lose. Yet, in Catalonia they still dared to dream. On this fateful day when it might come down to one second of individual brilliance to crown a season of hard slog and endeavor, how they would miss Maradona.

Sunday 29th April 1984. Last minute prayers were whispered as in Madrid, Bilbao and Barcelona, the whistles blew to begin the games. With seven minutes gone in the *Vicente Calderon,* the thousands of *cules* whom had travelled to the Capital in more hope than expectation suddenly erupted in joy, for on a rain-soaked pitch, Maradona's replacement Juan Carlos Rojo blasted their team in front. At that moment Barca were top. A crazy day of wonderful highs and desperate lows for all concerned was underway. The *cules* began a chant of *'Campione'* but far too early to tempt the Devil's eye. No surprise that Catalan ecstasy was to be short lived, for on seventeen minutes, yet another unfortunate fumble by Javier Urruti from a free kick, fell to Athletic striker Juan Rubio, who slammed the ball into the net from close range. Then, even before Barca had chance to recover composure from being dragged level, news filtered through from Bilbao of even graver tidings. The champions were in front.

The previous season Athletic Bilbao's La Liga triumph was won away from home in Mallorca, at Los Palmas.

Thus, meaning many Basques couldn't be present at the moment of coronation. This time around fate shown a little heart in granting them a home match to retain the precious title. Their opponents of all teams, on this day of days, their *compadres* from San Sebastian, only nineteen kilometers away. Basque neighbours Real Sociedad. A sporting occasion unlike any before witnessed in the region was unfolding at the *San Mames*. At stake, not just the championship of Spain, but fierce local pride. Amid fanatical scenes, deafening noise and against a spectacular backdrop around the stadium of a red/white sea of flags, Bilbao took the lead. Liceranzu, the defender nicknamed 'Rocky' who plied his trade alongside Andoni Goikoetxea at centre-half, lashed home from six yards high into the Sociedad net. Hysteria descended! Javier Clemente's warriors had one hand back on the trophy. Then, seven minutes later Barca were again in front! A wonderfully, brave, attacking run by a determined Carrasco, who cut through the heart of Athletic Madrid's' defence before finishing clinically over the keeper Pereira's head into the net. So, it went on, nerve shredding, fans of all three sides stood with head in hands. The tension unbearable. The radio bringing good, bad, and false tidings. Half time blew, with forty-five minutes left to play in La Liga, as it stood, FC Barcelona were second, still with a fighting chance of the title.

Catalan hopes were lifted further when ten minutes into the second half, a huge roar came from the travelling *cules,* as news came that Real Madrid had gone a goal down at Espanol! Their dear neighbours doing them a massive, but totally unexpected favour. As the drama continued unabated, the millions of neutrals were loving the pained expressions of those involved. They just wanting the fun, games and heart attacks to continue. It was a strange day and there remained many a twist before it was over. With just twenty minutes remaining of the season, the title race was again thrown wide open when Real Sociedad equalised in the *San Mames*. A goal that caused mayhem in the bars and clubs of Barcelona and amongst the Catalans in the *Vicente Calderon*. One more for Sociedad, heaven on earth would arrive for Barca. Then, the mood changed again as Real Madrid went level at Espanol. A dashing, young striker given his debut by Alfredo Di Stefano called Emilio Butragueno, swooped like a vulture to put the Madrilenos back in the picture. Another for them,

and they would be champions.

On eighty-three minutes, it broke in Madrid that Butragueno had got a second, the nightmare scenario secretly feared by every Barca *cule* was coming to fruition. Especially those watching their team live, if the unthinkable occurred, they would be stranded amongst the celebrating Madrilenos, as they danced in celebration. The Catalans were to be saved such torture, for only moments after Butragueno's goal, Athletic Bilbao went back in front at the *San Mames*. Again, it was their defender Liceranzu, whose flashing header from a free kick granted him legend status and sent the Bilbao fans into a state of euphoria. Javier Clemente screamed from the touchline at his team. The words and mannerisms clear to understand, 'Defend with your lives, your title and don't you fucking dare throw it away!' They never, come the final whistle, Athletic Bilbao were champions once more. Real Madrid and FC Barcelona had been left behind truly in their wake. The power base of Spanish football now definitely rested in the Basque country at the *San Mames*. The old order not just put in their place, but locked away in a box.

Barca were in mourning. So, close to touching heaven, but left at the end in the dark, murky, depths of footballing hell. They had a last chance to salvage something from yet another disappointing campaign, with a game against the now, twice champions Athletic Bilbao, in the King's Cup final. One that promised fireworks, for there were on both sides players whom had grown to hate the sight of each other. Scores to settle, vendetta's still lying unfinished. None more than Diego and the. A dark duel that would trigger an explosion of violence never before witnessed in Spanish football history.

Their remains just one last great tale to be told of Maradona in Barcelona.

CHAPTER FIFTY ONE
ALL THE KING'S MEN
'I can´t be held responsible for what happens if Maradona keeps talking.'
Pedro Aurtenetxe (Athletic Bilbao President)

Diego Armando Maradona's farewell, his last encore in Barca colours was on Saturday 5th May 1984, in the King's Cup final at the *Estadio Bernabeu*. Against, of all teams Athletic Bilbao. In the presence of special guest King Juan Carlos, two teams previously hell bent in their last encounter on killing each other would play out the season's royal finale better suited started by a bell, rather than a referee's whistle. Where a body count, not fouls would be deemed needed. On the game's eve, Maradona, seemingly now at war with the whole of Spain, turned his attention to another sparring partner, Bilbao coach Javier

Clemente, 'Clemente hasn't got the balls to look me in the eyes and call me names to my face. He is a coward.' Diego's bitter outburst saw Clemente hit back in equally strong terms, 'It is amazing how someone like him who earns so much money, can have absolutely no human qualities.' All of this going on before they actually got on the pitch? Dousing the flames further was a boasting Athletic retaining the La Liga title, not slow in reminding the Catalans of their own shortcoming, in a now torturous, ten-year drought. Rubbing even more salt into already open Barca wounds, Real Madrid stole second place off them at the last. Suddenly, winning the King's Cup for FC Barcelona, was so much more than just having a trophy to show for an otherwise barren season. It became a necessity, a matter of pride.

A fiery, smouldering, atmosphere existed on the touchline and as both benches glared, the insults were hurled. A smiling Javier Clemente took his place whilst lighting up a cigarette then inhaling. A picture of a man satisfied with a successful season of work done well. Content, knowing fully well the television cameras were upon him and these pictures were being seen in Barcelona-the message was simple. 'We beat you, live with it. Sending greetings from Bilbao!' In being able to retain La Liga at this fledgling stage of his career was a monumental achievement for Clemente. Winning one could well have been dismissed by his many critics, but twice? Time and again, they poured written diatribe on his footballing philosophy. Yet, to win two in a row when fighting against the likes of giants, FC Barcelona and Real Madrid? This could never be down played, also adding to the fact his hands tied by the Basque policy of local and ancestral recruitment, all only adding to the achievement. Javier Clemente was indeed darned of special cloth. Whereas Clemente's 'Athletic may never have won friends or prizes for its glittering football, they had in abundance a work ethic unmatched and a tenacity and tactical capacity to go play at any stadium in Europe standing their ground. Now, to finish off with the scalp of their greatest enemy-Athletic Bilbao had all but taken a blood oath in the dressing room, failure in the King's Cup final was not an option. The season was not yet over.

As for Cesar Menotti? The scenes in his pre-match dressing room of wound up players seemingly gearing up for a war, not a game of football concerned him. All the years working with Maradona, never had Menotti witnessed him so tense. This was not the bubbling, cocky, but loveable youngster who had enchanted, and enthralled him for the past eight years. More now a young man determined to seek vengeance on the one who so nearly finished his career.

Menotti's words beforehand, 'Stay calm Diego and don't get involved. Just kill them with your skill.' He could only pray Maradona had been listening.

The teams entered to an enormously, rousing reception. Two regions so proud, nations in their own right and ready to tear each other apart to win the King's Cup. The *Estadio Bernabeu* lay immersed in the colours of both. One end draped Bilbao red/white, the other Barca red/blue. Each determined to out shout the other, cheer their team to victory in a detested stadium. It was Athletic who began well with some bright attacking football. The striker twenty-three-year-old Guarrotxena Endika, almost scoring in the opening moments, as his chip over a stranded Urruti was cleared off the line by a chasing Migueli. However, it was to be short-lived luck for Barca, as moments after, the relentless, dangerous Endika got his just rewards when he burst through Barca's defence to chest down the ball and fire low-past a diving Urruti. 1-0 for Bilbao and the delighted Basque youngster celebrated wildly in front of his cavorting, jubilant supporters behind that same goal!

Barca hit back, first Carrasco coming so close to finishing a sweeping move, with Diego Maradona and Bernd Schuster. Then, a blistering low drive by Diego, from twenty-yards, hit straight at the keeper Zubizaretta. An entertaining first-half broke out as both teams continued to attack. However, just beneath the surface a fuse simmered and snarled. Slow burning maybe, but one certain to ignite. It was just a question of time, all would blow shortly in the second half, when Schuster took out Andoni Goikoetxea for crimes past, earning himself a yellow card. Retribution was swift when moments later, the butcher's defensive partner, the recently anointed Basque saint, after his two goals against Real Sociedad, Licarenzu, caught the German with a ferocious shoulder charge, that would have seen him arrested for assault on a public street. Amid the increasingly, violent fouls taking place, Bilbao's right-winger Argote broke away, only to be scythed down outside the penalty area by a desperate Alexanco. Another booking forthcoming for Barca. The free-kick came to nothing, but across the pitch attention was starting to drift from the actual ball to event happening elsewhere. Athletic Bilbao began to torment the Catalans with keep-ball. A thunderous roar of 'OLE!' coming from the Basque terraces greeting every pass. It was torturous for the Barca players, tempers soon became frayed, as tackles flew high and dangerous. An argument over a throw in, blew up at Athletics' end near the corner flag and the Catalans found themselves bombarded with cups, bottles, anything the fans could get their hands on. As the referee and his officials stepped in to calm tempers between the sides, Bernd Schuster inexplicably began lobbing back the items into the crowd! In what appeared a concerted attempt to lynch the German, the outraged Basque attempted to tear down the fences, only for riot police to move fast, blocking their path. They instead were forced to content themselves by launching a new hail of objects towards Schuster, who simply laughed at the sheer madness of it all. As the clock ticked down, Barca threw caution to the wind. Their great hope Diego Maradona went on a mazy run in the Bilbao box. A gang of Basques left dazzled, as Diego at full speed went careering through, only to be sent crashing to earth by the full-back Nunez. A clear penalty, but ignored by the referee Senor Martinez, who claimed Maradona had dived. Three Basque players surrounded and accused him of cheating, Nunez, in particular, the most vociferous. An irate Maradona put his head into the defender's face and leaned forward, refusing to back down. Only the swift intervention of the referee prevented possibly another red card for Barca's number ten. Still the arguments continued, the Basques looked to intimidate Maradona to such a point, he exploded. None more than the butcher. For by this time, Diego's head was close to boiling point. In an atmosphere of sheer hysteria, with only seconds remaining, the Catalans threw everybody forward. They bombarded the Basque goal in search of an equaliser that would not only have saved the game, but their season. As Athletic defended like devils denying the Catalans, means legal and illegal, the clock ran down and Senor Martinez's whistle blew for full time. For Barca, an ending of bitterness and frustration. It was Athletic Bilbao's day once more, clearly the season of the Basques.

Surrounded by cameramen thrusting microphones into his face, Javier Clemente headed onto the field to embrace his players for their glorious achievement of a League and cup double. The football game had ended and now the real battle was set to begin. The ball would be put away and all hell in its fire and fury would descend on the *Bernabeu*. The outrageous events that occurred from the last whistle onwards will be forever remembered with a shudder, of when all the King's men staged a battle royal.

Bilbao player Elizade Miguel Sola celebrated by sticking a raised two fingers salute right into Diego Maradona's face. Only then paying a painful price as an outraged Diego, never the best of losers, let fly a punch that knocked Sola to the floor and as the Basque lay cowering, Maradona quite shamefully set about finishing him off! Cue unadulterated madness, as the entire Athletic team rushed to extract revenge on Diego. Led by none other than the butcher himself, Andoni Goikoetxea, who for the second time in his career lashed out brutally at Maradona, with the sole intention of finishing off a job he began six months previous. The butcher caught him around the midriff with an outrageous high kick that knocked Diego off his feet-this was the signal for footballing Armageddon to erupt. In an eye blink, Maradona was joined by a blazing, wild-eyed wave of red/blue Barca teammates charging into their Bilbao counterparts, with an astonishing array of karate kicks onto opponent's chests. Flying through the air came Migueli landing feet first on a Basque stomach. His nickname of *Tarzan,* was well earned. Boots and punches flew as these two bitter adversaries quite literally went mad. It was carnage! Stood looking on in the VIP box was President Nunez. Grim faced, open-mouthed, not knowing whether to scream in horror, or burst into tears as Diego Maradona led the Catalans on yet another death-defying charge upon the Basque ranks. Alongside Nunez, King Juan Carlos watched the brawl below him unfold with incredulity etched upon his face. By this time baton-wielding riot police with their shields had ringed off the pitch area, where the assailants were battling, in what appeared a genuine ploy to keep the crowd safe from the players! Sporadic fights kept bursting out as private vendettas were settled in the glaring eye of public view.

Ripped shirts, bloodied faces, murderous glances and players knocked unconscious. Ever since the butcher first left his calling card on Maradona, this had been a bomb waiting to blow. Finally, slightly calmer heads from both sides prevailed, as officials and security staff successfully separated the warring parties, the bedlam eventually subsided. But, not before all involved had dragged their club's reputations through the mire. Maradona would claim, 'Bilbao were after me, Goikoetxea wanted to finish what he started.' Athletic Bilbao went up to collect their trophy, a bedraggled lot, cut and bruised, their pride smarting, but now determined to rub the Catalans noses even further in the dirt. Immediately, their players raced over to where their fans were, demanding they be allowed to join them on the terraces. Soon, the King's Cup was being joyfully passed around by thousands of joyful Basques. Waved in the direction of the depressed Barca fans that stood dumbstruck, after what they had just witnessed.

Shamefaced and disgraced in this of all places, Madrid, where no doubt in the boardroom, they would be roaring with laughter at the Catalan's humiliation. President Nunez knew he had to act in ridding his club of this Argentine pestilence. No more. Maradona had to go, blessed by angels they claimed.

For Nunez he had become the fucking, devil's spawn.

CHAPTER FIFTY TWO
ADIOS DIEGO

The fallout from the *Bernabeu* saw Diego Maradona receive a three month ban from all Spanish competitions. Again, Maradona felt an injustice, his mood not helped when Nunez claimed it was deserved. However, with Diego determined to quit, this only strengthened a desire to rid himself of all things Barca by escaping. Also, coach Cesar Menotti waved adios to the *Camp Nou*. Heartily sick of the Catalan desire to blame all but their own for what had occurred in the King's Cup, he could also no longer stomach the backstabbing and arrogance of Barcelona politics. Menotti returned to Buenos Aires a lot richer and with a tall story to tell, but thoroughly drained after all that had erupted in his short reign. The white smoke rising from the *Camp Nou* in the summer of 1984, meant a new leader had been chosen to replace Menotti and it was one that left many *cules* under-whelmed. President Nunez had done his homework. He had tried a dictator in Udo Lattek, the laid-back Father figure in Cesar Menotti. The German and the Argentinian. After long consultations and debates, it was time for an Englishman, one few saw coming.

Before the official appointment was made, the net was cast, others were also thrown a fish just to see if they bit. It was in the immediate, painful aftermath of the Old Trafford debacle that Nunez first approached Manchester United manager Ron Atkinson. The President was swiftly tiring of his Argentine contingent. Maradona was all but history, Cesar Menotti also set to be jettisoned, soon as a successor was identified. A discreet phone call was made to sound out Atkinson, who responded positively. Since that game, his stock had risen considerably amongst the Barca hierarchy. A man of good character, charismatic, tactically sound. Away from prying eyes, a secret meeting took place in a London hotel where Atkinson duly confirmed his interest. He insisted that if Barca could resolve a deal with the United board and hand him a three, instead of the on offer two-year contract, then Atkinson foresaw no problem going to Barcelona. They broke up with an understanding to speak again soon, but events elsewhere would see Ron Atkinson's hopes of landing his dream job end dramatically. Looking for advice on the best candidate, President Nunez sought out the recently appointed England team manager Bobby Robson. If Nunez thought it even slightly credible that Robson would have come he would have said name your price, but such was the Englishman's patriotism, the President knew there was no chance. Inevitably, the question was asked and Robson, as was his manner politely declined. Yet, there was another who might solve Nunez' problem? Robson threw in a name that fascinated the Barca President. He couldn't speak highly enough of a bright, enthusiastic, young London coach. Tactically exciting, innovative and burning with ambition.

Terry Venables.

There had been a growing consensus in the corridors of power at the *Camp Nou,* that Menotti's team had become over-reliant on Diego Maradona. Both physically and mentally, if he never played. It was felt someone of Venables ilk, a talent for improving players and building, highly watchable teams suited the profile to take Barca forward. Nunez was also under the misguided impression that the forty-one-year old Venables would be easy to control. His thinking, that due to the brash cockney's sheer appreciation of being allowed to manage this great club, he would ask how high when told to jump? For the President had grown weary of confrontation. The battles with Maradona had worn him out. Also, Venables came relatively cheap. Never a fact to be ignored. Helenio Herrera, Rinus Michels, Ladislao Kubala, Udo Lattek and Cesar Menotti. Now, a new name would be added to that esteemed list. The job criteria as ever from President Nunez was succinct, ruthless and straight forward. 'Win, win and win. Or pack your fucking bags.'

On Terry Venables' very first day in charge at the *Camp Nou,* he was tossed a live hand grenade, in the shape of a want away Argentinian, by Nunez. Venables knew it was a test, one he could ill afford to fail. Venables was challenged by the President on the extremely prickly subject of Diego Maradona and urged to make this top of his agenda. Nunez had been approached by certain, powerful Barca members, whom suggested maybe not enough was being done to try and mend bridges with Maradona? That despite what appeared at the moment an unbridgeable chasm, it may well be worth Venables speaking to the player and testing where the land truly lay? Nunez made known also his own personal opinion, Diego was poison, that if it was up to him he would already have cancelled his contract and sacked him after the King's Cup fiasco. But this was Barcelona, the scheming in-house politics meant even those opinions he vehemently disagreed with, had to be listened to. The feeling amongst some being that to sell now a player destined to become arguably the greatest of all time was madness. An act of folly, footballing suicide that would return to haunt them both on the pitch and financially off it, for a generation to follow.

Adhering to his President's wishes, Terry Venables met with Maradona, but before doing so, he also sounded out his team mates, trusted club officials and respected journalists, those not loyal to either man. What the Englishman discovered, especially amongst the players was overwhelming support, a love and respect in which he was still held truly surprised Venables, giving him hope that Diego Maradona could well stay on. Carrasco told him a story of when Barca were on a tour of South America, 'We had to play a game, but Diego was injured. The contract specified that if Maradona didn't play, the club could not charge as much, meaning we the other players got paid less also. Even though he was injured, Diego said he would play, because he wanted his team mates to have our full bonus. He played for the good of the group.'

With all this in mind Venables sought out Maradona, but very swiftly became of the opinion, there was next to nothing chance of a reconciliation. Far too much bad blood had been spilt between Maradona and Nunez. Even if a temporary truce could be brokered, nothing remained more certain that sometime in the near future the merest trigger would set off an eruption. Sadly, for Venables, he couldn't help but like the player. When sat one to one, he found it hard to believe this affable kid could possibly be the same notorious villain made out by Nunez? They talked for hours, as Maradona opened up his heart on the two years spent with Barca. How he wished things had turned out different, but the relationship with Nunez left him no choice. The broken promises, the lies that had been told meant life in Barcelona had become unbearable. Diego

choosing not to mention the small matter of his agent Cyterszpiler leaving them all but bankrupt. In different circumstances, Venables would have loved the opportunity to drag Maradona back from the abyss to once more enchant in the *Camp Nou*. But Diego Maradona and President Jose Luis Nunez were a marriage made in hell and that meant there could be only one answer. Divorce.
 A decision to sell had been made,
 and the man chosen by Nunez to oversee the transfer was forty-year-old Barca vice-President Joan Gaspart. There was only one instruction off his boss for Gaspart, 'To bleed Naples dry.' The Neapolitans sent to Barcelona their General Manager and former legendary player Antonio Juliano. Here was a favourite son of Naples, trusted by his club to bring the player home. The bargaining would take place with the Catalans, for Diego Maradona had already agreed figures. He and Cyterszpiler had settled on $6.4 million dollars over six years. This with ad-ons to see the numbers double over that same period. Maradona and Juliano bonded at first sight. Both hailing from similar backgrounds of poverty and hardships. The backstreet slums of Forcella in Naples, no different to the ramshackle, wastelands of Villa Fiorito. The prickly business of Barca's transfer fee sure to be astronomical lay in wait for Juliano. This was a task he couldn't afford to fail. Naples expected. Napoli first became aware of Diego Maradona back in 1979, but due to the Junta's refusal to even contemplate the notion of letting him move abroad, a deal was deemed impossible. Instead, the Neapolitans changed tact, they sent Maradona a Napoli strip with a letter insisting that soon as the rules changed they would come calling. Sadly, Barca beat them to his signature, but four years later they had returned and this time around were

determined to get their man. At any price. A deal had to be brokered. Antonio Juliano understood that footballers of Maradona's ilk were worth their weight in gold. For so long, too long Napoli had been the poor relations to the northern giants of Milan and Turin, the opportunity to sign Maradona had arrived heaven sent. For this kid who moved as if no one was ever in his way, truly special. So, it was Juliano felt his heart drop, when on first meeting with Jose Gaspart, he told him the asking price was a new world record of $13 Million dollars! The arrogant Gaspart had little time for the Neapolitans, considering them like Maradona, mere peasants in comparison to Catalans. He enjoyed watching Juliano squirm, as the Neapolitan stressed there was no way Napoli could afford such a monumental price. It was simply beyond them. There was a plan B for the Neapolitans, God forbid, it came to that, in the name of the great Brazilian Socrates, who stood waiting to come if the deal with Barca collapsed. A phone call was made and the doctor was told get ready, for Gaspart was adamant, he was not for turning, claiming to Juliano that there were others who could and would pay. Notably a name that turned even the most placid man from Naples into a spitting, snarling, lunatic. Juventus!

On hearing of the *Old Lady's* interest, Juliano immediately contacted Napoli President Corrado Ferlaino, to share the grave news about Juve and to inform him of Barca's demands. The Catalan's ruse, apart from infuriating Ferlaino shocked him to the core, sending cold shivers down Ferlaino's spine, for the world would not have been a big enough place to hide if he allowed Maradona to slide into Turin's grateful arms. Already at Juventus, was the great French playmaker Michel Platini. With Maradona alongside him? Losing Diego at this late

stage was not an option, for such a huge loss of face against Gianni Agnelli's Fiat-bankrolled giants could never be lived down. A car had already been blown up outside his home and at the San Paolo. A warning from those in Naples when leaving such calling cards meant business. The message succinct, clear.
Don't you fucking fail El Presidente!

A despairing Ferlaino was on the brink. There was no more money. He had bankrolled both his and Napoli's entire future on this one deal. The consequences of it collapsing around his ears couldn't be contemplated. There was one card left to play, but it resembled neither an ace nor a joker. In desperation and in an act totally unprecedented elsewhere, Corrado Ferlaino went for broke appealing directly to the citizens of Naples for the extra cash. It was a dangerous ploy, one that could easily have seen him hounded out of the city. The scenario of Ferlaino being frog-marched by a Neapolitan lynch mob to the summit of Mount Vesuvius and thrown into its abyss was real.

Luckily, for the President, the response to his desperate plea for help defied belief. The word spread quickly of Ferlaino's plight. In the crumbling tenements of the *Quartieri Spagnoli,* (Spanish Quarter), that stretched from the legendary Via Santa Lucia, to the over-hanging hills of Pizzofalcone, the collections began. This decaying, winding den of intrigue, blind alleys that spilt messily downwards to the seaport was home to the true hardcore of Napoli *tifosi* and a place feared by strangers and *Carabinieri* alike. So, named after the invading Spanish army who billeted there in the seventeenth century, it remained forever sheltered from the sunlight, by the endless sheets of flapping washing lines lying festooned across the cobbled alleys.

A world in the shade, a law apart.

In the ravaged slums of the Forcella district, a *Camorra* stronghold of the fearsome Giuliano clan for two decades, people gave all they could afford and more. Across the city, long queues gathered outside the Bank of Naples offices, all desperate to help. For the thought of seeing Maradona in the despised black and white Juve stripes would rip open their hearts. In less than a day the amount was raised, as Neapolitans rallied round. *Camorra* hoods helped collect the cash. No matter how small their donation people were determined to contribute.

In a place plagued by crippling unemployment and wretched crime, the sheer magnitude of this generosity shocked outsiders. But, such was the craving to have Diego Maradona amongst them, families went without food, women pawned their best jewellery, children sold their favourite toys. The more fanatical would have sold their soul to the Devil if it meant seeing Diego Maradona playing for Napoli. A miracle occurred in Naples and the begging bowl was filled. It wouldn't be the last. The patron saint of Naples San Gennaro sighed heavy from above-he know what was coming their way!

Late, on the evening of Saturday 30th June 1984, aboard President Ferlaino's luxurious yacht, moored off the beautifully lit-up island of Capri, Diego Maradona soothed Napoli nerves by finally putting pen to paper. Corrado Ferlaino welcomed Maradona in typical, Italian tradition by kissing him on both cheeks. Their embrace appeared to those unknowing of a Father embracing his long-lost son. In this city such an act held a hidden meaning, 'Don't ever cross me.' As the champagne corks popped, Napoli *tifosi* prepared for the biggest party in their history, for Diego Armando Maradona was on his way! In the days before, there had been nothing but sadness and despair. Now, a new era dawned. A sweet Neapolitan moon shone bright.

There were little tears shed in Barcelona when the deal was confirmed, the unbelievably joyful, if chaotic scenes as the Neapolitans greeted Diego Maradona shown on Catalonian television moved few. For their experiences with Diego, had been at best tempestuous, ugly even, though at times, as in any passionate relationship, there were moments of pure, unadulterated pleasure. The goal against Real Madrid when he stood on the goal-line waiting for the defender, before beating him also, then tapping the ball into the net.

That alone enough to see Maradona immortalised in Barca folklore. Sadly, Diego's opinion of President Jose Luis Nunez's arrogance and the inherent snobbery of FC Barcelona against him, meant there was never going to be a happy ever after. So, the story of Diego Armando Maradona's stay with Barca ends. His two years at the *Camp Nou* remain largely lost in the midst of time. Forever in the shade of the seven tumultuous seasons, he was set to have in Italy. But, once upon a time in Barcelona, Maradona did strut his stuff to leave an indelible mark. The journey of *El Pelusa* would continue under the volcano. In Naples,
 but, that's another story!

QUOTES ON DIEGO

1: ''In Argentine football there is a before and an after Maradona.''

Julio Grondona **(President of the Argentine FA)**

2: "The best of the lot, no question. In my generation, my era, he was simply the best. I saw Maradona do things that God himself would doubt were possible. He always had someone marking him, he always had someone hanging on to him, and yet he could still always conjure up wonderful pieces of magic. A genius." *Zico*

3: "What Zidane could do with a ball, Maradona could do with an orange." *Michel Platini*

4: "Maradona was absolutely the best player I ever played with."
Mario Kempes

5: "Maradona is like a little fat barrel, he'll never score against me."
Orlando Gatti

6: "When Maradona ran with the ball or dribbled through the defence, he seemed to have the ball tied to his boots. I remember our early training sessions with him... the rest of the team were so amazed that they just stood and watched him. We all thought ourselves privileged to be witnesses of his genius."
Lobo Carrasco

7: "He was only a little kid, but he made such an impression in training, playing like one of the kids far bigger than him. He was from another planet. He was different." *Francisco Cornejo*

8: "Maradona epitomized the mystique of the working class revolution: aloof and arrogant like the 1980s." *Manuel Vazquez Montalban* **(Spanish journalist)**

9: "The greatest player ever. I played with him when he burst onto the international scene as a teenager, but we'd all heard about him long before that. Phenomenally talented; just training with him was a joy." *Ricky Villa*

10: "The impressive thing about Maradona was his ability with the ball. He was very skilful, and had great vision." *Pele*

11: "Maradona is the fastest player I've ever seen running with the ball, and he kept it perfectly under control. His pace was absolutely frightening, you just couldn't stop him. And he always got himself into positions where he could score." *Sir Bobby Charlton*

12: "He was the best player I ever played against." *Lothar Matthaus*

13: "I wanted to be a soccer player, and I became the best of the best, the number one, better than Maradona, better than Pele, and even better than Messi, but only at night, night-time, during my dreams. When I wake up, I realized that I have wooden legs and that I'm doomed to be a writer."
Eduardo Galeano

14: "Bumping into him is like hitting cement." *Alfredo Di Stefano*

15: "Im going to have a word with Diego Maradona because all our fans want to see him play with efficiency on the pitch, and with unimpeachable behaviour off it." *Jose Luiz Nunez* **(President of FC Barcelona)**

16: "We always said that we would both start together, and we would both end together. It could not be, but I always thank God for everything he gave to Diego." *Goyo Carrizo*

17: "I think he going to be as good as Di Stefano and Pele."
Nicolau Casaus

18: "As a coach, (in reference to Maradona), you really are only a dancing bear for stars." *Udo Lattek*

19: "My Mother thinks I am the best. And I was raised to always believe what my Mother tells me" *Diego Maradona*

20: "When Diego was baptised, I only asked that he grow up healthy, and a good person." *Dalma 'Tota' Salvadora Maradona*

What came next…

Once upon a time.

It began on Thursday 5th July 1984...

A most beautiful day in the Italian South. With 70,000 screaming Neapolitans awaiting him, roaring out his name in the *San Paolo* stadium, Diego Armando Maradona arrived under the shadow of Mount Vesuvius, in Naples and for seven years all hell was let loose. For so long the ailing giant SSC Napoli criminally underachieved. Their fanatical support unequalled in both passion and size across Italy. None had ever been more feared or hated, but how they ached for success.

A history dramatic, explosive and so damned tragic. Like the finest Italian operas' it always ended in despair. Then, came Maradona. Blessed with a ball at his feet on the field, hopelessly cursed off it. When in the mood unplayable, but also a dark side. He mixed openly with the city's most feared and notorious gangsters, the Camorra. The feared

Giuliano clan. Untouchable, beyond reproach. A lifestyle fuelled by cocaine. A lawless idol with thorns so deep they pricked to make Maradona believe for a while he was a God.

Scarface in football boots. Nothing less.

When not enjoying the decadent excesses of this Babylon by the sea, there was magic to be made on the field, as the charismatic Argentinian inspired Napoli to their first ever Scudetto title. It was the stuff of Neapolitan dreams and Northerner's nightmares. Juventus, the Milan clubs, all despised as they mocked this last major European city before Africa.

'Welcome to Italy'.

'Vesuvio wash them with lava' claimed the banners on any journey North. In revenge, Maradona, this barbarian king, led the southern hordes against those who viewed Naples lower than the dirt on the Italian boot. A revolution took place every Sunday for seven years with battles raging both on and off the field, as the Napoli *tifosi* fell in worship at his dancing feet. Maradona continued to party on unabated. Sheltered from all prying eyes until the magic faded and he was tossed out like garbage. Once Upon a Time in Naples attempts to chronicle this unforgettable era of when Diego left his inestimable mark on Italian football and in Neapolitan's hearts. Whom he raised to the stars, only to ultimately break them. An alluring tale of wonderful football, glory, despair, betrayal, corruption and then came a moment many years later of redemption. In a city that lived for the day and chanced their hand on the forever changing moods of Mount Vesuvius, Diego Maradona became bigger than God himself. From a high their patron San Gennaro kept a watching eye, but even he couldn't promise to bring about a happy ending.

Miracles are one thing, Maradona another. For in this city, where the devil feared to tread, even the angels had dirt under their wings.

 Welcome to Naples!

 (Available to buy on Amazon book and kindle)

(Once Upon a Time in Naples was the basis for the Diego Maradona film directed by the Oscar winning Asif Kapadia, and produced by Paul Martin and James Gay Rees.)

THE END

JOHN LUDDEN

@Johnludds

johnludds@gmail.com

Printed in Poland
by Amazon Fulfillment
Poland Sp. z o.o., Wrocław

65981429R00237